PENNSYLVANIA AVENUE

PENNSYLVA

PROFILES IN BACKROOM POWER

RANDOM HOUSE   NEW YORK

NIA AVENUE
JOHN HARWOOD
AND **GERALD F. SEIB**

Published in the United States by Random House, an imprint of
The Random House Publishing Group, a division of Random
House, Inc., New York.

RANDOM HOUSE and colophon are registered trademarks of
Random House, Inc.

LIBRARY OF CONGRESS CATALOGING-IN-PUBLICATION DATA
Harwood, John.
    Pennsylvania Avenue : profiles in backroom power /
John Harwood and Gerald F. Seib.
        p.   cm.
    Includes bibliographical references and index.
    ISBN 978-1-4000-6554-7
1. Political culture—Washington (D.C.)   2. Politicians—
Washington (D.C.)   3. Power (Social sciences)—United States.
4. United States—Politics and government—2001–   I. Seib,
Gerald.   II. Title.
    JK1726.H39 2008
    320.973092'2—dc22   2007035797

Printed in the United States of America on acid-free paper

www.atrandom.com

9 8 7 6 5 4 3 2 1

FIRST EDITION

Book design by Simon M. Sullivan

TO FRANKIE AND BARB
PARTNERS, FRIENDS, COMPANIONS, SOUL MATES

CONTENTS

I. WASHINGTON WRIT LARGE

1. GRIDLOCK ON AMERICA'S MAIN STREET

PENNSYLVANIA AVENUE, the most celebrated mile of pavement in America, stretches northwest from the U.S. Capitol to the White House, along a path cleared through the Washington swamp two hundred years ago. Every important chapter of American history has played out, in one fashion or another, on Pennsylvania Avenue.

Pennsylvania Avenue is the capital's best address, the street of status, where the powerful work, and meet, and where the ambitious come to get things done. From the days when it was little more than a muddy path, the Avenue has been populated by smart people, men and women full of passion and drive and strong beliefs, many of them well meaning. Over the span of American history, the powerful have come together here to accomplish great things—to free the oppressed, to win great battles, to launch great public works, to comfort the downtrodden.

The people of Pennsylvania Avenue can be vain, greedy, downright nasty as well. Sometimes the Avenue is where they manage to stop things from getting done. Interspersed with the moments of great glory are those occasions when fear, mistrust, or simple disagreements run out of control to produce confrontation and gridlock on Pennsylvania Avenue.

In recent years, such occasions have become more and more numerous, to the point where, simply put, Pennsylvania Avenue doesn't work very well these days. For a complex set of reasons, it has become an avenue divided—divided by party, ideology, money, technology—

so that even the best of intentions these days often produce the worst of results.

To some extent, this complex of forces is well known to those who watch the nation's political machinations through the pages of newspapers and magazines or the shouting heads that have come to dominate political talk shows. What's less well known is the existence of a new kind of power broker on Pennsylvania Avenue, backroom power players who confront these forces and who strive to vault over them and, indeed, sometimes even succeed in doing so—in making Washington work.

Many of these people are new to the national scene, having moved into the power structure thanks to the political upheavals of the last two decades. Over that time, the old establishment in Washington has been pushed aside, starting with Ronald Reagan's conservative sweep into Washington in 1980, followed by the Bill Clinton years, the Newt Gingrich revolution in the House in 1994, and the Democratic comeback of 2006. The capital's old wiring has been ripped out, and replaced. It is the lot of today's power players to have assumed positions of import at a time when, by all accounts, it has become harder and harder to get things done in the nation's capital. Some of these backroom power brokers have mastered the new rules of the road on Pennsylvania Avenue, and perhaps profited from them; others have figured out how to get things done despite Washington gridlock, by breaking away from the traffic patterns that have produced that gridlock.

What all of these powerful people on Pennsylvania Avenue have figured out, amid great conflict along that 1.2-mile stretch of road, is a way to make their voices heard.

This is a book about some of those people on Pennsylvania Avenue, people who are rarely seen, often unknown. Through these profiles in backroom power, we mean to show how a new network operates in Washington today, and by a new set of rules.

. . .

But first a story, one that shows some of the changes that have transformed Washington, and some of the forces that have created gridlock on America's Main Street.

This story unfolded in February 2006, with a furor like that of one of those summer thunderstorms that periodically sweep across the nation's capital, seeming to arise out of nowhere, building rapidly to a loud and frightening climax, and then moving out again, leaving Washingtonians to wonder what had hit them. The episode became known simply as "the Dubai Ports deal."

The story began quietly enough: A company few in Washington had heard of, with headquarters in a country most Americans never thought about, agreed to a corporate transaction that once might have passed unnoticed. The deal involved the purchase of terminal operations at a handful of American seaports. In the modern global economy, overlaid by new national-security fears and today's instant and shrill political jousting, this particular transaction lit a fire of rebellion and disunity.

A firm called Dubai Ports World—DP World for short—had emerged as the winner in a bidding contest to take over a British firm, Peninsular & Oriental Steam Navigation Company, for $6.85 billion. Both companies were in the business of operating the giant oceanside ports that increasingly send and receive the massive shipments of goods that keep the new global economy running.

P&O, a firm with a long and illustrious history in shipping, had long-run shipping terminals at ports around the globe. DP World, in turn, was a company created and owned by the government of Dubai, a tiny Persian Gulf emirate, to do the same thing. Dubai had used some of its billions of dollars in oil money to build a world-class port of its own, and then created DP World to buy and manage other port operations. DP World was run largely by Westerners on the emirate's payroll.

What P&O owned, and what DP World coveted, were terminals at some key ports around the globe. Most important, P&O owned port operations in booming China. The fact that DP World would gain access to terminals at six American ports also run by P&O was seen largely as a fortunate by-product.

It was hardly a secret that P&O was selling out; that had been noted in *The Wall Street Journal* and other newspapers, though in routine stories on inside pages.[1] More important, the company approached the U.S. government in mid-October 2005 to inform it that a sale affecting American port operations might be coming.

That, too, was a routine move. Foreign firms attempting a takeover or merger that might affect national security must get a stamp of approval from a little-known group called the Committee on Foreign Investments in the United States, a panel of representatives from across the government run by the Treasury Department from its grand building on Pennsylvania Avenue, next to the White House. CFIUS, as the group is known, has representatives from twelve different Cabinet departments and White House offices. Under its procedures, lower-level career officials in the departments study proposed foreign investments to see whether they pose any security threats. If those officials agree among themselves, a deal is approved. If there are disagreements, a proposed investment deal is kicked upstairs, where higher-level officials, normally political appointees, can take forty-five days for a second investigation, and the decision is ultimately put on the president's desk.

As it happened, CFIUS had been racked by dissension in the previous year or so. Officials from the Defense Department and other security agencies, who tend to be more sensitive to foreign threats than are their counterparts at the government's financial agencies, felt that their views weren't being heard enough in the process. They wanted more scrutiny of deals. Their counterparts at the Treasury and elsewhere, in turn, felt they were under pressure from the White House to decide on deals without pushing them up the line where they would bother higher-level officials and land on the president's desk. In the months before the DP World deal arrived, the officials running CFIUS had been busy changing their procedures to better ensure that security agencies would have their views heard.

In the case of the ports deal, the question was whether foreigners operating American ports could be counted on to make sure the ports weren't being used by terrorists or rogue states to sneak into the United States either people or materials for terrorist attacks. So, when the ports deal arrived, CFIUS went into action. The Department of Homeland Security was chosen to take the lead in vetting the deal, because it was in charge of port security. P&O and DP World twice briefed officials from all the agencies and departments in CFIUS on the proposed deal. The Central Intelligence Agency and its sister intelligence services were asked to provide written assessments of whether the deal posed problems. Meetings were held, memos exchanged; the system did its job.

By mid-December, when P&O and DP World formally filed their request for government approval, the American government already had been considering the deal for two months. Questions had been asked and answered, security guarantees sought and delivered. In early January 2006, DP World sent a dense three-page, single-spaced letter to the Department of Homeland Security promising to abide by all the U.S. government's port-security programs already in place. More than that, the company agreed to keep its American port operations under management by American citizens "to the extent possible," to open up its files on the "design, maintenance of the Companies' U.S. facilities, equipment or services," and to give the government "any relevant records" it might seek regarding directions the port managers received from abroad.[2] Security officials felt that, if anything, they would end up having a tighter security arrangement with DP World than with any other port manager in the country. By mid-January, a poll had been taken of all the government agencies involved in CFIUS, and the decision was unanimous: The deal should be allowed to go forward.

It's not hard to understand why the bureaucrats saw no threat to American national security, given the way they viewed the deal. DP World was seen in the shipping business as a smart and well-run company—and one that actually had been very cooperative with Homeland Security in setting up a program to monitor shipping containers that are sent from abroad to U.S. shores. The tiny sheikhdom of Dubai, just a few years earlier known as a place that looked the other way as extremists transferred money through its banks and Iran shipped weapons parts through its ports, had transformed itself into the Gulf state most openly cooperating in the war on terror. Among other things, it publicly allowed the U.S. Navy and Air Force to use its ports and airfields. As such, Dubai actually was a favorite of the folks at the Pentagon who might normally be the most keen to suspect national-security threats in a foreign takeover.

Moreover, given the recent turmoil among the officials who ran CFIUS, if objections weren't registered by the Defense and Homeland Security officials, who had been so annoyed that their concerns weren't being heard on other deals, why should anyone else stand in the way of this one? At that point, perhaps 250 officials, at the second and third tiers of government, had reviewed the deal, and their consensus was that it didn't pose a problem.

The substantive, logical, and bureaucratic considerations all ignored one thing: the chance that the politics of the deal, inflamed by a polarized electoral system and media culture, could explode in controversy. Whether DP World was a safe partner or not, how would it look to Congress and the American public, in the midst of a war against terrorism emanating from the Middle East, to sell operations at some of America's most important ports to an Arab country? Worse, how would it look to sell those operations at a time when the administration was being criticized specifically for not doing enough to be sure terrorists weren't smuggling bombs, or even people, into America through the nation's ports?

This separation of political passions and bureaucratic decision-making wouldn't last. And it was a sign of the times that those passions exploded in the face of a man who had seen, in his life and career, the erosion of the sensible center, and the emergence of gridlock on Pennsylvania Avenue.

The DP World deal closed quietly on a Friday in February 2006.

That night, Robert Kimmitt, the deputy secretary of the Treasury Department, who recently had been assigned the task of overseeing CFIUS, got an e-mail message at home from one of his staff members alerting him to the deal. The message suggested it might turn into a problem.

Kimmitt, a big, bespectacled man with the build of the rugby player he once was and the calm air of one who was trained to keep his cool, had been around the block many times on the politics of national-security issues. In fact, the arc of his life reflects, almost precisely, a political transformation within Washington over the last generation. In the 1960s and 1970s, when Democrats ruled Congress, Kimmitt's father, Stan, was a fixture in the Democratic firmament. Stan Kimmitt, a retired military man, had worked as secretary of the U.S. Senate, meaning he had rubbed elbows with the barons who ran that chamber, and had become their friend and confidant. Young Bob Kimmitt grew up in army postings and then in Washington, and he proceeded to West Point to attend the U.S. Military Academy.

Bob Kimmitt embarked on an army career until, as is often the case with bright young officers who get spotted by outsiders, he was recruited into government work on the civilian side. The army sent him to Georgetown University's law school, where he was working on a paper on the legalities of American arms sales abroad. A friend of his father in the Ford White House knew of Bob Kimmitt and his work, and recruited him to take a summer job, while finishing law school, on the National Security Council staff. The summer job turned into a full-time slot—the kind of slot regularly filled by military officers on loan to the White House—which lasted through the Ford administration and into the first months of Jimmy Carter's term.

Bob Kimmitt then clerked for a federal judge for a year, and was recruited back onto the NSC staff. While he was on that White House tour, the partisan tide turned. Carter lost the presidency to Ronald Reagan, Republicans took over the U.S. Senate, and suddenly it was no longer his father's Washington. Kimmitt, who as a military officer didn't really have a political affiliation, stayed on the NSC staff and began to work for the new Reagan team. Eventually, he resigned his military commission, became a civilian working on arms-sales matters on the Reagan NSC staff, and was promoted to NSC executive secretary—the third-ranking job on the staff.

There he came into contact with James Baker III, Reagan's first White House chief of staff and a man on his way to becoming a dominant figure in Washington. The two clicked, and Kimmitt followed along as a top aide when Baker became secretary of the Treasury, and later secretary of state. Along the way, Kimmitt, although the son of a prominent Democrat, became a prominent Republican. Baker eventually named him U.S. ambassador to Germany. After his time there, Kimmitt took advantage of the new Washington's connection to the global economy to cross into the private sector, working as an executive for the Lehman Brothers banking firm, as an attorney in a prominent Washington firm, as a leader of a small software company, and as an executive of AOL Time Warner. But he yearned for a return to government, and was invited back in, during George W. Bush's second term, as the Treasury Department's second-highest official.

Thus, Kimmitt had seen many a political firestorm, from his perches in the White House, the State Department, and the Treasury Department.

And so, when he read the e-mail on that Friday night, about the DP World deal, he raised the kinds of questions that occur to one who's earned his scars from other Washington battles. Had the company alerted anyone in Congress about the deal, to sense reaction and prevent the anger that comes when lawmakers think they have been taken by surprise? Had anyone considered how to handle public reaction to the announcement of the deal? The answer was no on both counts.

Kimmitt sensed trouble ahead—and he was right—but it was too late to do much about it. A strange sequence of events was about to turn the deal into a Pennsylvania Avenue earthquake.

The sequence started, as such episodes often do in Washington, with a little-known lobbyist who knows how to push the right buttons.

As it happened, a small stevedoring company in Miami, Eller & Company, thought the sale was a bad idea, not entirely because of national-security operations but because the big Dubai firm, if it took over, might push the smaller company out of the work it was doing on Miami terminals under contract with P&O. Eller & Company decided to oppose the deal, and Washington lobbyist Joe Muldoon pitched in to start spreading the word about the proposed deal in Congress. Muldoon, a lawyer with deep roots in the northern-Virginia horse country west of the nation's capital, says he took on the task because one Eller executive was an old friend of his family. He began poking around congressional offices, starting with Senator John Warner of Virginia, a family acquaintance, and branching out from there. Notably, one of his conversations was with the staff of Democratic Senator Charles Schumer of New York, whose state is home to one of the giant port operations that would be affected by a sale.

Within days, the Associated Press ran a story on its news wire framing the debate in a new way: "A company in the United Arab Emirates is poised to take over significant operations at six American ports as part of a corporate sale, leaving a country with ties to the Sept. 11 hijackers with influence over a maritime industry considered vulnerable to terrorism."[3] The AP story stressed that some of the 9/11 hijackers had transited through the UAE. For comment on the story, the AP called Senator Schumer. Schumer had not only a giant port operation in his state, but also a penchant for seizing a political opening; he was, at the time, running the Democrats' Senate campaign committee, and he knew a good issue when he saw one.

The AP quoted Schumer criticizing the deal. That comment, in turn, caught the eye of Democratic Representative Rahm Emanuel of Illinois, who says he called Mr. Schumer upon seeing the story and told him: "Chuck, you have something here. Stay after this." The senator assured him he was already planning to do so.[4] Almost immediately, national-security analyst Frank Gaffney wrote and circulated a column criticizing the deal.[5]

Still, the story at that point was a second-tier item on the agenda in

Washington, which at that moment was caught up in another story: Vice President Cheney's accidental shooting of a hunting partner in rural Texas. Yet the DP World story had entered the New Age media echo chamber, in which news can be shaped and laced with opinion and attitude and given power no political leader—not even a president—can thwart.

Cable News Network anchor Lou Dobbs decided to make the story a cause. In a "special report" on his February 13 evening program, he informed viewers that "a country with ties to the September 11 terrorists could soon be running significant operations at some of our most important and largest seaports with the full blessing of the White House." That same day, conservative radio talk-show host Michael Savage also attacked the deal—which had doubtless escaped the attention of most of his listeners until the moment they heard him describe it as a threat to their security.

A routine business deal that had skated easily through the government regulatory maze was suddenly turning into a national-security scandal. Worse for the White House, the Savage report sent the issue racing through the circuits of the network of conservative radio talk shows, Internet blogs, and instant-reaction pundits.

That sort of brush fire can outrace the ability of even a disciplined White House message team to control it. Home for Presidents' Day weekend, lawmakers were especially attuned to any controversy that was raising the hackles among their followers.

Republican Bill Frist of Tennessee, at the time the Senate's majority leader and a man harboring his own presidential ambitions, was better plugged in than most. Addicted to instant communications, Frist carries his handheld e-mail device with him constantly, sending and receiving messages at all hours. Frist's BlackBerry began pinging with the sound of incoming messages from his Senate colleagues, staff members, and friends back home, all concerned about the growing story of a Dubai company about to take over some especially sensitive American real estate.

Frist was scheduled to appear that Sunday on *Face the Nation,* the

CBS Sunday-morning interview show, and he told his staff he wanted to be prepared for questions about it. To Frist's surprise, he wasn't asked on the air about the deal, but liberal Democratic Senator Barbara Boxer of California followed him on the show, and she was asked about it. Frist sensed the controversy was moving rapidly out of the conservative-talk-show realm into the mainstream.

By coincidence, Frist left after his CBS interview for Boxer's home state, where he was scheduled to tour the Los Angeles seaport and review new security measures aimed at preventing terrorists from slipping weapons materials into the country. It was inconceivable that the Dubai deal wouldn't come up, because it was being framed then as a transaction that might make it easier for terrorists to do precisely that. Frist and his aides concluded that the story was rapidly gathering momentum.

So Frist made the unusual decision to get out in front of the snowball himself—either to stop it, or to shield fellow Republicans from its impact. He issued a public statement in California proposing a forty-five-day hold on the deal for further review. The statement included an explicit threat to the White House: "If the administration cannot delay this process, I plan on introducing legislation to ensure that the deal is placed on hold until this decision gets a more thorough review."[6]

Frist gave the White House only the scantest advance notice of his challenge to the administration's decision. Soon his BlackBerry pinged again, with an angry e-mail from a White House aide chastising him for indiscretion.

Installed as majority leader with White House blessing three years earlier, Frist had rarely defied Bush so boldly. But his decision to do so in this case was one of the first big signals of how much President Bush's reputation and fortunes had eroded in his second term. The conflict in Iraq, which most Republicans had expected to be a closed chapter by then, was instead turning into a millstone around Bush's and the country's neck. If Iraq was a big problem for Bush, it was a big problem for Republicans in the Senate, too, just months before they would face voters in midterm elections. Simply tying themselves to their party's president no longer looked like a suitable re-election strategy.

Similar sentiments were building on the House side of the Capitol as well. Ron Bonjean, a well-wired communications aide to Speaker Dennis Hastert, Republican of Illinois, was getting worried e-mails from other congressional offices as members heard the early rumblings about the deal. The last image any Republican wanted to project was simultaneous support for an unpopular war in Iraq and softness on terrorism at home. That was the emerging picture among conservative opinion leaders.

Just as Senator Frist was preparing to speak out, House Speaker Hastert got a call from Representative Peter King, a New York Republican, who heads the House committee in charge of homeland security. King informed Hastert that he had just publicly blasted the DP World deal. He expected the Speaker to be angry about an unexpected breach of loyalty; instead, Hastert echoed his judgment that the deal was a bad one. Hastert, himself preparing to leave Washington for a California fund-raiser, ordered aides to draw up his own statement of opposition. When it arrived, he considered it too soft and ordered its language toughened up. He then called the White House to say he, too, was breaking with the president on this.

The significance wasn't lost on George W. Bush. He was traveling to make a speech in Colorado when word of Frist's declaration was relayed to Air Force One. Mr. Bush summoned his two most trusted White House aides, Karl Rove and counselor Dan Bartlett, to decide what to do. They sensed big trouble at the worst possible place: at the grass roots of their own party.

By now, the talk-radio hosts and political bloggers were making an uproar about DP World, among the very conservative activists the president once could count on. Bartlett and Rove knew that the relentless twenty-four-hour-a-day news cycle meant CNN, CNBC, MSNBC, Fox News, and their brethren would make DP World a giant story before the president even returned home.

DP World was "turning into a wildfire," Bartlett recalled later, and Bush's team decided to try to stop it. The president used the one legislative tool at his disposal whenever he decided to open his mouth: a veto threat. The president always travels with a small "pool" of reporters who function as representatives of the much larger group of newspaper, magazine, newswire, television, and radio correspondents who cover the White House. So Mr. Bush called the pool, a dozen or so strong, to the front of Air Force One for a rare in-air press briefing. The president declared that he would veto any legislation to block the DP World deal. A Republican president was digging in against the leaders of his own party in Congress, a sign both of how strongly Bush felt about making sure America was open to foreign investment and of how much leverage he thought he still had over fellow Republicans in Congress.

The veto threat didn't work; instead, it backfired. By the time Congress and the president got back to town, the universe of bloggers, conservative talk-radio hosts, and saturation cable-news shows had irreversibly shaped—or distorted, in the administration's view—public perceptions. The portrayal of Dubai as a friendly and helpful Arab state was drowned out by the fearful specter of Arab port managers letting terrorists' cargo slip through security. Even in a Senate then controlled by fifty-five of Mr. Bush's fellow Republicans, there were enough votes to override the president's threatened veto.

By the time Bush called congressional leaders to a private meeting at the White House a few days later, it was clear to all that the deal was dead. The only question was how it would be buried. Ultimately, the Bush administration performed the service itself. Several top officials told representatives of the company and the Dubai government that the deal seemed unlikely to survive the political heat. A White House official called a top official in the Dubai government to say that support for the deal was lost. On Capitol Hill, Senator Warner, one of the few leaders still willing to argue for the merits of the deal, got a call from a DP World official saying the plug was being pulled on the sale. Within hours, DP World announced that it would put the U.S. port operations it had just bought up for sale.

The episode damaged Bush and his party. It exacerbated forces of disunity within the GOP, and renewed questions about the administration's competence that Hurricane Katrina and the Iraq war had placed at the center of the Democrats' 2006 attempt to win back Congress. The aftermath of the debacle was angry and ugly. Kimmitt, nominally in charge of the CFIUS apparatus that oversaw approval of the deal, became the designated punching bag for a few days. At one hearing, Democratic Senator Paul Sarbanes of Maryland demanded that Kimmitt identify by name the underlings who had been involved in approving the deal. Kimmitt, steeped in West Point training on honor and an officer's need to accept responsibility for the actions of those beneath him, refused to do so.

The Washington furor died down, but its consequences took months to play out in the real world. True to its promise, DP World set out to slice off the American port operations it had just bought and sell them to a buyer more acceptable on Pennsylvania Avenue. That process took months, but in March 2007 the company announced that it had sold the American operations to AIG Global Investment Group, a New York–based asset-management company. The price wasn't announced, but *The Wall Street Journal* reported that the U.S. operations went for about $1.2 billion.[7] Few in Washington took note. The story had returned to its starting point, deep inside the pages of a few newspapers, largely ignored by everyone else. Pennsylvania Avenue had moved on.

The DP World uproar was precisely the kind of situation that a president once would have found relatively easy to control. In an era when members of Congress stayed in Washington over a long weekend, when communications were a little slower, and when the machinery for firing up grass-roots activists wasn't so technologically advanced, the president might have flown back to Washington, summoned congressional leaders to cocktails at the White House, and cajoled the lawmakers into backing down. But none of those conditions prevail in the modern Washington. Today, on an avenue divided, it's easier to stop something from happening than to make something happen.

Divisions have always been part of Pennsylvania Avenue's landscape, of course. Since the birth of American democracy, Americans have been split by their ideologies and their interests, their races and religions, their regions and their resentments. But today the divisions have taken on a new character. Power is so divided between the two parties that, in a very real sense, nobody has enough control either to paper over differences or to roll past them. Nobody is in charge.

Over the last generation, voters learned that the country's two main parties stood in quite different places—on civil rights, feminism, the sexual revolution, welfare, taxes and spending, the Vietnam War—and they saw those differences fall into consistent patterns. Campaign strategists grew ever more skilled at using the proliferation of information sources—newspapers and magazines, broadcast television and radio, direct mail and cable channels, the Internet—to underscore and inflame those differences to the benefit of their candidates.

Today, the result is partisan conflict in which ideological divisions are clearer and sharper. Once, the Republican Party combined practical, Chamber of Commerce Midwesterners with blue-blooded noblesse-oblige Northeasterners such as George W. Bush's grandfather; now the party is uniformly conservative. Once, Democrats brought together Southern white segregationists with Northern blacks, Jews, and Catholics; now it is unambiguously the party of the left. Conservative Southern Democrats and liberal Northeastern Republicans used to fill up the middle of the political spectrum, forming a kind of human bridge between the partisan extremes. Now many of those conservative Southern Democrats have become Republicans, and those liberal Northeastern Republicans have nearly been wiped out. The center is a much lonelier place.

And because the two sides are so evenly divided, the stakes of every battle appear high. Two remarkably close national elections, in 2000 and 2004, followed by a war in Iraq that became more bitterly divisive with every bombing of an American soldier's Humvee, have made the divisions all the more raw.

The art of modern politics has also made the divisions wider. Today, the lawmakers who ply their trade in the U.S. Capitol can be sure they are surrounded in their districts back home with like-minded constituents. Computer software allows politicians to pin-point, house by house, the voting tendencies of particular neighbors. Armed with that information, political demographers from both par-ties are able to draw increasingly safe, ideologically homogenous con-gressional districts when state legislatures back home recraft those districts after each decade's census. Instead of voters choosing their congressmen, Republican Representative Tom Davis of Virginia says, congressmen are choosing their voters.

Thus, conservative lawmakers can speak largely to fellow conser-vatives when they are trying to get re-elected, liberals to fellow liberals, minorities to fellow minorities. Members of Congress have less rea-son to reach out to the other side, and little reason to fear for their jobs, provided they simply keep their own partisans happy. The twenty-first-century art of redistricting has made it safe to remain highly partisan. In 2002 and 2004, for example, not a single seat in California's fifty-three-member congressional delegation changed partisan hands. Even in 2006, the year of what was popularly seen as a political earthquake when Democrats took over control of both the House and the Senate from Republicans, only a single incumbent, Republican Representative Richard Pombo, lost his seat. Put another way, recent elections show there's a less than 1 percent chance a Cal-ifornia House seat will change party hands in any given election.

The rise of niche media has accelerated the trend of each side's talking only to itself. The explosion of cable-news outlets, talk radio, e-mail communications, blogs, and Internet chat rooms has frag-mented public communications and fostered a more insular dia-logue.

At the White House, National Security Council official Elliott Abrams recalls a Reagan-era routine in which official Washington froze between 6:30 and 7:30 p.m. to watch the nightly newscasts on CBS, NBC, and ABC—whose monopoly on mass communication made them the most important megaphone for any political leader. By their choice and framing of stories from Pennsylvania Avenue, correspondents such as Sam Donaldson and Lesley Stahl had the ability to affect the national psyche.

Now network-news broadcasts have been swamped by cable-news outlets and Internet news sites, whose twenty-four-hour news cycle feeds political buzz nonstop. More than that, these new political news outlets are, in many cases, designed to feed partisans of one side or the other political information tailored to fit their preconceived ideologies and notions. Conservatives in Missouri can absorb Rush Limbaugh's worldview each day, while liberals in California can tune in with like-minded activists from around the country on Markos Moulitsas's Daily Kos website.

Now, Abrams says, "I don't even watch the evening news. Ever. It just isn't an important event."

He's not alone. Nielsen ratings indicate that when Ronald Reagan was running for president, 75 percent of television sets turned on in the early evening were tuned in to one of the three network-news broadcasts. By the time of George W. Bush's second term, that had fallen to 37 percent.[8]

These trends mean that the successful politician has become the one who rouses partisan passions rather than the one who soothes them. The price is erosion of the ability to achieve compromise on Pennsylvania Avenue.

In the past, the capital had social institutions that brought political rivals together, and helped them sand off the sharp edges of party divisions. But those social institutions have weakened or broken down entirely. Today, the social life of the capital provides fewer and fewer opportunities for lawmakers of the two parties to bond on a personal level.

In the era before travel made it relatively easy and cheap to jet home every weekend, most members of Congress and their families actually lived in and around Washington, where they got to know one another on a social level. Today, as members of Congress have increasingly retreated to their partisan corners, they have also increasingly retreated from Pennsylvania Avenue itself. Fewer and fewer lawmakers—especially in the House, where every member faces reelection every two years—stay in Washington for the weekends. They work a Tuesday-through-Thursday schedule in the capital and then go back home to meet with constituents and protect their seats.

Representative John Dingell, a powerful Democrat who has served in the House for half a century, and whose father served there before him, recalls that when he first came to Washington the only way to arrive was to endure a twelve-hour train ride from Michigan. Later, the preferred commuting route was a long car ride. Either was too painful and time-consuming to undertake too often. Instead, the whole Michigan delegation lived in Washington, where the members—Republican and Democrat—became well acquainted with one another. "People now don't know each other," Dingell says simply.

Consider the bifurcated lifestyle of Republican Senator Sam Brownback of Kansas. His wife and five children have never moved to Washington. Instead, they remain back home in Topeka. The senator's wife rarely comes to the capital—"once or twice a year, whether she needs to or not," he jokes.

So Brownback lives a bachelor's life in Washington during the week. After residing in a series of apartments rented with other congressmen, he finally invested in a small condominium a few blocks from the Capitol, which he shares with a colleague. On weekends, he flies out of Washington, heading back home or to campaign and party events elsewhere.

The House gym long was one place where lawmakers met informally. Young Republican lawmakers such as Donald Rumsfeld and George H. W. Bush played paddleball with young Democrats such as John Dingell. House-gym regulars held an annual informal dinner in which Democrats and Republicans got together, smoked cigars, played cards, and became friends. That annual dinner has faded away. Similarly, the wives of House members used to gather weekly for a lunch or some other social event. Now such gatherings occur perhaps once or twice a month, and are much more sparsely attended, because many spouses work or live back in their home states.

Journalist Cokie Roberts, herself the daughter of two members of Congress, once reflected, in a poignant commentary on National Public Radio, on how much the social atmosphere of Washington, and particularly Capitol Hill, has changed in a generation.

Roberts's father, Hale Boggs, was a Democratic majority leader in the House. When he died in a plane crash, her mother, Lindy Boggs, took over his seat. Roberts recalled growing up in a congressional social circle in which one of her best friends was the daughter of a Republican congressman named Bill Miller, who was his party's vice-presidential candidate in 1964. Roberts described a world in which partisan divisions were put aside at day's end, when the members "gathered in someone's office and broke out the bourbon and branch." Most members moved their families to Washington and called it home. "The wives knew each other well. They saw each other at the club for congressional spouses. I went to dancing school there with the Nixon girls. The wives joined PTAs and ran charitable organizations together. . . . None of that is true today." Fewer members really live in Washington, she noted, and more of them win campaigns in the first place by bashing Washington as "a sinful Sodom on the Potomac." The parties have become more ideological. And now, Roberts noted, "microphones go to the loudest, most outrageous voice. The boring guy in the middle hardly merits airtime or print inches."[9]

Money has changed Pennsylvania Avenue as well. The rise of the global economy has led more companies and industries to seek help from the American government, which retains unique powers to open trade and commerce around the world. As specific firms or industries seek an advantage, the ranks of companies establishing a Washington presence has grown exponentially, as has the money they devote to prodding the government.

In the first decade of the twenty-first century, the number of persons registered to influence the executive or legislative branches has doubled to thirty-four thousand.[10] And it isn't just American companies that are seeking to build or buy influence in Washington. Economic globalization has brought foreign-based companies to Pennsylvania Avenue in unprecedented numbers as well, because trade across borders and oceans required rules that only governments could set. Siemens, the German-based telecommunications firm, and Nestlé, the European food-products giant, have established lobbying offices within two blocks of the White House at 1600 Pennsylvania Avenue.

To a large extent, these lobbyists underwrite the rising price tag for the two parties' efforts. The new rivers of money flowing down Pennsylvania Avenue have financed the new politics that divide those on the Avenue.

The result of these changes: Within a generation, the way to get things done on Pennsylvania Avenue has been turned upside down. Instead of cutting deals in the political center, presidential aides and legislative leaders win by marshaling and arousing their own partisans. This upheaval has brought fresh blood and energy to the capital, and in some ways has made debate along the Avenue more open and honest. But debate has also become more brutal and less likely to unite the nation.

That is the norm. And then there are those who make Washington work, or who make it work for them. These people operate in a different, and very savvy, way. People like Ken Duberstein, the Fixer.

2. THE FIXER: KEN DUBERSTEIN

Exit through the White House gates onto Pennsylvania Avenue, walk four blocks to the west, and you'll find the office of one of the capital's pre-eminent wise men, Ken Duberstein.

A generation ago, that wise-man status was more commonly associated with Robert Strauss, a Texas Democrat with an easy manner and a baritone drawl. Operating from a powerful capital law firm and occasional stints inside administrations of each party, Strauss dispensed wisdom to the powerful, fixed problems, made money, and helped his clients make even more.

Today, that description applies to Ken Duberstein, a jovial New Yorker who entered political life as an aide to liberal GOP Senator Jacob Javits, whose strain of Republicanism has become all but extinct. Duberstein rode to prominence on the Republican wave of the 1980s, and he has succeeded by adapting. He has become one of the few people remaining in Washington trusted by those on the right yet also comfortable with those on the left.

He helped manage congressional relations for President Ronald Reagan, and eventually he was promoted to become Reagan's White House chief of staff. He got no small boost along the way from his close relationship with First Lady Nancy Reagan, a pragmatist who placed her husband's interests above any partisan or ideological causes.

When he left the White House, Duberstein knew he didn't want to start a traditional lobbying practice, so he created a new model for wielding influence. It was, paradoxically, a model not crafted strictly for shaping decisions inside the government, but more for providing service-for-hire from the outside.

Duberstein launched a one-of-a-kind boutique consulting-and-lobbying firm, with an elite client list of top corporations and a few nonprofit organizations. His clients pay a flat fee—hundreds of thousands of dollars per year—to get the advice of Duberstein and his handful of associates on how to solve problems in the capital and beyond, and to get the occasional bit of persuasion in Congress, or an entrée into the office of an important federal bureaucrat.

Though a lifelong Republican, Duberstein didn't want to be seen as a partisan figure. So he hired as his partner Democrat Michael Berman, a former aide to Vice President Walter Mondale and a veteran of every Democratic presidential campaign since 1964. Duberstein has come to personify an oddity of today's Washington: Bipartisan cooperation is more likely to be found outside the government than inside it. The model also meant that, when Democrats stormed back in the fall of 2006 to regain control of the House and the Senate, Duberstein ran an operation that, unlike lobbying operations run strictly by Republicans, didn't go into shock. Duberstein had thrived while Democrat Bill Clinton was in the White House at one end of Pennsylvania Avenue; he could thrive when Democrats were in charge in the Capitol, at the other end.

Duberstein and Berman structured their business to keep it small and manageable, with only about twenty clients. That allowed plenty of time for Duberstein to play the other roles his status could command. He serves on a handful of corporate boards, and is a lifetime trustee of the Kennedy Center for the Performing Arts. He spent months trying to help the quasi-governmental housing agency Fannie Mae work itself out of trouble in Congress and the courts of public opinion when its accounting practices and executive pay were under attack.

More than that, he has left himself time to become Washington's all-purpose man to see. In the first Bush administration, he was tapped to shepherd the troubled Supreme Court nomination of Clarence Thomas through the Senate. He won, in part by quietly negotiating—and then sternly insisting on enforcing—a deal with senators that ensured Thomas would be given a chance to rebut his critics on national television during prime time.

At the key moment in the dramatic confirmation fight, Thomas had been attacked by opponents in a day of testimony before the Senate Judiciary Committee that was splashed all over the network news. Democratic senators were about to adjourn the hearings for the night, which would have left the damaging testimony hanging unanswered. Duberstein went to Delaware Senator Joseph Biden, a leader of the Democrats on the committee, and reminded him of the agreement that Thomas would be given a chance to rebut critics on the same day. Duberstein backed up his plea with a subtle threat: If the hearings were adjourned, Thomas would hold a press conference in front of the locked committee-room doors to give his own statement. Thomas was allowed to testify that night, he forcefully rebutted his critics with his instantly famous declaration that he was being made the victim of a "high-tech lynching," and his confirmation was saved.

Now Duberstein is as likely to get calls from Democrats Ted Kennedy and Patrick Leahy seeking his opinion about how to deal with the Republican White House as he is to be called into that same Republican White House to consult about a big upcoming speech. He has come to be seen as credible, because he understands both parties' leaders and is honest enough to be a broker.

At one point during George W. Bush's second term, Duberstein drew upon his myriad connections to pull off an inside play that aptly illustrates how he works. Duberstein sat on the board of directors of the Boeing Company, the aerospace giant. Boeing had a Washington problem. Through its defense contracts, the federal government was one of Boeing's biggest customers. Yet the government's ties with Boeing had been strained by a series of ethics scandals in the company's defense-contracting business. The company's chief executive officer, Jim McNerney, wanted to do something to change Boeing's image.

An important job was about to come open at Boeing, the position of general counsel; McNerney hoped he could install in that position a newcomer who could impose new ethical standards for Boeing and help fix its image in Washington.

Duberstein knew a man who could help accomplish that. J. Michael Luttig was a prominent federal judge who, before being named to the bench, had worked in the Justice Department. There, he had worked closely with Duberstein to shepherd through the Senate the nominations of both David Souter and Clarence Thomas to the Supreme Court. The two became friends, before Duberstein went on to form his consulting shop and Luttig went on to the federal bench.

Luttig had achieved wide notice as a conservative jurist and had been on everybody's short list of potential Supreme Court nominees. But he didn't get an appointment from President Bush, and White House annoyance with his handling of a terrorism case made it seem less likely he ever would. So Judge Luttig was looking for something else to do.

Luttig would become Duberstein's solution to Boeing's problem. At a dinner in the back room of i Ricchi, a tony restaurant in downtown Washington, Duberstein suggested to Boeing's McNerney that he try to hire Judge Luttig to become the company's new general counsel, giving Boeing a tough and prominent figure well known around Washington as its top ethics cop. Duberstein then called Luttig to pave the way for the overture. McNerney approached Judge Luttig, who stunned the capital by agreeing to leave the bench to take the job.

The move was even shrewder than it appeared on the surface. Boeing's biggest problem in Washington was Republican Senator John McCain of Arizona, a prominent scourge of wasteful government spending who had been hammering the firm for its contracting practices. As it happens, Duberstein is a friend and confidant of Senator McCain. In brief, then, Duberstein understood Boeing's problem in Washington (a bad reputation), he was a friend of the man who was the source of much of the problem (John McCain), and he knew somebody who stood the best chance of becoming the solution to the problem (Judge Luttig).

It worked. A few months later, Boeing negotiated a settlement to the government's ethics complaints against the company that required Boeing to pay $615 million in settlement charges to the federal treasury.[1] Then, in hopes of really changing Washington attitudes toward Boeing, McNerney, Luttig, and Duberstein hatched a plan under which Boeing would agree not to take the tax deduction it could claim for paying the $615 million in charges. Duberstein arranged for McNerney to tell McCain privately beforehand about the decision to take a pass on the tax break. McCain responded as Duberstein had hoped; at a public hearing immediately after being told of the decision, he lavishly praised Boeing and McNerney for the company's new culture.[2] Before long, McCain's committee authorized a new order of C-17 transport planes from Boeing. Because of that new order, Boeing was able to drop plans to shut down its entire C-17 production line.[3]

This is what Duberstein likes to do, is good at doing, and is paid to do: know the right people, sense the nub of a problem, and quietly figure out how his connections can solve it. He gets some credit publicly for his fix-it work, but not too much. That's why people are willing to pay a lot of money to have Ken Duberstein be their friend in the capital. He likes the reasonable solution, and as a result he is sometimes troubled by the new Washington, which seems more drawn to conflict than to the artful fix. When Washington operators go on TV and yell at one another, which is increasingly the style of cable-news coverage of Washington, that artful solution is harder to find. Like Cokie Roberts, Duberstein notes, "If you say something moderate and reasonable you don't get on the TV show."

Though newspaper references to Duberstein inevitably refer to him as "former White House chief of staff for President Reagan," he wasn't a leader of the Reagan Revolution. In fact, he was an unlikely candidate even to be part of it, hailing as he does from New York rather than Reagan's California, and having come of age as a moderate Republican rather than as one of Reagan's army of conservatives. But Duberstein's story is a classic tale of how connections count, and how Washington's inner world of politics is like a game of "Six Degrees of Separation": Go back far enough and it isn't hard to find common links between the capital's old pros.

Duberstein is the quintessential Jewish kid from Brooklyn, where his family was involved in politics, but in an oddly bipartisan way: One uncle was head of the local Republican club; a cousin was head of the local Democratic club. So Ken Duberstein grew up hearing lots of talk of politics, much of it of the local, grass-roots variety.

He went off to Franklin & Marshall College—a small school in Pennsylvania, not far from Washington—and through his New York political connections got a job as a summer intern for Senator Javits, the very embodiment of the dying breed of liberal Republicans.

But the Javits connection was enough to lead Duberstein into the Ford administration. He took a job working on congressional relations for the General Services Administration, one of the capital's more mundane agencies, handling contracting, purchasing, property, and real estate for the vast federal bureaucracy. Normally, a GSA job isn't exactly a ticket onto Washington's fast track. But in one of those quirks of history, it fell to the GSA to handle former President Nixon's operations in San Clemente, California, and to process the former president's papers and the famous Oval Office tapes that had helped bring Nixon down in the Watergate scandal. That job brought Duberstein into contact with two of the movers and shakers of the Ford administration, Bill Timmons and Tom Korologos, a pair of longtime Washington politicos who were working in the White House.

That connection, in turn, led Duberstein into a higher-level job in the Labor Department, and then on to the Committee for Economic

Development, an independent nonpartisan organization of business and education leaders who want to weigh in on economic and social issues.

When Ford lost his bid for re-election, and presidential power changed to the Democrats, Duberstein went to work as a lobbyist for Timmons and Company, a government-relations firm run by Timmons and Korologos. Four years later, in 1980, when Reagan won the Republican nomination, Duberstein, Timmons, and Korologos all did what smart Republicans knew they should do: They fell in behind him.

That seemingly simple decision, in fact, illustrated why Reagan's 1980 campaign was one of the genuine turning points of politics over the last century. Until then, the Republican Party had two wings that barely coexisted. Gerald Ford represented one wing, the moderates, who tended to favor balanced budgets, détente with the Soviet Union, and a laissez-faire attitude toward abortion. Ronald Reagan represented the other wing, the conservatives, who favored big tax cuts, confrontation with the Soviet Union, and opposition to abortion.

The two wings came together in 1980, almost literally at the Republican convention in Detroit, when, for an entire tantalizing night, Reagan and Ford, through their aides, negotiated over the shocking and unprecedented idea that Ford, a former president, might actually agree to become Reagan's vice-presidential running mate. The idea, which almost certainly would have proved to be a disaster in real life, died. But the marriage of the Ford and Reagan wings of the party was officially blessed from on high, and it flowered.

Reagan became the vehicle for a Republican and conservative rise to power. At the same time, a whole group of capable and savvy members of the Ford wing rode into power along with him, after which they would come to dominate the Washington scene for more than two decades. George H. W. Bush, a Ford appointee as ambassador to China, became Reagan's running mate. Dick Cheney, Donald

Rumsfeld, Jim Baker, Colin Powell, Alan Greenspan, Brent Scow-croft—all had been part of the Ford team. They all became, to some extent, members of the Reagan world that year.

As did Ken Duberstein. When Reagan won, Timmons and Korologos were enlisted to help run the Reagan transition team. They, in turn, recruited Duberstein to join the Reagan White House staff, handling relations with the House of Representatives.

There wasn't much debate about whether Duberstein and his colleagues in the new Reagan administration would take a bipartisan approach to dealing with Congress. They didn't have much choice. Reagan had defied the odds and all predictions by helping Republicans pick up a stunning twelve seats in the Senate, to take control there for the first time in twenty-eight years. But the House remained an unshakable Democratic redoubt. Though Democrats lost thirty-three seats to the Reagan onslaught, they still continued to hold a daunting fifty-one-seat advantage in the House as Reagan took office. For Duberstein and the rest of the Reagan team, working across the aisle with Democrats was as much necessity as virtue.

So Duberstein set out to find ways to work with the same Democrats Reagan had spent two decades belittling and excoriating on what he always called the rubber-chicken speaking circuit. Duberstein found that the task involved building personal relationships as much as institutional ones. Early on, Duberstein went to visit William Ford, a blunt-spoken Democratic warhorse from Michigan then in his sixteenth year in the House. Ford seemed as unlikely as anyone in Congress to be friendly to Duberstein's cause. But when Duberstein came calling, Ford gave him a lesson in how important the human side of politics can be.

As they sat in Ford's office, the congressman buzzed his secretary and asked her to bring the file of letters from the man who had held Duberstein's job handling White House relations with the House in the just-departed Carter administration. In that file were two letters, one dated the first week of the Carter presidency, the second dated the last. "And I never heard from the son of a bitch in between," Ford said. Ford's point was clear: I want to be consulted. "I don't like Ronald Reagan, and I disagree with him on everything," he told Duberstein. "But my door is always open to you." Duberstein took the cue and made a point of talking to Ford regularly. He never got his vote on an important issue, but always got good intelligence on where House Democrats were going.

Similarly, a young, boyish-looking Democratic congressman from New York named Tom Downey came onto the White House radar screen when he said something unflattering about First Lady Nancy Reagan on the House floor, and a very unhappy President Reagan noticed. He sent Duberstein up to talk to Downey. Downey blew off Duberstein; they seemed destined to be adversaries.

But the personal side of political relations again entered the picture. At one point, Duberstein was the White House representative on a trip a congressional delegation made to the Caribbean to study the impact of a proposed free-trade initiative for the region that Reagan was promoting. Dan Rostenkowski, the gravel-voiced, old-school lord of the powerful Ways and Means Committee and a master at the art of Washington deal-making, walked up to Duberstein before the group took off, pointed to Downey, and declared: "Before this trip is over, you two guys will spend time together and you'll get to be friends."

So, when the group landed in the Dominican Republic, Duberstein took Rostenkowski's cue and sat down next to Downey on the back of the bus that carried the delegation away from the airport. They talked New York baseball, and found they liked each other. They grew into friends. Later, when Democrats were driving to pass a nuclear-freeze initiative, which would have stopped the Reagan administration's plans to deploy new nuclear weapons, Downey voted for the freeze but gave Duberstein good intelligence on how Democrats were playing the issue. That intelligence helped Duberstein construct a legislative strategy to stop the proposal.

In substantive terms, Reagan was a shock to the established order from the start. He started by changing the location of his inaugural, ordering it moved from the East Front of the Capitol building to the West Front, where he could deliver his inaugural address looking down the sweep of Pennsylvania Avenue and, beyond that, toward the rest of the country. Why face across the Atlantic Ocean looking east, Reagan asked his aides, when you can face west and look out across America?

After that, Reagan proceeded single-handedly to change the terms of debate up and down that same Pennsylvania Avenue. When he said the United States should spend more on defense to show the Soviet Union it couldn't outgun America, he meant billions more, right now. When the Reagan administration presented its first defense budget, in 1981, reporters in the Pentagon gasped when they got a look at it. The Reagan Pentagon passed out photocopies of the defense budget the Carter administration had left behind; the old spending numbers had simply been crossed out by hand, with higher numbers written in above them, row after row.

For Duberstein, the principal challenge was getting the combination of that giant defense budget and an equally elephantine tax cut passed simultaneously through Congress. The Reagan team succeeded by identifying and then assiduously courting a group of conservative Democrats, largely from the South, who were sympathetic to Reagan, and who came from states and districts whose voters had shown they were also sympathetic to Reagan. These became known as the Boll Weevil Democrats, and Duberstein and his boss went after them hard.

At one point, the White House put a group of them on military helicopters and ferried them all out to Camp David, the presidential retreat in the Catoctin Mountains, not far from Washington, for a Sunday barbecue with the president. Two nights before a key vote, the White House tracked down one conservative Democrat so he could be lobbied personally by Reagan over the phone. They found him at dinner with a group of his Boll Weevil colleagues. Reagan took the opportunity to lobby each one.

The Reaganauts, forced to adopt bipartisanship as a tactic, made the most of it. When the crucial first vote came on the Reagan budget plan, it passed with every Republican vote and a whopping sixty-three Democratic votes. Follow-up votes gave Reagan a giant tax cut and the defense spending he requested. Each passed only because Reagan had won over Democratic votes.

For Ken Duberstein, the Reagan years allowed him to evolve into a kind of master of the new Washington universe, a position he has been able to retain through the partisan wars that followed. When Reagan left office, Duberstein seemed most likely to return to his life as an influential but conventional Washington lobbyist. But he had a yearning to strike out on his own instead, and to do Washington influence-peddling in a new and different way. So he consulted a man who needed lots of help in Washington: Steve Ross, the chairman of Time Warner Inc. Ross knew something about the Washington influence game because his firm, as a then-new communications giant, had plenty of business before regulatory agencies such as the Federal Communications Commission and the antitrust cops at the Justice Department and the Federal Trade Commission. Ross encouraged Duberstein to set up his own firm, and assured him he could be successful. "I'm so sure I'm right I'll cover your costs for the first year," he told Duberstein.

So the Duberstein Group was created, billing itself not as a lobbying firm but as a strategic-planning-and-consulting company. It set up shop on Pennsylvania Avenue, and Time Warner became its first client. By and large, the Duberstein Group doesn't do the normal Washington lobbying-for-hire work, roaming the halls of Congress to buttonhole members of Congress and their staffers to plead for a favorable piece of legislation or an "earmark"—a provision in a spending bill sending a federal contract in a specific direction.

Instead, Duberstein's small coterie of Washington insiders essentially contract out their knowledge of how Washington works, and not on a case-by-case or crisis-by-crisis basis, but as virtual Washington ad-

juncts of the companies with which they contract. Duberstein also refuses to represent foreign governments—too controversial, too ripe
for uncomfortable publicity—and refuses to do the bread-and-butter
work of so many Washington firms, which is seeking specific government contracts for his clients.

In essence, Duberstein sells his brain and his Rolodex, not his shoe
leather. Each of his clients knows it can have access to the advice and
help of the Duberstein Group whenever the need arises.

Thus, when a top official of the De Beers diamond company was
visiting Washington and hoping to resolve a trade problem, Duberstein could place a quiet call and arrange an appointment with the
U.S. trade representative. When IBM sold its laptop-computer business to a Chinese firm, Duberstein could advise the new business on
how to resolve a big problem: the reluctance of U.S. government
agencies to buy sensitive computer equipment from what had suddenly become a foreign firm run out of a nation many saw as more
rival than ally.

In the process, Duberstein has developed especially close relationships with the companies he has served, to the point where he is regularly invited to join corporate boards of directors.

Duberstein's seeming ability to be involved in every important
event in the capital—sometimes on the fringes, sometimes in the
heart of the action—was perhaps best illustrated by the prolonged
saga of the leaking of the name of an undercover Central Intelligence
Agency official, Valerie Plame, to syndicated columnist Robert
Novak. As is often the case in Washington, Duberstein was a friend of
both the figures who would emerge as the central players in the
drama: Novak and former Deputy Secretary of State Richard Armitage. At one point, Novak wanted to talk with Armitage about Iraq.
He didn't know Armitage well, but he did know Duberstein well, having covered him in a variety of settings, including during Duberstein's time as White House chief of staff. And Duberstein, in turn,
knew Armitage well. Duberstein is close to former Secretary of State
Colin Powell, from their days together in the Reagan White House,

and Armitage served as Powell's right-hand man in the State Department.

So Duberstein helped put Novak in touch with Armitage for a conversation.[4] At the end of that conversation, the two men discussed the controversy over Joseph Wilson, a former U.S. ambassador who had undertaken a mission for the Bush administration to investigate reports that Iraq had tried to buy uranium yellowcake, a precursor for producing materials for a nuclear bomb, from the African country of Niger. If the reports were true, they constituted clear evidence of an active Iraqi program to produce weapons of mass destruction. The Bush administration, in fact, had used those reports as one of its justifications for invading Iraq. But Wilson was publicly charging that the Bush team had distorted the results of the mission he undertook to investigate the reports; he said he failed to find evidence to back up the charges. Wilson had begun publicly attacking the administration over the Niger matter, asserting, essentially, that his story showed that the Bush White House used flimsy and false pretenses to justify invading Iraq.

In discussing the matter, Armitage told Novak that Wilson's wife, Valerie Plame, was an official at the CIA, which may have explained why the agency chose Wilson to investigate Niger in the first place. Novak put that in his column, after confirming it with a second source. The CIA was incensed, asserting that the identity of Plame, who had served for years as an undercover agent, was still a classified secret, and that its revelation was a crime. That led the Justice Department to appoint Patrick Fitzgerald as a special investigator, and Fitzgerald spent more than two years tearing through the Bush administration, ostensibly in search of the leaker.

As it turned out, Armitage told Fitzgerald early on that he probably had been the original source of the leak.[5] Fitzgerald seemed to have decided that the unwitting slipping of Plame's identity hadn't been a premeditated act and didn't constitute a crime. He spent most of his time trying to find out whether others were involved or had tried to cover up their involvement, ultimately charging—and eventually convicting—only Vice President Cheney's chief of staff, I. Lewis "Scooter" Libby, with misleading investigators and the grand jury about his conversations with journalists.

As Duberstein's prominence illustrates, presence in Washington's inner circle begets opportunities that allow one to stay in Washington's inner circle. His role as a trustee of the Kennedy Center for the Performing Arts, the capital's premier venue for cultural events, for example, ensured that he would be invited by President Bush to a White House dinner one night in late 2005 to commemorate a Kennedy Center festival on Chinese culture.

Duberstein mingled at a reception in the White House foyer before the event with an A-list of capital celebrities. Chatting nearby were President Bush and Federal Reserve Chairman Alan Greenspan, along with Greenspan's wife, NBC News correspondent Andrea Mitchell. The two men were discussing golfer Tiger Woods's performance in a golf tournament that day, and the president was regaling the group with recollections of a conversation he had had with Woods about exercise routines. The first President Bush was moving about the crowd, greeting old friends, and radiating pleasure at being back in the White House. Chinese Ambassador Zhou Wenzhong was nearby, as were National Security Adviser Stephen Hadley and actress Bo Derek.

Duberstein took advantage of the opportunity to pull aside the current President Bush, who was sliding into his second-term political slump, and discuss steps the Reagan team had taken to revitalize that administration, which had been similarly troubled in its second term.

For Duberstein and others like him who came to prominence in the Reagan Revolution, the arrival of the second Bush term had been a happy turn of events. George W. Bush himself had made it clear that, in political terms, he modeled his tenure at 1600 Pennsylvania Avenue more on Reagan's than on his own father's. Duberstein isn't exceptionally close to the younger Bush; his ally Nancy Reagan had famously strained relations with the Bush family; and he works hard at being bipartisan. Still, continued Republican control of all the levers of political power, which came with Bush's re-election, was a comfortable state of affairs for all Republicans.

It was only natural, then, that all Republicans, certainly including Duberstein, became increasingly chagrined as the second President Bush went into a long and deep political slide soon after he entered his second term. The war in Iraq, where the civil strife moved steadily from troublesome to consuming, was the biggest reason, obviously. A related question was whether the Bush White House was aware of how deep its troubles were, and whether it knew how to respond.

In addition to his private chat with the president himself at the dinner marking the Chinese cultural festival, Duberstein found other ways to send flares up to the White House. He subsequently wrote an op-ed piece for *The New York Times*, discussing how the Reagan team had rescued that president from his similarly alarming second-term slide. One of the things Reagan did, Duberstein wrote, was to shake up his White House staff for his second term. The readership that really mattered for the piece was very small; it consisted of the president and a few of his closest friends and advisers. Duberstein's hope was that they would get the hint and act—and, indeed, he got calls from two assistants to the president and one assistant to Vice President Cheney after the piece ran, all wanting to talk about the advice it carried.

Privately, Duberstein would recount to friends how tricky it is to persuade presidents that they need to recognize when they are in trouble and to make uncomfortable changes to adapt. When Reagan was sliding in his second term, his wife had to choreograph a kind of show for him to persuade him to act. She arranged for two political graybeards to be called in to meet with the president. One was Stu Spencer, a political consultant with deep California roots and perhaps Reagan's most enduring political adviser, and the other was Democratic wise man Bob Strauss, the Ken Duberstein of his time. Nancy Reagan saw to it that she would be in attendance as well, to be sure the act played out according to script. They counseled a shake-up in the staff surrounding the president. The meeting led directly to the departure of then–White House Chief of Staff Donald Regan, the arrival of a new chief of staff, Howard Baker, and the choice of Duberstein to be deputy chief of staff, a position of new prominence.

In Reagan's case, the shake-up had worked wonders. His administration both turned over a new leaf in its second term and, perhaps as important amid the Iran-Contra scandal and a welter of other problems, was seen as having turned over a new leaf. The tone of the White House changed—it appeared less defensive and began reaching out to Congress more openly and aggressively.

That was more or less what Duberstein hoped President Bush would do once his problems set in. But whereas Reagan was thought to be stubborn and a believer in loyalty, it turned out that Bush trumped him on both counts. For a long period, Bush resolutely refused to take the hints that his troubles were deep and that a shake-up of his team might be needed to alter the dynamic of his second term. Republicans across Washington became increasingly concerned. Iraq was becoming a disaster. But more than that, there was a growing feeling that Bush was becoming insular.

The kinds of changes Duberstein was advocating ultimately came, but not immediately, and not because Bush set them in motion. The changes began when White House Chief of Staff Andrew Card initiated a changeover in the White House staff. Card walked into the Oval Office in early 2006 and told Bush he was ready to go.

That led to the elevation of Josh Bolten to become White House chief of staff, and a mini-shake-up of the Bush team. None of that was enough to stop Bush's steady political slide, which caused his job-approval ratings to slide into the 30-percent range and Republicans to lose both houses of Congress in the 2006 election—in significant measure because of unhappiness over the war in Iraq. The kind of second-term revival that a change in staff produced for Reagan wasn't so easy to spark in the wartime atmosphere of the Bush White House.

All of which turned Bush into a true lame duck, and led Washington's political actors to turn their attention to the 2008 campaign early and hard. Republican presidential contenders began courting Duberstein, and political observers began looking for signs of which way his support might go. At one point, *The Hill*, one of three newspapers that chronicle comings and goings in and around Congress, reported that McCain had been spotted holding "a one-on-one conversation with former White House chief of staff and Republican superlobbyist Ken Duberstein on a Capitol veranda."[6]

Yet Duberstein wasn't quick to pick a candidate to support, and chose to bide his time as the Republican scramble to replace Bush unfolded. He was better positioned than most for the uncertainty. Typically, Duberstein seemed to have some connection to every one of the top Republican candidates. He had been a friend of John McCain's for years. He shared a New York background with Rudy Giuliani. He had an Olympics connection with Mitt Romney: Romney managed the 2002 Salt Lake City Olympics, and Duberstein once served as head of the U.S. Olympic Committee's ethics committee. And he once worked in the Reagan White House with former Tennessee Senator Howard Baker, the political godfather of presidential contender and Tennessean Fred Thompson. Duberstein's Zelig-like nature—his ability to know just about everybody important and to be part of just about everything important—showed no sign of failing him as the Bush era was drawing to a close.

3. THE BUSINESSMAN: DAVID RUBENSTEIN

PRECISELY MIDWAY BETWEEN the Capitol and the White House along Pennsylvania Avenue stands a grand building that houses the office of a kind of Washington operator that didn't exist a generation ago. His name is David Rubenstein. He is an alumnus of Jimmy Carter's White House staff, and, like others up and down the Avenue, he is a deal-maker.

But the deals Rubenstein strikes now are economic rather than political. Though they involve hundreds of millions of dollars, the money comes from investors rather than taxpayers. As a result, in his own unobtrusive way, Rubenstein symbolizes a giant but little-appreciated change in Washington over the last generation: the arrival of really big money.

Rubenstein is a founder of the Carlyle Group, one of the world's biggest private-equity investment firms, meaning it pools large bundles of money from big investors—wealthy individuals, investment houses, pension funds—and uses the money to buy underperforming companies. Neither the Carlyle Group nor anything like it had existed in Washington until Rubenstein decided to create the firm in 1987. Yet now a world-class financial power center sits inside the gleaming office building at the corner of 10th Street and Pennsylvania Avenue.

Carlyle generally runs the companies it buys for a few years, until they turn around, and then sells them off, whole or in pieces, for a profit. The Carlyle Group manages more than $58.5 billion on behalf of more than a thousand high-dollar investors in sixty-one countries.[1] It's fair to say that virtually none of the Washingtonians scurrying by on Pennsylvania Avenue just below realize they are passing the office of a firm that owns, solely or jointly, Dunkin' Donuts, Hertz Rent A Car, Baskin-Robbins, and the world's largest car-wash company, along with a host of other firms and properties.

All this is happening just a few floors above the Avenue mostly because David Rubenstein, bored and unsatisfied as just another Washington lawyer, figured out how to build a financial machine in part by tapping the expertise and connections of both political parties. Rubenstein is a Baltimore native who grew up in a family of modest means, then went to Duke and the University of Chicago Law School. He practiced law for a prestigious New York firm for a couple of years, then came to Washington to become chief counsel to a Senate Judiciary subcommittee. The Senate at the time was firmly in the control of the Democrats, and he was introduced to the world of big-time Democratic politics. So, when Jimmy Carter won the White House in 1976, Rubenstein was asked to join his staff. He became the young White House aide who started earlier and stayed later than anyone else, and who mastered the flow of memos that are like blood coursing through the veins of a White House operation.

Like most Carter aides, he was out on the street after his boss lost the 1980 election, and, like most veterans of that administration, he wasn't exactly considered a hot property after Republicans took control of the White House and the Senate in 1981.

He took a job with a Washington law firm, but was restless. "I realized I wasn't a great lawyer," he says. "I didn't have the passion for it." Nor did he have much taste for the career path taken by many of his more gregarious colleagues in the Washington legal firmament, schmoozing their way through the lawyer-lobbyist world of the capital: "Ultimately, I didn't want to be part of the revolving door. I didn't want to be a lobbyist."

For a smart young man in his position, there weren't a lot of options. Washington's economy at the time was, to put it kindly, stunted. "Washington had one business, government, and one commercial enterprise, real-estate development," Rubenstein recalls. "No one came here to make money. . . . The only role models were lawyers and lobbyists and trade associations." But Rubenstein decided that making money might be a challenge he would enjoy, and he got the idea and inspiration he needed by reading about a Republican former Treasury secretary, William Simon, who ran an investment firm after leaving government. At one point, Simon bought a company called Gibson Greeting Cards, investing only $1 million of his firm's own money in the card company, then oversaw its turnaround and initial public stock offering and made $200 million in eighteen months.

Rubenstein found a couple of partners and opened his own merchant-banking company, taking the Carlyle name from a hotel in New York. His company would be in the business of finding companies that could be bought for a reasonable price, turned around, improved or broken up, and eventually sold for a profit. Immediately he confronted a basic difference between the cultures of New York and Washington. In New York, status has always been measured in dollars, which he lacked in any truly impressive way. "People in New York didn't take us seriously," Rubenstein says. In Washington, however, power is the currency that matters. So Rubenstein took early steps to gain credibility by accumulating power.

First, he found a building with an impressive address — 1001 Pennsylvania Avenue — and a grandiose lobby that, though part of a new office building, was designed to evoke visions of old money. Luckily, there was space available within the building; one floor had just been used as a set to film the movie *Broadcast News* and now was vacant. The Carlyle Group moved in. Rubenstein told the landlord he didn't want a lease giving him the right to expand, as is standard, because he figured the odds of expansion were slight.

Second, Rubenstein set out to capitalize on the Avenue's biggest asset: prominent politicians. They could offer Carlyle the early credibility the firm needed to build momentum. If the strategy worked, Carlyle could offer the kind of lavish compensation that so many successful politicians crave but cannot accumulate in long careers in public service.

So Rubenstein reached for names. His first big catch was Frank Carlucci, a former defense secretary for Reagan. There followed a who's who of leaders moving through the Carlyle office: former President George H. W. Bush, former Secretary of State James Baker, and former British Prime Minister John Major all affiliated with Carlyle. Carlucci helped identify some defense companies for Carlyle to buy, which helped establish its presence and created an aura that, because it was a Washington private-equity firm, it must know special secrets about how to buy and run companies involved in defense and government contracting. Bush, Baker, and Major opened some doors. Indeed, some of Carlyle's early deals were in buying and selling defense contractors.

In truth, though, the political titans were largely window dressing. They were hardly equipped, by training or inclination, to conduct the financial analysis of companies that was needed in order to discern which were worth acquiring, and at what price. But they helped Rubenstein find a handful of initial investors, including the Mellon family. He and his partners began to assemble a stable of finance experts and young MBA's to do the nitty-gritty work of private investing. By being both smart and conservative, Carlyle began providing an average return of 30 percent annually on its investors' money, in a business where the investment risks are, by definition, higher than average.

Now Carlyle has more than four hundred investment professionals on its payroll, and operates out of eighteen countries.[2] Rubenstein himself is worth, it's safe to estimate, several hundred million dollars. The company doesn't have to operate out of Washington but does because its principals like the city and the lifestyle.

Increasingly, Carlyle is emerging as a player on the city's landscape. That represents an evolution for the firm. For most of its existence, Carlyle has operated in the shadows of the capital, and Rubenstein himself was hardly a social animal. In fact, his name appeared in *The Washington Post,* as good a barometer as any of the Washington social and political scene, only twice in all of 2006.[3] Those who know him consider him to be personally reserved and a workaholic of almost mythic proportions. He has reported to acquaintances that he sleeps just four to four and a half hours a night, and he works sixteen-hour days, a habit that has remained consistent since his time on the White House staff.[4] He often does Carlyle business on weekends.

Christopher Ullman, a Carlyle aide who handles public affairs, recalls once sending an e-mail to Rubenstein while Rubenstein was at a Super Bowl game, and getting back a response in five minutes. With his enormous wealth, Rubenstein has bought a beautiful house in Colorado ski country, at Beaver Creek. His wife and children like to ski — but Rubenstein never does. He's more likely to be found working in the office of his Colorado house, say those who have visited there. One acquaintance remembers calling him in Colorado and asking how the conditions were on the slopes. "I hear they are fine," Rubenstein replied dryly.

To be sure, the company was eventually taken seriously in financial circles in New York, and, to downplay its image as a firm that merely specialized in buying government contractors, Carlyle went through a period in recent years of soft-pedaling its Washngton connections. It shied away from partisan affiliations; "I describe myself more as a capitalist than as an active Democrat or Republican," Rubenstein says. It formed no political-action committee to contribute to campaigns, and Rubenstein himself eschewed personal campaign contributions.

But some connection between the worlds of private equity and government is inevitable. For one thing, some 60 to 70 percent of all private-equity funding comes from state pension funds. For his part, Rubenstein has come to think Carlyle may have gone too far in downplaying its Washington ties. Like most companies, the firms that Carlyle buys increasingly have issues with the government, or a desire for government help in the global economy. By not taking advantage of its Washington locale, Rubenstein has come to feel, Carlyle may be depriving its companies of a natural asset. So, by mid-2007, he was pondering hiring an associate to handle government relations for the firm and its companies.

For a long while, Rubenstein's workaholic hours and obsession with his business made him nearly invisible in the Washington celebrity world. While some billionaires and would-be billionaires in New York have made attracting attention into an art form, Rubenstein's inclination was the opposite: to avoid publicity that might make it appear in the world of finance that the upstarts from Washington were more sizzle than steak.

As an extension of that view, he avoided using his money to make a splash by supporting philanthropic enterprises that would have brought him both attention and the admiration of the Washington social circuit. "In the beginning, when Carlyle really started to make money, David wouldn't support anything," one friend recalls. "David used to say, 'Once you start getting into this, you'll never stop. If you do one, you have to do the other.' " Then, a few years ago, that began to change. "It is my sense," the friend recalls, "that at some point David decided that he had made enough and wanted to now start to reach out and branch out in different ways."

Slowly, step by step, Rubenstein is emerging as a figure in the capital's social scene. He has, among other things, become a significant supporter of Washington cultural institutions. He sits on the boards of the Kennedy Center for the Performing Arts, the Smithsonian Institution's National Museum of American History, and Ford's Theatre. (In another sign of how the worlds of Washington and money are growing more intertwined, the chairman of the Kennedy Center board of trustees is another private-equity pioneer, Stephen Schwarzman, the co-founder and chief executive of the Blackstone Group of New York.) Rubenstein has also branched out to become a player in the think-tank world, serving on the boards of the Center for Strategic and International Studies, the Institute for International Economics, and Freedom House, all significant participants in Washington intellectual debates on international policy.[5]

Taken together, the combination of money, social power, and intellectual influence is turning Rubenstein into a significant figure in the Washington firmament. What he intends to do with his new kind of capital clout is hard to know.

On the one hand, he muses as he talks about the future that he may want to back away from his Carlyle Group work and use his fortune to become a philanthropist of the Bill Gates variety, perhaps using his money as seed capital for good works just as private-equity investors use capital to enter new business arenas. "I hope to give it all away before I die," he says.

On the other hand, he also has told associates that he may be serving on too many boards, which pull him away from company business, and will cut back to reduce the distractions. In fact, a mess in credit markets caused by the bursting of the national housing bubble pulled Rubenstein back into core business problems in a rude way in early 2008. He was compelled to rush back to Washington from an investment conference in Utah to oversee the near-collapse of a Carlyle Group offshoot known as Carlyle Capital Corporation, which owned a portfolio of mortgage-backed securities that were falling in value rapidly. The problems in the capital group, only partly owned by Carlyle Group executives, represented a public-relations black eye for Rubenstein and Carlyle Group, but not any immediate threat to the larger enterprise.

In either case, simply by putting the Carlyle Group in place on Pennsylvania Avenue, Rubenstein has subtly changed Washington. "A lot of people who may have come from other cities and had finance skills, or never had financial skills and would like to get them, now can say, 'Aha, I don't have to be a lobbyist, I don't have to be a lawyer, I don't have to sell access. I can be in the financial world and live in Washington, D.C.' "

There has also been a political impact. The capital city traditionally had been, by and large, ignorant and mistrustful of what the big-money managers in New York do. In one sign of just how much

Pennsylvania Avenue can affect Wall Street if it chooses to do so, the two top tax-writers in the Senate, Democrat Max Baucus of Montana and Republican Charles Grassley of Iowa, moved in the summer of 2007 to raise the tax rate on private-equity firms that become publicly traded companies. The move was at least in part a populist reaction to stories reporting that Schwarzman, the Blackstone Group's leader, could make as much as $677 million initially and then see his personal stake in Blackstone soar in value to $7.5 billion, by selling stock in his firm to the public.[6] In an indication that the private-equity industry recognizes that its world will inevitably be affected by Washington, the leading private-equity firms put aside their normally intense competition with one another to form something called the Private Equity Council, a lobbying organization to represent the industry's interests in Washington.[7]

But there's little doubt that the presence of the Carlyle Group, literally in the center of the nation's capital, has tempered the political view of big money in general, and private-equity firms in particular. In recent years, for example, some consumer advocates have called for more government regulation of the private-equity business and hedge funds. And some liberals in Congress have beaten the drums for exactly that. Yet Congress has resisted the urge to regulate.

Is that coincidental? Maybe. More likely, the presence of Carlyle — led by, of all things, a onetime Democratic White House aide — just down Pennsylvania Avenue from the Capitol, has lessened Washington's tendency to demonize big money, and colored the course of government-business relations.

"What we have done by showing people how we make this kind of money, in terms of buying companies and improving them, has probably given people on Capitol Hill and maybe in the administration the sense that, yes, what Wall Street people do isn't so foreign to them after all," Rubenstein says. "It may be the case that people understand a little bit more about what we do than would have been the case had we been in New York. Maybe there's a better understanding of what Wall Street culture is."

II. WORKING THE SYSTEM

THE WATERGATE SCANDAL, which foreshortened Richard Nixon's presidency, taught many lessons about power on Pennsylvania Avenue and its abuses. Among the most enduring was the phrase written for dramatic effect for the movie version of *All the President's Men*, the book by *Washington Post* reporters Bob Woodward and Carl Bernstein: "Follow the money."

That advice remains crucial to understanding how things function on Pennsylvania Avenue. Those who work the system know that a lot of forces are in play every day, but money is always one of them. How much money is needed to gain power? How much to keep power? And who will make money once control of power is decided? The only change from the Watergate era is that the sums involved have grown so large it's sometimes hard to see over them.

At heart, the business of Washington is dividing the federal pie in all of its forms: taxing, spending, contracting, regulating. Even in periods of ostensible retrenchment, that business has grown. Since 1990, scholar Paul Light has estimated, direct and indirect federal-government employment has swelled to 14.6 million from 12.6 million.[1]

New Economy businesses, like high technology, have increasingly concluded what old-line industries such as autos and oil had long known: Decisions made on the Avenue can help or hurt—a lot. So they in turn have fueled the growth of Washington's lobbying industry to the benefit of legions of former lawmakers, aides, and executive-branch employees.

With the emergence of the global economy, multinational corporations have concluded the same thing. Whether their headquarters are in Detroit or Düsseldorf, they sooner or later have business to conduct in Washington, where rules of international commerce are written. Wayne Berman, one of the most prominent lobbyists on the Avenue, says corporations now consider having a presence in Washington simply another form of "risk management."

Japan-based Shinsei Bank once hired Berman's firm to lobby U.S. officials to press their Japanese counterparts to permit the purchase of the bank by American investors. Motorola Corporation hired him to help persuade the government of Russia to release a large shipment of cellular telephones that it had seized on dubious "safety" grounds. The giant oil firm Chevron Corporation, which is based in the United States but operates in more than sixty countries, hired Berman for assistance in its bid to acquire California-based Unocal—and to stop the rival Chinese oil firm CNOOC from besting its bid. Berman's efforts, which pitted him against an army of Washington lobbyists for CNOOC, succeeded.

All this has made the Avenue conspicuously richer. As Richard Nixon's presidency began in 1969, the Washington metropolitan area ranked twelfth in the nation in per-capita income. By 2004, it ranked fourth.[2]

Glossy magazines, heavy with photos of charity events and ads for upscale goods and real estate, now cater to the Avenue's growing taste for power and celebrity. One of them, *Capitol File*, boasts that 99 percent of its readers earn more than $200,000 annually; 78 percent have a net worth exceeding $1 million; 70 percent own luxury cars.[3]

Even more telling, 54 percent of *Capitol File* readers make political contributions. As the stakes of decisions made in Washington have risen, so has the cost of winning office on the Avenue. The campaign fund-raiser has become the Avenue's tollbooth. And the traffic never stops—or even slows.

In a real sense, the money chase has become the central organizing principle of life along the Avenue. It shapes the capital's workday.

Each party designs political agendas that take aim at the other side's benefactors. Republicans try to constrain the activities of the trial lawyers and labor unions who underwrite the Democratic Party by curbing the flow of damage awards and worker dues; Democrats, in turn, try to blunt the profits of the oil, tobacco, and pharmaceutical companies that finance the Republican Party.

And that in turn fuels the capital's nightlife. In tony restaurants and hotel ballrooms, it revolves around fund-raisers at which those whose interests are threatened, and their lobbyists, ante up in search of protection or reward.

For lawmakers, the chase for money is simply an accepted part of getting into and staying in office. So Democratic lawmakers weren't surprised in March 2007, just four months after midterm elections swept them into power, to be told by their party's leaders exactly how much money they would be expected to raise to finance the *next* campaign, in 2008.

The word came down in this memo:

TO: House Democratic Caucus

FROM: Member Participation Task Force

APPROVED BY: House Democratic Leadership

DATE: March 9, 2007

RE: 2007–2008 Member Participation Program

CAUCUS REPORT IN THE MAJORITY

In order to change the direction of the country, we must build on the momentum of the last election. This will require the active participation of every Member of our caucus in the DCCC 2008 election effort. As a result of our historic success last November, we have many more Members in challenging districts. Additionally, we are aggressively on offense and working to put a large number of Republican seats in play. The new Member Participation Program is critical to this mission.

The Member Participation Task Force has reviewed and discussed our Member Participation program taking into account our new majority. After extensive discussions, a consensus was reached on how Members should participate in maintaining and growing our majority. Together, with approval from Leadership, we are proposing the following for the 2007–2008 Member Participation program.

MEMBER DUES

Members' dues obligation will increase from last cycle. Dues obligations are based on factors including leadership positions and committee assignments. Members' dues reflect the ability to raise money as a Member of the majority and the new challenges we face in protecting our majority even as we seek to expand the playing field.

Members' dues constitute $\frac{1}{3}$ of the overall DCCC budget and are critical to our efforts to sustain and expand our majority. Members will continue to receive quarterly invoices asking them to pay their dues in order to help Members plan their own fundraising and, in turn, their contributions.

MEMBER RAISING FOR THE DCCC

In addition to paying dues, we are asking Members to raise money directly for the DCCC. Like dues, the amounts to be raised for the DCCC by each Member are based on a variety of factors. Members will be asked to fulfill this responsibility during the 2007–2008 cycle. For example, those who are assigned a $75,000 raising responsibility will have the 2 year cycle to complete this raising component. If a Member chooses not to raise his or her share for the DCCC, he or she may make up the difference by making additional dues payments.

The DCCC will partner with the Members and provide them with the necessary resources in order to ensure the success of this new obligation. DCCC regional fundraising staff will work directly with Members and their staff to assist in all aspects of fundraising directly for the Committee.

Members may raise money for the DCCC in a variety of ways including:

- Host an event in their district or in Washington, DC for the DCCC
- Call time to targeted donors
- E-mail solicitation
- Mail solicitation
- One-on-one meetings with targeted donors

DCCC staff will help you with the following:

- Research targeted donors
- Create call sheets
- Set up meetings
- Schedule events
- Assist in securing surrogates
- Draft solicitations
- Conduct all follow up on events, calls and pledges

PAC and individual contributions will be credited to a single Member. A Member will receive credit for a contribution he or she delivers or if a check comes to the DCCC with a letter of credit from the contributor. Credit allocation must be made when the contribution is received. The DCCC will no longer "back credit" contributions out of fairness to others.

When a Member hosts an event to benefit the DCCC that includes another Member as the special guest, those Members should decide how to apportion credit among themselves for the funds raised.

MEMBER PARTICIPATION

We also recommend implementing a point system to ensure that Members who travel and host events on behalf of Frontline Members and "Red to Blue" candidates are appropriately credited. The Task Force will work with the DCCC to develop a point system to properly acknowledge those efforts.

To successfully sustain and expand our majority, we are counting on your continued support. Thank You

---

Such instructions now are routine for both parties. On an Excel spreadsheet, the Democratic Congressional Campaign Committee listed precise individual fund-raising targets, calibrated to each member's power and hence to his or her ability to extract checks from special interests.

The minimum ante, applicable even to those representing the poorest rural or inner-city districts, was $200,000. Members of powerful "exclusive" committees, such as Charles Rangel of the tax-writing Ways and Means Committee, were directed to raise $1.5 million. House Majority Leader Steny Hoyer's tab was $3.3 million; Democratic Congressional Campaign Committee Chair Chris Van Hollen's: $10.4 million. House Speaker Nancy Pelosi was asked to raise $25.8 million. For the entire two years from Election 2006 to Election 2008, that worked out to $35,342 every day. By mid-2007, she was well on her way to achieving that goal.

Like Muzak in an elevator, the effort required to raise those sums represents the background noise along the Avenue. Still, it's only the starting point. Against the money backdrop, Washington's savviest operators move out to battle one another for political advantage, knowing that the costs and stakes are large. What follows are the stories of a few of the most intriguing people who work the system.

4. THE DEMOCRATIC STRATEGIST: RAHM EMANUEL

It was the last Friday in September 2006, and Rahm Emanuel was tired. He is a member of Congress representing his native Chicago and, of more immediate importance, had months earlier been put in charge of the Democratic Party's crusade to take back control of the House of Representatives. The battle was sufficiently intense to drain the energy from even this youthful politician fit enough to compete in triathlons.

Late on that Friday afternoon, Emanuel sat behind a small desk inside his small corner office at Democratic Party Headquarters, a short walk from the southern exit of the Capitol, his face drawn, eyelids drooping, and voice weary. He rarely slept through the night anymore, instead waking frequently, with his mind racing, trying to calculate his next moves to counter White House political maestro Karl Rove and other Republican strategists intent on preserving the GOP's grip on Pennsylvania Avenue. He had raised more money, by far, than any Democrat who had held his job before, and was about to take out a loan for millions more, for the party, to get to the finish line.

But this afternoon brought news that shocked Emanuel with its potential for suddenly altering the election's outcome. The news flashed across cable-television broadcasts and, soon afterward, the BlackBerry devices that had become ubiquitous on Capitol Hill. Representative Mark Foley, the gregarious and talented Republican who represented Palm Beach County, Florida, in the House, had abruptly resigned.

Washington gossip had long since pegged Foley as a closeted gay;

his sexual orientation was the sotto voce explanation for his refusal a year earlier to run for the U.S. Senate, when all outward appearances signaled that he was the strongest GOP candidate. Now ABC News had disclosed on its website that he had sent a series of lewd computer messages to an underage male former House page.

Thus, the country was learning that a Republican House member had made sexual advances to underage boys under the care of the House of Representatives—a House controlled by the party that had exploited issues of "moral values" to maximum advantage. Worse for the GOP, it became clear that members of the Republican leadership had an inkling of what was going on and had done little about it.

No one quite knew how sordid the scandal would become as Emanuel sat at his desk late that Friday afternoon. But Emanuel did know that, in a House campaign with few genuine takeover targets, he suddenly had a prime new opportunity in Florida's Palm Beach County. To oppose Foley, he had earlier recruited a respectable candidate, a wealthy and energetic former high-tech executive named Tim Mahoney, who was thought to have little expectation of unseating a Republican incumbent who routinely garnered 60 percent of the vote.

At the instant Foley resigned, though, Mahoney's long-shot campaign leapt to the top of Democratic priority lists. As a small television to Emanuel's right carried CNN's nonstop coverage of the unfolding scandal, aides darted in and out of his office with direct intelligence. Emanuel took a phone call from Representative Debbie Wasserman Schultz, a rising star among Florida Democrats who had taken on the task of determining how frantic Republicans in her home state would choose a replacement for Foley. "Who do you think they'll go with?" Emanuel asked, phone cradled between his ear and shoulder. "What's your assessment? . . . Well, get ready."

Emanuel had instructions for Wasserman Schultz as well—on how to start a fresh, rapid stream of donations into Mahoney's campaign. Collecting campaign donations on the House floor violates House rules; but distributing cards with information on where money can be sent does not. "No, it's not unseemly," Emanuel told her. Another call came in from a party lawyer, explaining how Florida election laws would work. In a good turn for Democrats, it was too late for Republicans to take Foley's name off the ballot. In a not-so-good turn, any votes cast for Foley would go automatically to whatever candidate Republicans chose to take his place.

Sarah Feinberg, Emanuel's communications chief, walked in with a slip of paper listing two Florida Republicans who seemed most likely to take Foley's place in the race. The rumor in Florida was that both had gotten recruiting calls from the Bush White House. "I need background information ASAP, OK?" Emanuel barked out. Feinberg was back out the door and on the case seconds later.

Even in the Friday-afternoon chaos, other business didn't stop. Emanuel received a call from another candidate he had recruited: Joe Sestak, a former military aide and colleague at the White House who was seeking a House seat from Pennsylvania. Emanuel greeted Sestak with a friendly hello, and promptly shifted into campaign-chief mode. He told Sestak that he was dispatching former Clinton White House Press Secretary Joe Lockhart and Communications Director Joel Johnson to advise Sestak on his forthcoming debate with Republican Representative Curt Weldon—another scandal-weakened incumbent Emanuel could see falling behind.

"I'm sending them down to help prepare you for this debate," Emanuel declared. "I want you to want them, and I want you to listen to them." He warned the retired three-star admiral of fierce impending attacks. "They're going to open up the hood on you," Emanuel declared. But he reassured the political novice that he could survive, because "you're comfortable as a former military man."

Suddenly the potential for Democratic victory was beginning to appear far stronger than either the White House or top Democrats could have imagined at the outset of the two-year election cycle. Democrats had a trifecta of powerful issues going their way: unhappiness over Iraq, high gas prices, and corruption among Republican lawmakers. The Foley scandal was rapidly shining a bright spotlight on that last GOP vulnerability. Yet Emanuel aimed to stay cautious. Democrats needed to gain fifteen new seats to win back control of the House. That afternoon, he confided, the range of projected outcomes lay between eleven and seventeen seats.

By the time votes were counted six weeks later, that wave carrying Democratic prospects had grown bigger than Emanuel could have dreamed. He led his party to a gain of thirty-one seats—without losing a single one that Democrats already held. The importance of the Foley episode was borne out; White House strategists later concluded that their Republican Party lost a full ten seats because their members were tainted by scandals and corruption. More startling to the political establishment, Democrats defied pre-election predictions and captured six new seats in the Senate. That was precisely the number they needed to gain control of that chamber, too.

In many ways, Emanuel was bred for the job of leading Democrats back to power, for he has a fierce competitive streak. The son of an Israeli immigrant, he danced ballet as a youth and also lost part of his right middle finger after slicing it with a meat cutter in high school. He worked in Chicago politics for the second-generation Mayor Daley, then briefly volunteered to help in the Israeli Army during the first Persian Gulf War.

After the war was over, he joined then-Governor Bill Clinton's 1992 presidential campaign, which fought to pick what many electoral strategists believed was a Republican "lock" on the White House. Inside the Clinton operation, he offended some colleagues with his intensity but impressed them by creating a state-of-the-art fund-raising machine. Soon after leaving the White House in 1998, he amassed a New Economy fortune. Entering investment banking with former Clinton donors, Emanuel left just a few years later having made more than $16 million.[1] Those riches freed him to pursue an open Chicago House seat in 2002 and indulge his love for political combat.

He won his race for a seat in Congress, and within two years he had a seat on the Ways and Means Committee—the cockpit from which all tax legislation is directed, and hence the focus of action for financial interests of all varieties.

More important, he was made chairman of the Democratic Congressional Campaign Committee, the party organization in charge of winning House elections. With uncommon energy and zeal, he began vacuuming political contributions that would eventually reach a record $125 million—fully 50 percent more than the same committee had raised two years earlier.[2] When funds seemed insufficient in the campaign's homestretch, he borrowed another $11.5 million.

He recruited scores of new candidates to run for the House, many of them new kinds of Democrats, who broke the familiar mold. They included veterans and business executives and social conservatives, all selected individually to match the proclivities of the districts produced by the nation's technocratic new political class.

One of those new-wave Democratic candidates was Heath Shuler, who once explained his childhood religious practices by telling an audience in Asheville, North Carolina, "When the church door opened, I was there with my grandmother." The surrounding Smoky Mountains had stopped being friendly territory for Democratic politicians. But Shuler's Baptist faith and opposition to abortion were just part of his extraordinary package of attributes that allowed him to thrive as a Democrat in a conservative state.

Shuler had long ago gained fame as a teenage star in the South's secular Saturday religion—football. He starred as quarterback for Swain County High School in Bryson City, North Carolina, and at the University of Tennessee; in 1994, the year Republicans won control of Congress, he was the top draft pick of the National Football League's Washington Redskins. After football, as he made a career in the real-estate business, his partisan affiliation remained fuzzy enough that Republicans also recruited him to run for Congress.

But Emanuel recruited Shuler to run as a Democrat, and his recruiting style was at least as relentless as that of the University of Tennessee coach, Philip Fulmer, when he lured Shuler to play for the Volunteers. Shuler initially demurred, fearing political life might require too much time away from his two young children. Emanuel argued back fiercely—by example, and via the cellphone that is ever at his side. Himself a father of three who returned to Chicago nearly every weekend, Emanuel began peppering Shuler with cellphone calls to prove that politicians need not abandon parenthood: "Heath, I'm at my daughter's swim meet now"; "Heath, I'm taking my son to a birthday party. . . ." It worked. Shuler entered the race against an eight-term Republican incumbent. Angry at being spurned, the GOP's campaign committee vowed to "destroy Heath Shuler." But by early fall, Shuler was leading, and he went on to win.

Abrasive and cocksure, Emanuel sometimes despaired over the competence and political reflexes of prominent colleagues. He feared that House Minority Leader Nancy Pelosi, a liberal from San Francisco, would be unable to resist pressures from the Democratic left that would undercut the party's national appeal. He fought privately and publicly with the Democratic National Committee chairman, Howard Dean, who sat in an office just above Emanuel's at DNC Headquarters, over how to spend their party's money. In Emanuel's view, Dean was wasting millions by spreading money to conservative bastions such as Utah and Idaho, where Democrats had little hope of winning, all because Dean had won support among DNC members by pledging to invest in every one of their states in pursuit of long-term competitiveness. Emanuel's idea of "long-term" extended only through Election Day—and he wanted all ammunition directed at the political targets Democrats could realistically hit in 2006.

To maximize resources, Emanuel changed the structure of the Democratic campaign. He broke down the traditional central campaign command into smaller guerrilla units. Each unit had one pollster, one media consultant, and one expert in using direct mail to boost candidates. Every unit was assigned a handful of key races to oversee, a subset of the fifty or so around the country that Emanuel

considered the best opportunities to unseat Republicans running for
re-election. "He didn't want some race to fall off the map, or to lose a
race by a point or two" because somebody in Washington wasn't paying attention, explained Feinberg, his communications aide.

In the end, Democrats scooped up almost all the seats that the outside analysts thought they had a shot at winning, and picked up a few
more surprise victories as well. In historical terms, the Democrats'
advance on the southeast corner of Pennsylvania Avenue wasn't particularly large. It didn't approach the sweep of the 1994 Gingrich
revolution, in which Republicans smashed Democratic control by
gaining fifty-four new seats. Nor did the Democratic margin of victory
in the races that mattered most suggest a vast realignment of the electorate. In the two elections that tipped the Senate into Democratic
control, Democratic challengers Jon Tester in Montana and James
Webb in Virginia defeated Republican incumbents Conrad Burns
and George Allen by a combined total of about thirteen thousand
votes.[3] That was the thin thread by which Democrats held control of
Congress. The election hadn't put Democrats in power so much as it
had splintered power.

But in the closely divided politics of contemporary Pennsylvania
Avenue, that still constituted "a thumpin'," as a chastened President
Bush described it the afternoon following the election. As a result of
the Democrats' triumph, the horizons that stretched so broadly in
front of the president as he began his second term had become dra-
matically constrained. The Republican dream of an enduring majority that might stretch on for a generation—in Congress, and among
American voters at large—was gone.

The voters' verdict produced one sharp and immediate change:
That same day, Bush announced the departure of Defense Secretary
Donald Rumsfeld, the man who had attracted the anger of so many
lawmakers in both parties for his management of the Iraq war. Bush
pledged to pursue another, broader change, in the bitterly polarized
environment that had come to define life on Pennsylvania Avenue.
"The message yesterday was clear," he declared from the Avenue's

most famous address. "The American people want their leaders in Washington to set aside partisan differences, conduct ourselves in an ethical manner, and work together to address the challenges facing our nation."

That raised at least two questions. One was whether Bush and his Democratic adversaries genuinely desired to work cooperatively, after so many earlier failures. The second was whether the partisan divisions on Pennsylvania Avenue—now deeply etched by powerful new ideological, financial, and technological forces—would even permit them to do so.

Iraq would prove to be the issue that ended any thoughts that the election of 2006 would produce some bipartisan nirvana on Pennsylvania Avenue. Iraq would also show exactly what Emanuel's victory in the race for the House had and hadn't done for the Democrats. It didn't allow the Democrats simply to take the initiative, or to take control of Washington's agenda, away from Bush. Particularly on a foreign-policy issue, the president simply has too much authority and control for even a determined congressional majority to roll over him. And on Iraq, President Bush was determined to use every bit of control and authority at his disposal to keep American troops on the ground and fighting at full strength against the insurgents who were making Baghdad and much of the country a shooting gallery.

But what Iraq showed is that a congressional majority can slowly and methodically grind down a president's power if it is determined and patient.

That process began within the first few months of Democratic control, and it started when Senate Democrats tried, and failed, to pass a resolution expressing disagreement with President Bush's strategy in Iraq, specifically with his decision to send a "surge" of additional U.S. troops there. Under the Senate's rules, Republicans could and did use the chamber's sometimes obtuse rules to extend debate, clog up the works, and stop a vote on such a resolution.

That kicked the action to the House, where simpler rules make it simpler for a determined majority to move. Emanuel, in his typical bulldog style, began pushing for the House to step in on Iraq, and in the most damaging way possible for the Bush White House.

He operated in large measure from his hideaway office on the Capitol's ground floor. Like all House leaders, Emanuel has both a public office in one of the mammoth office buildings across the street from the Capitol and an unpublicized hideaway, down one of the Capitol's labyrinthine corridors and stuck in one of its countless nooks and crannies. Emanuel's private office happens to be the one previously occupied by another gregarious Chicago politician, Dan Rostenkowski. It has exactly one window, but that window affords a spectacular view of the National Mall, framing, as if in a painting, the Washington Monument and, in the distance and slightly off to the side, the Lincoln Memorial.

Emanuel's desk in his hideaway office sits directly in front of that window and allows the congressman to take in the breathtaking view while he is on the telephone—which is where he is more or less non-stop. When the Senate ground to a halt on Iraq, Emanuel was on that phone instantly, pushing his idea of how the House should go on the record on the war.

The approach Emanuel was pushing was disarmingly simple but intentionally blunt. He wanted a stripped-down resolution that didn't offer alternatives or critiques but simply said: "Congress disapproves of the decision of President George W. Bush . . . to deploy more than 20,000 additional combat troops to Iraq."[4] His belief was that if he could get something close to three hundred members of the House— the people's House—to vote for such a simple and direct statement opposing Bush on the war, the impact would be enormous in the country at large, to say nothing of in the Senate.

Emanuel had originally been content to let the Senate go first, be-cause it seemed at the outset that some prominent Republicans there were going to vote with Democrats in opposing Bush on the war. "We wanted them to go because it was so clear from the beginning that there was a bipartisan move there," he said. It appeared the Senate wouldn't be as tough on Bush as the House would be, but it would make a bipartisan statement of concern about the war, and Emanuel was happy to let that set the tone. But now the Senate had failed, and Emanuel began the tedious task of nudging all the House's various Democratic factions behind a common approach. His task was to get people to put aside other ideas on how to make a war statement— resolutions that would be more nuanced, or that would lay out alternative strategies or complicated formulas for sending new troops—and unite behind the simple approach.

Toward that end, Emanuel made strategic calls to leaders of the ideological factions among House Democrats. To pull the party's liberal wing behind him, he called Representative Howard Berman of California. To get the House's Southern pro-military members in his camp, he called Representative Allen Boyd of Florida, a Vietnam veteran whose district is chock-full of retired veterans. To get the party's moderates, he called Representative Ellen Tauscher of California, a leader of the House centrists, who is influential with the "Blue Dogs," the loose association of more conservative House Democrats.

When all that was done, he had secured commitments from each faction to unite behind the approach he preferred. And at that point, he called Speaker Nancy Pelosi to tell her exactly that. The stage was set for a week-long House debate on a statement of simple, direct, unmistakable opposition to the Bush Iraq strategy. In the House, unlike in the Senate, a minority can't block a vote; there is no need for a supermajority to call for an end to debate. Instead, House leaders can simply force a vote. And that's precisely what Pelosi, Emanuel, and the other Democratic leaders did at the end of the week allotted for Iraq debate. The Democratic resolution opposing the troop surge passed, 246 to 182.

It was a largely partisan vote, and set the tone for the Iraq debate, and even more strictly partisan votes, that would unfold throughout the rest of the year. Later, the House would pass an amendment calling explicitly for troops to be withdrawn from Iraq; Democrats passed the amendment with a mere four Republicans going along. Meanwhile, the Senate never managed to pass a resolution expressing its disapproval of the troop surge in Iraq, but instead began attaching provisions calling for troop reductions to bills funding the Defense Department. President Bush vetoed the first of those bills, so his hand wasn't forced, but his support was eroding. By guiding Democrats back into control of the House, Rahm Emanuel—the boy-wonder politico with the cellphone that never stops—had set off tremors that spread not only up and down Pennsylvania Avenue, but across the globe to the Middle East as well.

5. THE PARTY CAPTAINS FOR 2008: CHRIS VAN HOLLEN AND TOM COLE

FROM THE TONE of daily combat along the Avenue, one could imagine the leaders of each side's congressional-election army as figures out of a World Wrestling Entertainment broadcast—blustering furiously, hurling chairs, leaping into one body slam after another.

One could surely not imagine those leaders as soft-spoken, cerebral figures such as Chris Van Hollen and Tom Cole. Yet both are highly effective political combatants charged with leading their parties' fight for control of the House in the 2008 election.

Van Hollen, the congressman from Maryland who succeeded Emanuel as chairman of the Democratic Congressional Campaign Committee, is the son of Foreign Service officers. He was raised at diplomatic embassy outposts around the world, and later in the good-government suburbs of Washington, which are filled with federal workers and steeped in policy debates.

Cole, the congressman from Oklahoma who chairs the rival National Republican Congressional Committee, is a member of the Chickasaw Indian nation. He's a student of history who holds a master's degree from Yale and a doctorate from the University of Oklahoma.

But their skills and ambition, however improbably, place them atop the forces battling for power for the post-Bush era. If neither seems bred to the media spotlight, each has won the confidence of his party for handling the unseen inside work of the Avenue that counts most on Election Day. For both, the margin between victory and defeat would be narrow. In 2006, Democrats won control of the House by gaining thirty-one seats. By gaining just sixteen seats in 2008, Republicans could return to power.

When Chris Van Hollen started in politics, it wasn't even as a Democrat. He served as a Senate Foreign Relations Committee staffer for Charles "Mac" Mathias, the sort of moderate Republican that his home state of Maryland then elected. When Van Hollen later won office in his own right, as a Democratic state legislator, he earned a reputation as a policy maven who could patch together political deals like a skilled repairman. His nickname in Annapolis: "Mr. Fix-it."[1]

Still, moving to Pennsylvania Avenue wasn't easy for Chris Van Hollen. In his 2002 campaign for Congress, Van Hollen was largely in sync with his opponent, incumbent Representative Connie Morella, one of the dwindling number of moderate Republicans left in the House; among other things, she was a Republican who favored abortion rights. His campaign argument centered on the fact that other House Republicans were out of step with her and her constituents in the moderate suburbs of Montgomery County, and therefore, re-electing her, Montgomery County voters would be keeping the conservative Republican majority in power. Morella argued that she could accomplish more with Republicans in charge than a Democrat could. But the argument worked well enough for Van Hollen; he defeated Morella narrowly, even though the Democrats weren't able to dislodge Republicans from control of the House.

Van Hollen showed some of the same legislative acumen on Capitol Hill that he had displayed in Annapolis. His greatest triumph came on the floor debate over an appropriations bill, a rare opportunity for members to offer amendments that need not be cleared by the Rules Committee. Alarmed over the Bush administration's increasing reliance on federal contractors—which reduced the number of jobs available to federal workers in Van Hollen's district—he offered an amendment designed to limit the administration's freedom to use such contractors. Because no proposal could pass without bipartisan support, Van Hollen cultivated Republicans whose districts included big contingents of government workers.

The outcome was remarkable: Van Hollen drew enough support from majority Republicans as well as Democrats to pass his amendment over the opposition of both the White House and House Republican leaders. It died in the Senate, but Van Hollen was emboldened enough to try again in 2004. Notwithstanding the pressures of a presidential-election year, the amendment this time became law. Some two dozen Republican lawmakers voted for it, withstanding lobbying by Republican leaders; the bill went to Bush's desk.

On a separate track, however, Van Hollen set out after partisan goals. Democrats considered his 2002 victory over Morella a model for unseating entrenched Republicans in suburban districts, so they tapped him to recruit suburban Democratic candidates for the 2004 elections. Democrats lost ground in the House that year, as Bush won re-election to a second term. But Van Hollen entered the 2006 midterm campaign as one of Rahm Emanuel's top deputies in the quest to knock off enough vulnerable Republicans to restore Democratic control. He worked on the formulation of the election-year agenda Democrats drew up to catch the voters' attention: "Six for '06," a list of legislative priorities they pledged to enact. The list included raising the minimum wage, enacting ethics reform, passing a package of security recommendations from the 9/11 Commission, reforming pension laws, cutting college loan costs, and enhancing support for alternative fuels.

Embedded in his partisan tasks, of course, was conflict with his legislative work. Van Hollen was actively seeking the defeat of some of the same moderate Republicans who had sided with him on his contracting amendment. He found that a price worth paying. "If we're committed to making progress on the big issues, we need as many people on the team who support that agenda as possible," he says.

Three of his Republican allies on the contracting amendment were defeated; others remained in the DCCC's crosshairs once Van Hollen succeeded Emanuel as chairman of the committee.

It's nothing personal. After four years in office, Van Hollen had still never had a colleague over for dinner. With three young children, he has little time, and most other members are regularly traveling back to their districts when they aren't working. One of his casual friends is Representative Tom Davis of Virginia. When Davis headed the National Republican Congressional Committee in 2002, he had worked unsuccessfully to keep Van Hollen from winning election in the first place.

All sides agree on this much: Close-quarters political combat represents the only sensible political strategy at a time when a handful of close races determine which party holds the reins of power. Genial relations across party lines, Van Hollen reasons, take place when a dominant majority party feels free to act magnanimous toward a feeble minority—not when a near-even balance makes the majority fearful and the minority hungry. That's why he got along well with the minority Republicans in the Maryland Legislature, and why the lopsided Capitol Hill majorities of an earlier Democratic era had smooth relations with Republicans who were badly outgunned.

But that's not the shape of today's Pennsylvania Avenue. With the two parties nearly equally divided, both have concluded that unstinting partisanship—targeting members and using the levers of power to control the House floor, control the agenda, and push a national message—is the only rational approach for both sides. As Democrats prepared to take power, that meant a collision between their oft-stated commitment to open debate and their determination to enact their "Six for '06" on their promised timetable of the opening hundred hours of the new Congress. There was no doubt how that collision would be resolved: Whether Democrats or Republicans are in control, controlling the Avenue's political narrative overrides any procedural imperative.

"I'm a pragmatist," Van Hollen says. "We committed to move forward on a broad array of issues. We're going to do our best to open the process—without losing control of the floor. The point of being in the majority is being able to move an agenda. . . . That's going to be a continuing tension."

"Tension" is an understatement. And the result is a long chain of unresolved grievances that is now nearly impossible to untangle. Well before Democrats complained bitterly about Republican abuses of power after the 1994 election, Republicans were screaming in identical terms about their treatment in the latter stages of the Democrats' forty-year House reign. In those days, says Vin Weber, a Republican House member turned lobbyist, Democrats talked to Republicans "like the plantation owner talked to the slaves."

That's why Republicans felt such urgency about holding on to the House in 2006. And it's why, having failed, they turned to Tom Cole to try to win it back in 2008.

Cole, a burly man with a gentle demeanor, is the only Native American serving in Congress. He was born with the politics gene; his late mother, Helen, a member of the Chickasaw nation's Hall of Fame, served in the Oklahoma Legislature. Tom was born with the competition gene as well; he was an all-conference lineman at his high school in rural Oklahoma. Not gifted enough for the University of Oklahoma Sooners, a perennial national power, Cole was recruited to play at tiny Grinnell College in Iowa.

For an Oklahoman, the liberal Grinnell campus produced a certain amount of cultural whiplash. "We warmed up in the lotus position doing Buddhist chants, had players with hair out of their helmets hitting their shoulders, elected a male homecoming queen, and had a pep squad that marched around the field singing 'The Internationale,' " Cole recalls. "But I never quit taking winning and losing seriously—in football or any other endeavor."

Over the years, he acquired a range and depth of practical political experience that few members can match. After studying history and politics at Grinnell, Yale, and the University of Oklahoma, Cole went on to chair the Oklahoma Republican Party, serve in the State Senate, work as district director for a GOP congressman, and become secretary of state.

Developing a reputation for savvy, organization, and calm under fire, he was tapped to run the staff of the National Republican Congressional Committee in the early 1990s, as the GOP accelerated its drive to break the Democrats' grip on the House of Representatives. He subsequently worked as a political consultant before winning an Oklahoma U.S. House seat for himself in 2002.

Throughout 2006, Cole found himself enmeshed in two campaigns at once. Neither involved his own survival in Congress; like most of his colleagues, Cole enjoyed a lopsided partisan advantage that meant he was unlikely to face any general-election challenge for his own seat. In his 2004 re-election, Cole received 78 percent of the vote.

But even the large number of safe seats like his wasn't enough to assure Republicans a national majority in a seventh straight House election. So Cole and other safe Republicans, through campaign advice and fund-raising help, spent much of 2006 in crisis mode, trying to keep their majority in the House alive.

Cole's second campaign was to advance his own rise through the Republican ranks. He was seeking the chairmanship of the NRCC, the campaign committee on which he had once served as top staffer. The job requires two overlapping qualifications. One is a talent for running campaigns; the other is the ability to raise money to fuel those campaigns.

On the former, Cole had a clear advantage over his principal rival for the NRCC chairmanship, Representative Pete Sessions of Texas. While Cole was amassing experience as a party operative, Sessions was working as a district manager for the Southwestern Bell telephone company.

But Sessions's base in Texas, home of Majority Leader Tom

DeLay, made him the early front-runner for the job. He had worked alongside DeLay in pushing the Texas Legislature toward a second redistricting following the 2000 election, which delivered an additional four seats for the Republican Party in the 2004 election. Perhaps more significant, Sessions's affluent North Dallas congressional district represented a far more lucrative fund-raising base than did Cole's rural-Oklahoma district. The $4.5 million Sessions raised to stave off a stiff 2004 challenge to his re-election was nearly four times what Cole had raised in his hard-fought first election to Congress in 2002.[2]

The primacy of fund-raising placed an extra burden on Cole. It meant paying the NRCC's minimum $100,000 "assessment" on Republican members, and then some; Cole actually ended up sending $145,000 to "the team." On spare afternoons, Cole would walk down Capitol Hill from his office in the Cannon House Office Building to the NRCC, where members ply the phones to hit up potential donors. As a "captain" for the NRCC's March 2006 fund-raising gala, Cole was expected to solicit at least $75,000 in donations for that event. After lunch one warm February day, he phoned his friend Scott Reed, who had built a career as a lobbyist after running Bob Dole's 1996 presidential campaign. Reed agreed to find $25,000 in donations for the dinner, which in turn would be "credited" to Cole's fund-raising target.

Cole also took risks to demonstrate his electoral pragmatism. Nevada congressional candidate Dean Heller—whom Cole considered the most electable Republican in Nevada's Second District— faced opposition from antitax conservatives for being insufficiently zealous in supporting tax cuts. Cole sent him a $2,000 check anyway; Sessions, who had burnished a reputation for economic conservatism, did not.

By the end of the campaign, Cole had held his own. His "leadership PAC," with the help of prime donors such as Reed, had distributed $531,611 to Republican members, compared with $672,500 handed out by Sessions's PAC;[3] overall, Cole could point to $2 million that he had directed to "the team" by various channels. Even more important, worsening political conditions for Republicans increased the value of Cole's practical political experience. Congressional Republicans felt increasingly alienated from, and endangered by, the weakness of the Bush White House.

The Election Day loss gave a major boost to Cole's candidacy to run the campaign committee. "We need to act decisively—starting right now—to restore our majority," Cole wrote his colleagues a few days after the election returns were in. The appeal worked. With solid support from newly elected Republican freshmen—among them Dean Heller of Nevada—Cole won the race.

Cole set out to recruit new candidates and raise money for the fresh election cycle that immediately opened for business. He knew it wouldn't be easy. The zealous Republicans who won the House in the 1994 Gingrich revolution ended up damaging their own political standing with hard-edged challenges that President Clinton eventually turned back. The new crop of Democrats—taking cues from the likes of Emanuel, who knew that story well from his years in the Clinton White House—wasn't likely to repeat that mistake.

But soon Cole was more sanguine, concluding that the partisan imperatives of the Avenue were kicking in to the GOP's favor. "The Democrats are beginning to drive us together by overplaying their hand," he said. For the wounded, divided tribe of Pennsylvania Avenue Republicans, the specter of marauding Democrats was precisely the goad they needed to rally their own forces.

The political arguments of 2007 droned on inconclusively. Democrats shoved through their minimum-wage hike, and built a double-digit lead in polls asking voters which party they favored to control Congress in 2008. But with other "Six for '06" promises stalled, Republicans cried, "Broken promises." They accused Democrats of being more interested in investigating the Bush administration than in legislating on the voters' behalf. Public approval of Congress sank below even President Bush's low levels.

But the Avenue's bottom line is unsparing. The only numbers either party considered solid were in counting cash.

Van Hollen didn't excuse even the most endangered incumbent from fund-raising chores. Democratic Representative Diane Watson, who represents poverty-stricken South Central Los Angeles, had less than $3,000 in her campaign bank account at the end of 2006. But she still faced a $200,000 DCCC obligation.

African American Democrats, especially, complain that the financial arms race has gotten out of hand. Not only do they tend to represent low-income districts, but they also rarely get DCCC assistance for themselves. The committee cares almost exclusively about districts that could change partisan hands, and most minority legislators represent safe Democratic districts, where the only competition takes place in the primary. If Democratic members decline to hit their allocations, it can harm their ability to move up to choicer assignments within the House.

Cole imposed similar discipline. The Republican fund-raising plan was tied to a specific series of events on the party's annual calendar: debt-reduction goals to be met by the time of a January party retreat, ticket sales for a gala March dinner, more tickets for the summer-season "President's Dinner" attended by Bush, then a scheduled payment for "incumbent support" due on September 30. The GOP also duns according to the power of members to pay. For 2007, members of the leadership faced a tab of $375,000, ranking members of the more powerful A-list committees $255,000, and ranking members of the Appropriations Panel, the principal crossroads for heavily lobbied "earmark" spending, $205,000. Even freshmen still learning their way around the Avenue were obliged to collect $60,000 apiece for the NRCC.

Before the President's Dinner, held on June 13, 2007, Cole's committee distributed a twenty-eight-page instruction packet listing companies, trade associations, and lobbyists to target. It even offered sample scripts to use in soliciting them, noting: "The opposition will be fully funded, so we must set our fund-raising sights high in order to be fully competitive."

But loss of political power creates burdens that aggressiveness can't always overcome. The President's Dinner raised $15.4 million for the Republican House and Senate campaigns—down from $27 million a year earlier, when Bush's party held the majority.[4]

In that respect, Van Hollen's fortunes were the mirror image of Cole's. By mid-2007, Democrats had raked in $36 million, up from $24 million a year earlier, as they languished in the minority.[5]

The distorting influence of this process is undisputed. Democratic presidential candidate Bill Richardson, a former member of the House leadership, offered a rare public acknowledgment in June 2007 as he struggled to remain financially competitive in his White House race. "Does somebody get a little bit of an edge because they helped a politician? Probably," Richardson said after a Los Angeles fund-raising breakfast. "Because the politician remembers that person . . . I don't give any extra access to somebody that contributes. But I'll remember that person, and I'll say, 'Jeez, that guy helped me. Maybe I can help them.' "

Van Hollen, in fact, supports funding election campaigns with taxpayer dollars. He calls the grip of moneyed interests on political Washington the most surprising and dispiriting discovery since he won his congressional seat.

"We'd all be better off in the long run" with public financing, Van Hollen says. "But as long as we operate within this system, our guys need the resources."

6. THE FUND-RAISING PHENOM:
DEBBIE WASSERMAN SCHULTZ

IN THE FALL OF 2006, the National Cable and Telecommunications Association, a major business trade group, hosted a fund-raiser for a first-term congresswoman from Florida. In some ways this kind of campaign support didn't make sense. The NCTA was headed by a conservative Republican and Representative Debbie Wasserman Schultz was a liberal Democrat.

Stuck in the House minority, Wasserman Shultz didn't even sit on the Energy and Commerce Committee, or the Judiciary Committee, where the cable industry's legislative interests tended to reside.

But in another way the event at Charlie Palmer's steak house made perfect sense. For Debbie Wasserman Schultz had rapidly made herself a Democrat that nearly anyone with interests on Pennsylvania Avenue needs to know.

Debbie Wasserman Schultz was still in high school when Ronald Reagan opened the doors to power for a new generation of Republicans. Born in Queens and raised on Long Island, she settled in South Florida after studying political science at the University of Florida. Tireless and vivacious, she fell in love with public life on the Gainesville campus. Her signal achievement: helping to create a new campus political party that challenged the establishment Blue Key organization, and managing its successful campaign to elect the president of the student body. "It was really my first attempt at going to bat for people who didn't have a voice," she recalls.

After college, she landed a job as an aide to a state legislator named Peter Deutsch, then won his seat in the Florida State House of Representatives when he moved on to the U.S. House of Representatives. And twelve years later, in 2004, when Deutsch ran unsuccessfully for the U.S. Senate, Wasserman Schultz set out to capture his Twentieth District U.S. House seat, representing parts of Broward and Dade counties. Both are Democratic bastions in the state; Wasserman Schultz's district backed both Al Gore and John Kerry over George W. Bush, giving the Democratic ticket more than 60 percent of the vote in 2000 and 2004.

Having gotten a heads-up from Deutsch of his intention to leave the House, Wasserman Schultz moved early to cement support in the district and foreclose the options of potential Democratic primary rivals. She won a prompt endorsement from the National Women's Political Caucus. Even more significant, she won the pre-emptive backing of then–House Minority Leader Nancy Pelosi. Even before the primary-filing deadline had passed, as other Democrats pondered jumping in, Pelosi came to South Florida in February 2004 to headline a Wasserman Schultz fund-raiser.

That helped to set up the extraordinary scene that unfolded weeks later inside the U.S. Capitol. It was an election-season custom to bring Democratic congressional candidates to Washington to be introduced to their potential future colleagues. Many of the contenders offering their brief remarks to the Democratic caucus were hoping to win some assistance for their campaigns. Yet they had no assurance they'd ever make it to Washington, because they were attempting the difficult feat of ousting an incumbent Republican.

But Wasserman Schultz was different: She was a Democratic nominee whose district was so tilted in her party's favor that her election was guaranteed. And her message was different, strikingly so.

"I'll be writing a hundred-thousand-dollar check to the DCCC," she said. Instead of asking for money from the party, Wasserman Schultz was giving to the party, before she had even won a seat. Both stunned and thrilled, Democratic members responded with a standing ovation. That moment established that Wasserman Schultz was a "team player" and a prodigious fund-raiser, working out from her wealthy Florida district to a national stage.

Soon after taking office in January 2005, she displayed another strength of exceptional value—a sprightly presence on television. Democrats at first were unsure how to handle controversy over Terri Schiavo, the comatose Florida woman on life support whose family was battling over whether to let her die. The Democrats were wary of another "values" debate that could boomerang on the party. But Wasserman Schultz had worked on end-of-life issues in the Florida Legislature, and was confident that Republican politicians were badly overplaying their hand by injecting themselves into a family crisis and trying to dictate that Schiavo be kept on life support. She took it upon herself to prepare fact sheets for fellow Democrats, distribute them on the House floor, and then help lead the debate on the issue. Two months after being sworn into office on Capitol Hill, Wasserman Schultz appeared on the CBS Sunday talk show *Face the Nation* to debate the issue with religious-right leader Tony Perkins.

It wasn't long ago that first-time lawmakers faced a long wait in line before gaining any significant attention. Former House Speaker Newt Gingrich tells the story of the time 1950s-era House Speaker Sam Rayburn expressed his displeasure with a young congressman from New Jersey, Frank Thompson, by making Thompson wait three hours for a meeting.

"There were thirty congressmen who mattered" then, Gingrich reflected. Now, every member with talent and ambition can matter, if only because someone treated as badly as Thompson was would rapidly "be on television attacking the Speaker."

In 2006, Wasserman Schultz didn't face a challenger from either party, but that hardly slowed her down. She became co-chair of the Democrats' campaign to turn "red" Republican districts to "blue" Democratic ones by funneling money to the races of Democrats running against vulnerable Republicans. She claimed credit for helping raise $11 million for that program, as well as another $2 million for Rahm Emanuel's Democratic Congressional Campaign Committee. After the 2006 election, she became chair of the DCCC's "Frontline" program to help vulnerable Democrats hold their seats in 2008, and by April 2007 had already raised a healthy $1.2 million for that effort.

Her reward: an astonishingly fast rise up the congressional ladder. By 2007, Wasserman Schultz was not only a "chief deputy whip" within the House Democratic power structure, but also had captured the chairmanship of a subcommittee of the powerful House Appropriations Panel. That made her one of the thirteen influential "cardinals" who controlled all spending legislation in the House.

"I work my butt off," she says. "I live, eat, and breathe this stuff. I am not going to lose because I got outworked."

Her rapid rise doesn't make her more fond of Washington than she is of her old political haunt of the Florida Legislature in Tallahassee. "It's exponentially more venomous here," she says.

In the state capital, legislative members are mostly sequestered for a two-month session, living in the same apartment complexes, eating at the same restaurants, and working in close quarters on legislation. But Pennsylvania Avenue "is a much more disconnected environment." Because members don't know each other, "the pain isn't felt as directly when you're shooting at somebody here. It's hard to have friends on the other side of the aisle." On weekends she returns to Florida, where her banker-husband and three children live. During the week, she shares an apartment blocks from the Capitol with two Democratic colleagues, Carolyn Maloney of New York and Melissa Bean of Illinois.

She knows how to play the money game to legislative advantage, leveraging her status as a go-to ally for Democrats seeking to reach out financially to women's groups and Jewish groups. Sometimes that works across partisan lines. Once, during her first term, as Wasserman Schultz struggled to amass Republican support for a resolution declaring "Jewish History Month," she devised a strategy to break through. "I called every major Jewish donor" to President Bush and the GOP, seeking support for the resolution. With help from Senator Arlen Specter, a Jewish Republican from Pennsylvania, she eventually steered the proposal through Congress.

But her role as a "team player" in Democratic election strategy can also impede her legislative work. Among the principal initiatives of her first term was a pool-safety bill designed to set more stringent rules for barriers around pools, and the kinds of drains manufacturers are permitted to install. Battling uphill in a Republican Congress, she obtained support from the swimming-pool industry and a prominent Republican co-sponsor—Senator George Allen of Virginia.

In the run-up to the 2006 election, Senate Democrats wanted to hold up progress on the bill for a singularly partisan reason. Allen was in a dead-heat race against Democratic challenger Jim Webb; with partisan control of the chamber potentially hanging in the balance, Democrats didn't want to provide ammunition favorable to Allen, which he could use with Virginia voters against Webb.

Senate Democratic leaders "didn't want to give Allen a victory before the election," Wasserman Schultz says matter-of-factly. And she was in no position to object. "I was co-chair of the 'red to blue' campaign. It was hard for me to say, Give one of your most targeted members a big victory." The result: A bill that had majority support in both chambers of Congress didn't become law. Wasserman Schultz insisted she'd win passage of the bill later in any case.

Her upstart's disregard for conventions of bipartisanship emerged in tense election-year relations with a Florida Republican colleague, Representative Clay Shaw. When Wasserman Schultz's friend from the Florida Legislature, Ron Klein, moved to challenge Shaw, a veteran of a quarter-century in Washington, Shaw went to Wasserman Schultz and invoked a long-standing Florida tradition that members of Congress from one party would not campaign against members of the other party within the state. But Wasserman Schultz wasn't interested in the "old, stale" traditions of seniority or deference; in her view, there was too much at stake politically. Even as Shaw publicly complained that her partisanship would hurt the state's interests, Wasserman Schultz helped Klein amass a $4-million war chest and end Shaw's congressional career on Election Day.

In an era of mounting attacks on "pork-barrel" spending for special-interest projects from watchdog groups, colleagues, and the White House, her ascent to become one of thirteen House Appropriations "cardinals" carried some risk. With Republicans in charge, Democrats used an out-of-control spending process as an emblem of Republican incompetence and corruption. Conservative Representative Randy "Duke" Cunningham went to jail for accepting bribes in return for helping steer federal money to a defense contractor.

But many critics found that the broader scandal lay in perfectly legal "earmarks," or specific spending orders, delivered by lawmakers to growing legions of Pennsylvania Avenue lobbyists at taxpayer expense. Then-Representative Harold Ford of Tennessee, mounting his historic bid for a Senate seat, pointed to "a whole parallel government" plied by lobbyists who seek individual appropriations "earmarked" so they go to specific projects—lobbyists often hired by special interests because of their connections to a single key member of the Appropriations Committee—and the flak began flying.

And it began flying at Wasserman Schultz and her colleagues, almost immediately after they assumed the majority. George Bush and House Republicans sought to regain some political traction by accusing Democrats of abusing earmarks to reward their own supporters. They succeeded in forcing the overall Appropriations Committee chairman, David Obey of Wisconsin, to abandon his plan to delay public identification of thousands of earmarked requests until committee staffers could evaluate them.

Americans for Prosperity, a voluble conservative advocacy group, mocked Wasserman Schultz, accusing her of sending a "Porky Valentine" in the form of a memo instructing fellow lawmakers in the method for requesting earmarked spending.[1] In March 2007, Citizens for Responsibility and Ethics in Washington, the same group that had hounded Tom DeLay and Jack Abramoff, raised questions about an earmark that Wasserman Schultz herself had pursued.

The earmark in question was a $50,000 grant for an autism school in Miami whose advisory board included Robin Parker, a donor of $8,000 to past Wasserman Schultz campaigns. Some $1,850 of that money came on June 12, 2006, three weeks before Wasserman Schultz announced House approval of the earmark. CREW also questioned the $450,000 that Wasserman Schultz obtained for Nova Southeastern University, where she had once worked while serving as a part-time state legislator in Florida.

"It looks like she's trading campaign contributions for earmarks," said CREW executive director Melanie Sloan. "You don't go to Congress and earmark for your friends and your former employer."[2]

Wasserman Schultz dismissed the criticism as "ridiculous." Parker is a longtime friend; Wasserman Schultz said she didn't even know Parker was connected to the autism school. Though Nova Southeastern University is indeed her former employer, she has no current ties to the school. If Nova is to seek federal money as other universities do, "they have to go to me," as the representative of the district in which the school is located.

"The thing that bothers me is when the media says there's something wrong about pursuing appropriations for supporters," she says. "I have pursued appropriations for contributors," but "I put my name next to them" and justify them on the merits. "You should have transparency.

"If you are an unethical person, there's definitely some risk," she goes on. But "the sleazy stuff is a very small percentage." And she says it "really burns my butt" when critics complain about earmarks on the grounds that the relevant federal agencies haven't requested them. "Last time I checked," she snaps, "the bureaucrat at HHS [the Department of Health and Human Services] who controls that budget didn't run for office."

Wasserman Schultz makes no apology for the role money plays in the process, calling allegations of corruption on Pennsylvania Avenue "overrated." Campaign donations simply become one device among many, she explains, that help members decide how to spend their time. If she returns to her office to find thirty phone messages, "of the thirty, you're going to know ten of them. Anyone is going to make phone calls to the people they know first. I'm going to call the people I know. Among the people I know are donors." Many of her most prominent donors, she says, want no favors at all. When they meet at political gatherings, "they want me to know their name."

More corrupting than money, she says, are the distortions of the reapportionment process. Gerrymandered election districts leave most members of Congress ensconced in politically safe territories, beyond the reach of partisan foes, and thus largely beyond accountability to voters. Wasserman Schultz holds one of those safe districts.

"I could kill somebody" and still win re-election, she jokes—unless, that is, the victim was exceptionally popular in South Florida.

7. THE REPUBLICAN STRATEGIST: **KARL ROVE**

SITTING in his windowless White House office as he neared the end of almost seven years there, Karl Rove, President Bush's political guru, pondered the battle between the two major parties for control on Pennsylvania Avenue and concluded: "This is like two boxers fighting to the point of exhaustion."

Rove has plenty of allies and plenty of enemies up and down the Avenue, but nobody on either side doubts his acumen or his sense of American history. And in his boxing analogy, he is describing a moment in political history that he, perhaps as much as any single individual, has helped to create.

Rove is at once the pre-eminent Republican strategist of his era, and a man whose job is nearly impossible to describe or define. He was the most important figure on George W. Bush's two successful presidential campaigns, but he wasn't the campaign's manager, or its chairman, or a fund-raiser, or a communications director. He did something more elemental: He figured out the strategy to win, so others could execute it.

Similarly, after President Bush moved into the White House, Rove was widely considered the most important person on the president's staff, but he wasn't chief of staff, or even political director. Others held those jobs. Rove instead became the all-purpose thinker, planner, and architect—"Bush's brain," in the capital's shorthand and the title of a popular biography; "boy genius," in the somewhat sarcastic nickname used by his boss, the president.

Such figures emerge from time to time on Pennsylvania Avenue:

Mark Hanna served that role for President William McKinley, ushering in a generation-long period of dominance by Republicans and their pro-business agenda of protective tariffs for America's manufacturing industry. Harry Hopkins played a similar role for Franklin Roosevelt, and helped usher in a generation-long period of domination of the capital by Democrats and their New Deal programs.

Rove, in fact, rose through his party with a similar vision: His goal has been to lay a foundation that would allow today's Republican Party to control American politics for the next generation, and his life has been spent in pursuit of that vision. As the end of the Bush term drew near, with power exquisitely divided between the two parties, the dream seemed to be slipping further away, but Rove was hardly prepared to let it go.

Rove was born in Colorado and raised in Nevada and Utah. He attended the University of Utah but dropped out to become executive director of the national College Republicans. With help from a friend named Lee Atwater, he ran for the presidency of the College Republicans, and won, in a race filled with controversy and charges of dirty tricks.[1]

That race brought him into contact with George H. W. Bush, who at the time was Republican national chairman, and later with his son George W. Bush. A lifelong bond was formed between Rove and the Bush clan. Rove moved to Texas, home of the Bush family, and became a political consultant, helping all kinds of Republicans win elections. His specialty became the art of the direct-mail campaign, which involved assembling and categorizing massive lists of addresses and preparing mailings to solicit money or action. He formed a highly successful company that did direct-mail campaigns for political candidates as well as for private organizations. A voracious reader of history and political history in particular, Rove also taught at the University of Texas in Austin, where he had set up his shop.

Along the way, Rove also helped the elder Bush win election as president, and masterminded his son's two successful campaigns to be elected governor of Texas. So, when George W. Bush decided to run for president in 2000, Rove was the logical choice to be the chief campaign strategist. He played the same role when Bush ran for and won re-election in 2004.

The Rove strategy in both cases was marked by two characteristics.

The first was his dream to use the campaigns to help build a durable Republican coalition that would hang together over time and give the party national dominance for years to come. This vision assumed that the country was, in the broadest sense, already moving toward the Republican message of low taxes, conservative social values, a muscular military, and an activist government in some limited areas, such as education. The goal was to bind together the voting groups that most strongly agreed with that message.

The coalition was assembled in the South, where Republicans had already become dominant in the years since Ronald Reagan was elected; in the mountain West, where conservatism seemed to come naturally; in the suburbs and exurbs, those extended areas of growth outside cities where conservative churches were proliferating and drawing together voters who tended to be Republican; and among Hispanics, the fastest-growing American minority group, where the Democrats' traditional advantage could be eclipsed with a message of conservative social values that many Hispanics shared and a welcoming posture toward immigrants.

The second Rove hallmark was a campaign strategy that has become the defining characteristic of recent campaigns in both parties: Win by mobilizing your own base first. In other words, the top priority isn't to woo voters who lean toward the opposite camp, but, rather, to focus on energizing and then turning out at the polls the maximum number of voters already on your side.

The 2004 re-election campaign that Rove oversaw stands as the preeminent, state-of-the-art example of the base-driven strategy. Midway through Bush's first term, Rove knew that the circumstances of the Bush presidency precluded a substantial broadening of Bush's political appeal. The national reaction to the 9/11 attacks, which initially united Americans behind the president, wasn't as powerful as the forces of division: the bitter circumstances of Bush's first election, when he prevailed despite losing the popular vote to Al Gore; the ambitious conservatism of the president and his team; and a war of choice in Iraq that would eventually bring a highly polarized partisan reaction. In 2003, shortly before the invasion that toppled Saddam Hussein, Rove concluded that it would be a "mobilization election"— that is to say, the goal of turning out the partisans already on your side would be even more important than normal.

One key element of the mobilization strategy was the "Target Voter Index" developed by Will Feltus of National Media, a top Republican consulting firm. Feltus's long career in Republican political activity tracks the geographic and technological roots of his party's national rise. Feltus grew up in Natchez, Mississippi, when the South was still solidly Democratic. But he inherited the Republican proclivities of his parents, both active in the then-tiny Mississippi GOP.

After studying organizational behavior (and playing varsity tennis) at Yale, Feltus went to work in the Mississippi GOP himself. In 1978, laboring alongside a young operative named Haley Barbour—now Mississippi's governor—Feltus helped to elect Thad Cochran as the first Republican U.S. senator from the state since Reconstruction. He later worked on Cochran's staff before earning a Harvard MBA and going to work as a researcher with prominent Republican pollster Robert Teeter. Through one of Teeter's clients, then Vice President George H. W. Bush, Feltus sampled some of the Avenue's most rarefied privileges, such as playing on the White House tennis court.

At National Media, Feltus directed a research project that aimed to fine-tune Republican advertising strategies. The project amassed comprehensive information about the people behind the "Gross Ratings Points"—the raw numbers of people watching any particular political ad, the unit of measurement for campaign media buyers. Instead of relying on Nielsen ratings, the traditional industry standard, Feltus purchased data from a New York–based firm, Scarborough Research, that combined viewing habits, demographic information, and political preferences in television markets across the country.

It was no surprise that the data showed that more Democrats watch *Face the Nation* and Republicans prefer *Fox News Sunday*. But the research also showed that Republicans are more likely to choose cable television over network programming. Within the realm of cable, Democrats gravitate to the likes of Court TV, Nickelodeon, and CNN, whereas Republicans were more likely to watch Outdoor Life, the Golf Channel, Country Music Television, and the Fox News Channel.

The data had a profound effect on the Bush campaign. In 2000, the campaign bought no advertising at all on cable television. In 2004, Bush operatives spent 20 percent of their advertising budget on cable, and another $5 million on radio.

"If you vote, you pick a side and you root for a team," Feltus explains. The Republicans were refining their ability to find the members of their team.

Meanwhile, the Bush team also was sharpening techniques for more direct forms of voter contact. Its "micro-targeting" program began with massive voter files showing the party identification and propensity to vote of individual Americans. Then it would merge those data with information about some of those same people purchased from consumer-research firms—which ones, for instance, preferred red wine to white, which ones preferred Ford over Chevy, which ones subscribed to *Sports Illustrated* and which to *Newsweek*. Finally, the program would conduct a poll of voters in particular lifestyle categories, which in turn would determine the issues that the campaign would use in reaching those voters via direct mail, telephone banks, and door-knocking by volunteers.

The Bush campaign had been methodically preparing for the homestretch of the 2004 campaign since the outset of his administration. Concerned that Democrats had outgunned Republicans in the final days of the 2000 race, Rove and his deputies used subsequent special elections and the 2002 midterm campaign to experiment with the precise combination of contacts—phone calls, mail pieces, door-knocking visits—most likely to motivate allies to turn out.

The result was the so-called 72-Hour Project, named for the cli-mactic three days of the general-election campaign. In particular, the GOP high command aimed to maximize voter turnout in fast-growing exurbs beyond the suburbs of big cities. Married families with children, many of them conservative Christians, have flocked in recent years to these exurbs in places such as Lake and Osceola coun-ties, outside Orlando, Florida; Scott County, outside of Minnesota's Twin Cities; St. Croix County, outside Eau Claire, Wisconsin; and Deschutes County, around Bend, Oregon.

"It takes them time to get settled, pick the right grocery store, the right church, and then get registered to vote," says Rove. "These are places we've got a lot of natural support that we've got to energize and turn out."[2]

The Bush team built its efforts around more than one million com-mitted volunteers. In crucial states such as Ohio, those volunteers, working in carefully targeted areas to turn out the vote, made the dif-ference and were the reason Bush—and Rove—prevailed.

That election kept alive the dream of a lasting Republican elec-toral majority, and Bush and Rove entered the second term hoping to use the president's remaining time in office to make it a reality.

But before long it began to appear that the increasingly unpopular war in Iraq was consuming the Bush presidency, and just two years after Bush's re-election triumph, Democrats took control of both the House and the Senate in the 2006 midterm elections. Rove liked to point out to visitors that the losses Republicans suffered weren't large by historical standards. A president's party tends to lose seats in the midterm election during his second term, as the country tires of the party in power. The average loss by a president's party in a second-term midterm election is twenty-eight seats in the House and five in the Senate. Bush's Republicans lost thirty in the House and six in the Senate—almost precisely the historical norm. Bush also didn't do too badly when measured against other presidents ruling in wartime. In midterms conducted during wars, the president's party loses an average of thirty-two House seats, and five Senate seats.[3]

Still, the 2006 election, which also saw Democrats make gains in gubernatorial and state-legislative races, produced a picture of the two parties' having battled to a virtual draw, rather than a picture of growing Republican dominance. In Washington as well as in statehouses across the country, power was evenly divided between the two parties. A period of Republican dominance had been followed by a Democratic resurgence.

The overall balance can be seen in the cumulative results of recent elections. In the seven presidential elections that began with that first Reagan victory in 1980, Americans have cast more than 655 million ballots for the presidency. They have cast 51.6 percent for Republicans, and 48.4 percent for Democrats. Over the same period of time, Democrats have controlled the House of Representatives—the people's House, the institution of the federal government closest to the pulse of the nation—for fifteen years, the Republicans for twelve years.[4]

The broader question, of course, is whether closely divided power helps or hurts the country—in other words, whether it produces actions in Washington that are beneficial, or merely an endless stream of bickering and posturing. Rove, putting on his historian's hat, isn't convinced that divided power must be a bad thing. Nor is he convinced that moving to the center for compromise—the course of action many high-minded observers urged upon both parties after the 2006 election—is necessarily a good thing.

"Divided government is at times a benefit to the country and at other times a disadvantage," he says during a long discussion about the state of politics. "Similarly, at times unified control of the government is an advantage, and at other times it is a disadvantage. James Buchanan presided over a divided congressional environment, and it

was bad for the country. Ronald Reagan presided over a divided congressional structure, and it was good for the country."

More than that, Rove thinks the temptation to pine for the days
when there were more "centrists"—that is, more moderate Republicans and conservative Democrats who resided somewhere in that
loosely defined political center—is misplaced. Even when they were
more plentiful, he argues, centrists rarely drove policy. They proved
decisive mostly on new issues (a plan to contain nuclear materials in
the former Soviet Union, for example), when there weren't clear ideological positions on the left or right, or when those positions hadn't
formed yet. President Bush, he contends, actually has managed to
bring the denizens of Pennsylvania Avenue together in the center on
a handful of issues, such as education reform and energy, where there
was middle ground to be had.

Moreover, Rove argues, if a majority of Americans clearly resides
in the center on an issue, the political system will follow them there.
But in fact the country is divided on such issues as Social Security
and Medicare, on providing health coverage to the uninsured, and on
the turmoil in Iraq.

"The view that we have to meet in the middle assumes that that's
where everybody is, and they're not," he says. "If you look at the people who do not participate [in politics], they are spread all over the
political spectrum. In fact, if there is anything that ties them together,
it is the amount of political information they are willing to consume,
and when they're willing to act on that information, and how coher-
ently they organize that information. It's not that, 'We're all sitting in
the middle and we're sitting it out because we have two parties who
are on the extremes.'" That view was borne out by the conundrum
both presidential tickets faced in the homestretch of the 2004 election. The relatively small group of swing voters Bush and Kerry were
pursuing fell into two sharply different groups: upscale suburbanites,
and blue-collar voters without college degrees. In the end, both
groups split their votes.

Rove and Bush often are accused of having helped produce the polarized atmosphere in which the two parties retreat to their corners and lob bombs at each other, rather than meet in the middle for reasonable compromise. By throwing raw meat to the Republican base to mobilize core voters, the argument goes, Rove and like-minded political strategists have created a nasty environment that works against productive debate.

Rove agrees that political debate along Pennsylvania Avenue has grown coarser, and he says he regrets that. But he also points to another cause: the modern media world. He laid out the case in a speech at Washington College in Chestertown, Maryland, a few months into Bush's second term.

President Bush did not cause this polarization. Four things contributed to this condition. First, an explosion in the channels of communication. Second, an even larger increase in the demand for content by those channels. Third, the competitive conditions these two factors create for working journalists. And fourth and finally, the oppositional attitude of the press.

Think about this. Thirty years ago, most news was delivered by a couple of wire services, printed in local newspapers, perhaps printed in two or three papers of national significance, and dissected on three national television stations. Outside of Paul Harvey, radio was meant for music and sports, not commentary.

Today we have the Internet; more national newspapers; more wire services; a plethora of cable TV channels 24/7, 365 days a year; and always present AM talk radio. News and commentary permeates even the Comedy Channel. This dramatic increase in the number of ways news is communicated has led to an even larger increase in the demand for content.

The result? Rove concluded: "The press is drawn to political conflict like moths are drawn to a flame in the night forest. They cover it, encourage it, provoke it. And once it occurs, they high-mindedly condemn it—they lament how polarized, uncivil, and unserious our politics has become."[5]

Still, even Rove thinks the current fine balance of power and persistent polarization can't last. It's almost an unnatural state. "Equilibrium never lasts forever," he says. "Something always happens." The question is how a realignment of the country, leftward or rightward, toward Democrats or toward Republicans, will take place.

Some contend that a powerful, charismatic political figure could emerge to force realignment. Rove doubts that's the case. The forces needed to move the country off dead center have to be bigger than those that any individual can muster. In Rove's view, realignment might require a big event—an economic convulsion, perhaps a change in the world order—that changes the way Americans look at themselves and their nation. Alternatively, "you also have realignment that takes place by demographic, economic, and cultural changes that work their way through the political system and are acted upon by the political actors in such a way that one party gains an advantage and the other party is put at a disadvantage."

The Depression was such a difference-making event, as was the Industrial Age. The current question is obvious: Could the Iraq war turn out to be one as well?

Rove has a different guess. He thinks the era of the microchip is the giant cultural event of the times. Not surprisingly, he also thinks it will shift the political balance toward Republicans for years to come, because it creates a society that functions according to the individual-first view the Republican Party holds.

He contends that the digital age empowers individuals to do more things and decide more matters for themselves. Conversely, because people can use digital power to do so much on their own, it decreases the need for people to have giant organizations—unions, government bureaucracies—do things for them. The Internet also is creating more pure markets for Americans—eBays where they can buy and sell their own goods, eTrades where they can manage their own fi-

nances, current-affairs websites where they can trade ideas and arguments. Because Republicans stand for the power of markets and
against big-government and big-union solutions, Rove argues, they
will benefit. "This is why I think the Republicans will have, in the
years ahead, a narrow dominance that may grow with time."

Rove himself will push his vision from beyond the White House,
which he left in the summer of 2007. But he is likely to continue to
evangelize on the forces of history as he sees them. The "power of the
microchip," he says, will "allow people to be more in control of their
lives and the decisions that flow from the information that they ac-
crue during that process. . . . It's caused people to be more accepting
of the market. It's caused people to be less inclined to be in a union,
more inclined to feel like they are in command of their lives, and
more willing by their behavior to act on it."

III. POWER OUTSIDE THE SYSTEM

THE POPULAR IMAGE OF WASHINGTON is of a city populated by bombastic politicians and faceless bureaucrats, with a few judges in black robes thrown in for good measure. Those insiders are the only people who matter in the nation's capital, in this image, because they are the ones who move and shake and get things done.

That image always was a stereotype, but it's becoming more so over time. Today, much of what happens in Washington occurs not because of the work of those in official positions of power, but because of the efforts of savvy operators who reside outside the government, or who straddle the border between the government and the outside world.

These operators are the lobbyists, the journalists, the socialites, the advocates, the bloggers, the business representatives, and the big thinkers. Their ranks have grown over the last generation, as has their influence. Though they don't fit neatly into any civics-textbook description of how Washington works, they are collectively some of the most important people on Pennsylvania Avenue.

Consider the rise of just one kind of outsider, the private contractor. When Republicans rose in power over the last generation, they carried into government offices their belief that private businesses can almost always do things more efficiently than the government. As a consequence, they increasingly turned to private contractors to deliver all kinds of services, particularly in the mushrooming realm of homeland security since the 9/11 terrorist attacks.

As a result, these private contractors increasingly do work once performed by bureaucrats in Washington's warrens of nondescript government buildings. Between 2002 and 2005, the number of federal civil servants—that is, those people employed directly by the federal government—has remained nearly flat, at just over 1.8 million, according to a study by New York University Professor Paul C. Light. But over the same period, the number of outside contractors doing work on behalf of the federal government has soared by 47.8 percent, to more than 7.6 million from about 5.2 million. Private contractors, in other words, now outnumber civil servants by more than three to one.[1] The representatives of the companies providing these services to the governments—or those lobbying to get a piece of the action—are also helping fill up Pennsylvania Avenue.

For further evidence of the rise of outside players on Pennsylvania Avenue, one need only look at the largest government building of all, the International Trade Center, dedicated in the name of Ronald Reagan in 1998. At 3.1 million square feet, the Reagan Center is the largest building in Washington. It is a cavernous structure, distinguished by a large rotunda visible from the outside, an eight-story foyer inside one of its entrances, and a skylight that uses an acre of glass.[2] Though owned by the government, it is expressly dedicated to private-sector use as well as government use. It houses, among other private firms, the Washington offices of Volkswagen of America, Inc. In its ample meeting and conference rooms, government officials and business executives meet to discuss opening wider the doors of commerce between the United States and markets around the world.

Outsiders make their impact felt in dozens of other ways as well. Washington's idea machine—which consists of think tanks that house academics and former politicos and churn out policy proposals designed to advance particular agendas—forms a kind of alternate brain working alongside the policy-makers inside Congress and the White House.

Occasionally, these outside forces insert themselves directly into the government's decision-making. A prime example unfolded in late

2006 and early 2007, when a powerful group of outsiders arose to try to alter the course of the war in Iraq.

As the war was dragging on, amid mounting public anxiety and unhappiness, Representative Frank Wolf of Virginia, a Republican who represents the far-western suburbs of the Washington area, decided it was time to shake up the status quo. Wolf started by telling Bush-administration officials that there was a need for a fresh look at war policy. But he felt he was getting no response.

So Wolf decided to turn up the heat from the outside. Wolf is a member of the Appropriations Committee, the panel that writes the checks that actually fund the activities of the rest of the government. More specifically, he's the top Republican on the subcommittee that oversees the State Department. So Wolf inserted language into a State Department spending bill that created and funded an independent "study group" of outsiders to examine American policy in Iraq and issue a report on possible alternatives.

To execute this notion, Wolf turned to what remains of the foreign-policy establishment in Washington. He called on an old friend, David Abshire, a veteran of the Washington policy-making and think-tank circuit. Abshire had worked in the Ford and Reagan administrations and now runs a think tank called the Center for the Study of the Presidency. Wolf also contacted Richard Solomon, a former assistant secretary of state who now operates a government-funded think tank called the United States Institute of Peace, and John Hamre, a long-time congressional defense expert and later deputy defense secretary under President Clinton. Hamre is head of the Center for Strategic and International Studies, a national-security think tank that Abshire had helped start years ago. Together, the three, though outside the government, know everybody who has been a significant figure in national-security thinking in Washington for the last generation.

They agreed to help launch what they called the "Iraq Study Group." They had been around long enough to know that the task would be easier if they got the cooperation of the Bush-administration officials actually running the war. So they went to the State Department for a meeting with Condoleezza Rice, by then the secretary of state. They hoped to convince her, and by extension the president and the rest of the administration, to bless the effort. It was awkward; they were asking Rice to endorse the efforts of a group of outsiders that was being created only because of deep doubts about the war policies being pursued by her own administration.

Understandably, as Solomon and Hamre recall, Rice was resistant. We don't need this, she said; you can't come up with any options we haven't thought about already. At another point in the conversation, she asked the men to give the administration some time to come up with new options on its own: If we don't come up with anything satisfactory, she suggested, then you may have a role.

But in the end, she promised, grudgingly, to take the notion of a study group to the president. A few weeks later, word came back from the White House: Bush had accepted the idea. The national-security outsiders moved ahead. Though they were all deeply versed in foreign policy, they thought it better that they not run the exercise but have well-known political figures take charge. That would give the group's findings more credibility with both the public and Washington's political system. They considered various names—former Republican Senator Robert Dole, for instance, and former Democratic Senator Sam Nunn—but ultimately decided on former Secretary of State James Baker, a Republican, and former Representative Lee Hamilton, a Democrat with long experience on international policy.

Hamilton accepted the idea, but Baker was more problematic. Baker had been close to the Bush family for decades, and had served the president's father as political counselor, private confidant, and secretary of state. Putting him in charge of a panel that might ultimately criticize the way the younger Bush was running Iraq policy was delicate. Baker said he would take on the task only if the current President Bush wanted him to do so. He called the president, and got his blessing.

Baker and Hamilton then recruited a group of wise men and women with long histories of public service — half Republicans, half Democrats — who knew government but had left it behind. The list was illustrious: former Secretary of State Lawrence Eagleburger, longtime civil rights leader and Washington lawyer Vernon Jordan, former Attorney General Edwin Meese, former Supreme Court Justice Sandra Day O'Connor, onetime White House Chief of Staff Leon Panetta, former Secretary of Defense William Perry, and former U.S. Senators Charles Robb and Alan Simpson. They launched their work with a press conference on Capitol Hill, then moved into months of meetings behind closed doors. The goal of the group was to break out of the highly polarized public debate that was swirling over Iraq. They began getting briefings from experts — forty-four of them, assembled by Solomon and Hamre and divided into four working clusters.

The group met for months, even as the debate over the Iraq war grew more intense outside their meeting room and came to dominate the 2006 congressional campaign. Eight of the ten panel members flew to Iraq for a firsthand look. They returned sobered by the level of violence and uncertainty they encountered there.[3]

Slowly, the Baker group began to creep into the news. Baker himself, as it happened, had just finished a book, a biography of his public life, and he went on a book tour. Inevitably, the radio, TV, and newspaper interviewers he encountered asked him about Iraq, and, inevitably, he talked about the work his study group was doing. Speculation began that the Baker-Hamilton group was going to come up with a plan that President Bush could seize upon to get American troops out of Iraq.

The group worked toward issuing a report shortly after the 2006 election. The one recommendation the group most clearly agreed upon was that the United States should begin talking with Iran and Syria — both seen by the Bush administration as outlaw states unfit to be negotiating partners — in hopes of getting them to cut off their support for the Iraqi insurgency. That recommendation would be contro-versial, because it called for a complete about-face in the Bush ad-ministration's diplomatic strategy.

Beyond that, Hamilton insisted on a stark opening statement in the report, describing Iraq's situation as "grave and deteriorating."[4] That opening phrase would set the tone for the rest of the report. The two who worked most strenuously on the policy details were Baker and former Defense Secretary William Perry, who engaged in a debate near the end that almost kept the group from being able to issue a re-port at all. Perry wanted a deadline to withdraw troops from Iraq. Baker, knowing that would be unacceptable to the White House, re-sisted.

They compromised: The report would set a goal of withdrawing combat troops by the end of the first quarter of 2008, leaving open the possibility that training and support troops could remain after that. Overall, the report called for "new and enhanced diplomatic and po-litical efforts in Iraq and the region, and a change in the primary mis-sion of U.S. forces in Iraq"—to training and aiding Iraqi forces so they could assume the fight against insurgents themselves. "We believe that these two recommendations are equally important and reinforce one another," the report said.[5]

Finally, in December 2006, the group released its report, amid a glare of media coverage that generally speculated that Bush would seize on it to change his course in Iraq. Some two hundred cameras and five hundred journalists showed up for the press conference un-veiling the report.

Some of those in the Baker-Hamilton group also expected that the White House would publicly embrace the report and proclaim that it opened the door to a new beginning. But that isn't what happened. The White House praised the Baker report in a kind of pro forma way, while openly and pointedly rejecting immediately its suggestion for talks with Iran and Syria. Beyond that, the White House said it would come up with its *own* new Iraq strategy. Basically, the White House, rather than allow the appearance that it had ceded control of

Iraq strategy to this group of outside wise men and wise women, let the public's fascination with the Baker-Hamilton effort fade.

Within weeks, President Bush effectively buried the Baker-Hamilton report by offering his own version of a new Iraq policy, one built around a "surge" in the number of American troops sent there for one massive push to squash insurgents and restore order.

Over time, though, a strange evolution began to occur. As Bush's "surge" strategy failed to produce quick, meaningful change in the level of violence in Iraq, Washington began drifting back to the Baker-Hamilton report for answers. The Bush administration actually held a few tentative conversations with representatives of the Iranian and Syrian governments, as the study group had recommended. Bush told visitors that he was a "Baker-Hamilton guy," meaning he hadn't dismissed the group's recommendations after all. Presidential candidates began outlining Iraq strategies that resembled the Baker-Hamilton approach. Some senators drew up a piece of legislation that actually would have ordered the Bush administration to implement the Baker-Hamilton report's recommendations. Presidential candidates began talking favorably of the group's findings. As the Bush administration and Congress groped for an Iraq strategy that could last, the Baker-Hamilton formula of a troop drawdown, a shift to a mission focused more on training than on fighting, and diplomacy to get help from other countries in the region, didn't look so bad. The "surge" strategy, which eventually paid dividends, began melding with elements of the Baker-Hamilton plan.

The lesson: What happens outside the halls of power often helps steer what happens inside. What follows are the stories of some who know how to make that happen.

8. THE ADVOCATE: HILARY ROSEN

THE PICTURE-BOOK VERSION of the Avenue's power lineup is found in the caricatures on the walls of the Palm, an expense-account steak house a few blocks from the Avenue. There's Vernon Jordan, there's Karl Rove, there's Larry King, there's Hillary Clinton. Near the 19th Street entrance, where manager Tommy Jacomo greets regular patrons, is a drawing of the late Senator Philip Hart of Michigan, a legislator so revered that Congress named a Senate office building after him.

And next to Hart's image is a drawing of Hilary Rosen. That's one emblem of the stature Rosen has achieved as a $1-million-a-year Washington lobbyist. Yet Rosen is rare along the Avenue for something different. After rising in the world of Washington money and influence, she has also become a significant force in the evolving values debate.

Rosen's Washington story began modestly: She worked as a waitress at another Northwest Washington restaurant when she was a student at George Washington University in the 1970s. The daughter of an insurance agent, she was studying business then. But her mother was active in Democratic politics back in her hometown of West Orange, New Jersey; she was the first woman elected to the city council there. She knew the state's Democratic governor, Brendan Byrne. That got nineteen-year-old Hilary Rosen a part-time job as a Washington lobbyist for the state of New Jersey. The work wasn't glamorous; it involved, she recalls, "sitting in a cubicle crunching numbers" about federal aid, at 400 North Capitol Street, the Hall of States Building, in the shadow of the Capitol. And that was just fine for a young woman still more interested in business than in Pennsylvania Avenue politics.

She waded in a little deeper after meeting Liz Robbins, a lobbyist for the city of San Francisco. Robbins was just then setting out to build a business representing a wide range of state and local entities seeking slices of the growing pie of federal largesse. "It really took off, because there was money to be had," Rosen says. That led Rosen to a job at the Recording Industry Association of America, the lobbying arm of the music business in Washington. Technological changes had made the late twentieth century a time of intense challenge for the industry, as the rise of Internet file-swapping programs threatened to erode the value of copyrights in the United States and around the world. Rosen's job, as a lobbyist for ten years and, beginning in 1998, as the RIAA's chief executive officer, was to fend off those threats. "I didn't feel . . . 'lobbyist' was a dirty word," she says.

But the political aspirations of the entertainment industry and Hollywood were growing. They had become a target in the values debate from politicians in both parties—among them Al Gore's wife, Tipper—over the coarseness and vulgarity of material produced by some leading artists. Though the RIAA ran a relatively small political-action committee, never topping $100,000 in annual contributions, it acquired an outsized influence in arcane debates over issues such as digital copyrights, in part because of the glamour associated with the entertainment business.

In her early years at the RIAA, Rosen was navigating what had become a familiar Washington power arrangement—a Republican White House and a Democratic Congress. "Your lobbying work wasn't defined by your partisanship," she says. Though she personally associated with Democrats and donated to them, "you kind of did that on your own time." She had solid relations with powerful Republicans such as Orrin Hatch, a prominent member of the Senate Judiciary Committee who had produced his own music CDs.

The climate changed after the Gingrich revolution of 1994.

Through their K Street Project, Republicans began monitoring the political donations of those seeking to influence the Congress. A young Republican staffer Rosen had hired returned from a meeting of the "Wednesday group" of conservative activists run by an antitax crusader named Grover Norquist. The staffer reported that Norquist had read aloud from campaign-finance reports listing Rosen's donations to Democratic candidates. When a disturbed Rosen called Norquist later, the brash GOP activist downplayed the incident. "He said, 'You and Valenti get a pass,' " because of the industries they represented. (Jack Valenti, a former White House aide to Lyndon Johnson, was the movie business's longtime lobbyist as head of the Motion Picture Association of America.) But political heat continued to rise once Republican George W. Bush replaced Democrat Bill Clinton in the White House, giving Republicans control of both the executive and legislative branches. "The change contributed to a really unhealthy money grab," Rosen says. "Their lobbyists got greedy, and members of Congress got greedy." Monthly retainers for top lobbyists drifted up from $25,000 a month to $50,000 or more.[1]

As a Democrat, Rosen found herself battling more than just the Napster file-swapping service; her midday sojourns for chopped salad at the Palm, a couple of blocks from RIAA headquarters, became a respite from partisan wars. "The last two or three years it got sort of ugly," Rosen said. In 2003, Rosen stepped down as head of the RIAA. She did not, however, step out of the Pennsylvania Avenue maelstrom.

Rosen had never hidden the fact that she's gay; indeed, her then partner, Elizabeth Birch, with whom she had adopted two children, was head of the gay-and-lesbian advocacy group Human Rights Campaign. When President Bush and his party made a constitutional amendment banning gay marriage a key part of their 2004 appeals to so-called values voters, Rosen became a key adviser in the effort to fight back. It was a challenging campaign for gay-rights advocates. Both halves of the Democratic ticket, John Kerry and John Edwards, declared their opposition to gay marriage. So did most other mainstream Democrats, even though the party had identified itself as culturally progressive. The gay-marriage issue "had a depressive effect on some of the Democrats," Rosen says, while "energizing the volunteer base" of Republicans.

Rosen's main goal became persuading Democratic progressives that their path to political success lay in affirming their own values of tolerance and acceptance, rather than in a fruitless attempt to court opponents of tolerance. "Values mean different things to different people," she says. "It's the Democrats' lack of embrace of their own values that contributed to the problem. If you're more unabashed about it, you are better off. Democrats are getting smarter about that." Rosen acknowledges that, in pressing gay-and-lesbian demands for greater rights, advocates, including herself, raise the temperature of the debate and repel conservatives. "Do I think we're also part of the polarization? Yes. That's happening in the society."

Still, the power of gay votes and financial donations is significant, and Rosen sees the broader values dynamic tilting to her advantage since the 2004 elections. President Bush dropped the gay-marriage issue as the constitutional amendment went nowhere; Republicans who had crusaded against gay marriage, such as Tom DeLay and other House leaders, fell out of power. Vice President Cheney's daughter Mary, in a committed lesbian relationship with her partner, Heather Poe, wrote about coping with the Republican Party's stance and later announced that she had become pregnant by artificial insemination. "I think we've used her very effectively," Rosen says. "We've made the point that we're in every family. In this day and age, two-thirds of the American people know or love someone who's gay or lesbian."

Rosen herself, meanwhile, is working outside the narrow boundaries of Pennsylvania Avenue politics to advance the tolerance agenda in a different way. She keeps a foot in the entertainment business with a consulting firm that advises clients such as XM Satellite Radio, Viacom, and video-game manufacturers. More important, she has moved to harness the power of social networking on the Internet through

OurChart.com, which has become a leading destination for gay and lesbian Web users. Her partner in the venture is Ilene Chaiken, executive producer of *The L Word*, a Showtime series popular among gay television viewers. The show's star is Jennifer Beals, who gained fame from the 1983 movie hit *Flashdance*. That Beals herself is not gay, and is willing to play that role and maintain a personal page on OurChart.com, represents another sign of the increasing acceptance of gay lifestyles within American society. So is the success of the movie *Brokeback Mountain*, with two gay protagonists.

"We're clearly winning" the debate, Rosen says. Far from a constitutional ban, Rosen sees American society edging inexorably toward marriage rights in one form or another. "In ten years, we're probably going to have a mishmash of federal and state laws that approximate marriage." But she acknowledges that progress will come slowly, and will include some setbacks. Even as the policy debate drifts toward greater gay rights, most elected Democrats continue to be wary. "They still see us as more of a liability," Rosen says.

9. THE SOCIAL SECRETARY: LEA BERMAN

LEA BERMAN, a petite woman with an easy smile and a confident air, was caught squarely in the middle. It was the spring of 2006, and the leader of China was coming to call at the White House. And Lea Berman was in charge of making everyone happy.

Berman held one of the most difficult yet least understood jobs in Washington: White House social secretary. The social secretary, who technically works for the First Lady rather than the president, is in charge of all social events and entertaining at the White House. It is at once an enviable job—ingratiating its holder to legions of Washingtonians as well as to others around the country who measure their status by invitations to 1600 Pennsylvania Avenue—and an enormously demanding one. The social secretary is, in many ways, the White House's link to the powerful, the famous, and the rich who live outside the bubble of the federal government. Social events draw those people into the rarefied air of the White House, if only for a few hours. For the social secretary, that means dealing with the biggest egos in the world, a task that carries its own special kind of stress.

The stress is particularly high when the guest of honor is a foreign leader. Getting the arrangements for an event just right—the food, the table settings, the guest list, the seating chart, the entertainment—has not just social implications but diplomatic and even national-security ones as well. That was never more true than when Chinese President Hu Jintao paid a much-anticipated visit to Pennsylvania Avenue in April 2006.

The American and Chinese presidents can fairly be called the most powerful men on the planet, overseeing the two most important economies in the world, yet they don't often meet. America's relations with China are so complicated that they can make the tax code seem simple by comparison. The two nations waver between being adversaries and allies, and the tensions in their ties swing back and forth between security and economic issues. And at the time of this particular visit by China's maximum leader, relations were especially tense, over charges that China wasn't playing fair on trade, and over a Chinese effort to buy an American oil company that had gone bust because of protests in Washington.

Berman came to the job well equipped, because she had seen the Washington power scene from the inside for a long time. She had arrived in Washington more than two decades earlier, fresh out of Miami University in Ohio with an interest in politics and instructions from her parents that she had just one week to find a job. If she didn't succeed, she was to head back to Ohio for a job as a teller in a bank.

Berman found work at a Republican-leaning think tank, the Center for Strategic and International Studies. Though she didn't know it then, she was about to become a permanent Washingtonian.

Her initial job led to later stints working for Henry Kissinger's consulting firm and the National Republican Senatorial Committee. She married Wayne Berman, at various points a lobbyist, fund-raiser, campaign operative, and top Commerce Department official. Wayne Berman would become one of those Republicans who know how to collect big money for candidates, which would make him a figure whose support candidates coveted. Together the Bermans would become a Washington power couple.

Lea Berman stopped working after they had children. But by the 2000 campaign, she was ready to return to the workforce and joined the Bush campaign to help with fund-raising. After Bush was elected, a friend put her in touch with Vice President Dick Cheney. Cheney's wife, Lynne, hired her to run the vice-presidential mansion. When Mrs. Cheney fired her chief of staff in a dispute, Berman happened to be in the room at the time—and Mrs. Cheney promptly tapped her for that job. She then helped with the Bush re-election effort, and at the beginning of the second Bush term, Laura Bush hired Berman as social secretary to increase and improve entertaining at the Bush White House.

A good social secretary is like a good spy: She is most successful when nobody notices she is there. The job required Lea Berman to be shrewd, diplomatic, and, more often than an outsider might imagine, very tough. Nothing would tax her skills in all those areas like the visit of President Hu.

The importance of the event was no mystery. Cheap imports from China are critical elements in the American economy's ability to deliver continued economic growth with low inflation. China has become America's factory floor. The benefits are mixed, to be sure; business leaders harmed by competition complain that China doesn't play by the same economic rules as do other economic powers.

Thus, China wants an open American market to sell in the United States the goods its 1.3 billion people manufacture, just as any industrialized nation has. But it also retains the right to suppress the value of its currency artificially, so that it's harder for American companies to make a profit by selling their goods in China for the Chinese yuan.

China wants access to modern technology, but claims it can't control its country when asked to stop the massive pirating of American software on its streets. On track to pass the United States as the world's largest economy in the mid-twenty-first century, China already finances the U.S. budget deficit through its purchase of U.S. Treasury bonds. By midway through Bush's second term, the Chinese government held $1 trillion in American Treasury bills.

So, when the Chinese president visited, the most powerful business interests in America would be watching closely, hoping politics could help rather than hinder commerce. The meeting had been scheduled to occur much earlier, but Hurricane Katrina, which swamped President Bush and his White House staff in crisis management, forced its rescheduling.

The Chinese were eager for all the ruffles and flourishes that the world's only superpower can provide at the White House, which would help cement China's new image as a full member of the world's top-drawer economic and political club. But the White House, leery of giving full symbolic blessing to the world's largest communist nation, one that still had a spotty human-rights record, wanted something less than full honors. So the United States offered a compromise: President Hu would get a big White House welcome, but not an official "state visit" with all the honors and the lavish nighttime state dinner that accompany that distinction. Instead, it would be an "official" visit with a White House luncheon.

The Chinese weren't happy with the lesser status. Their displeasure showed a few weeks before President Hu's arrival, when U.S. and Chinese delegations met to plan the visit, at Blair House, the official government guesthouse for visiting dignitaries, across Pennsylvania Avenue from the White House. During a tense four-hour meeting, the Chinese made it clear that they would consider the event a "state visit" whatever the United States called it. They went on to challenge virtually every decision the American side had made over the arrangements, starting with precisely what time the motorcade carrying the Chinese leader would pull up to the White House. Later, the group moved across Pennsylvania Avenue to the White House to walk through the site of the visit. When the group got to the East Room, the large room on the White House's main floor where the lunch would be held, one Chinese official walked over to the large windows overlooking Pennsylvania Avenue and began tugging on the large curtains there, trying to close them. A White House official rushed over and asked the Chinese visitor what he was doing. The curtains would have to be closed, the Chinese representative said, so nobody in the room would be able to see anti-China protesters across Pennsylvania Avenue, in Lafayette Park. The U.S. side brushed off that demand; the curtains would remain open following usual practice, they informed the Chinese.

Chinese prickliness extended even to the seating chart for the lunch. Normally, a visiting male head of state sits next to the First

Lady, and the visitor's spouse sits next to the American president. The Chinese rejected that custom, insisting that President Hu, as a sign of honor, sit next to Bush. They got their way.

All those demands were problems for Lea Berman. Beneath the surface, she suspected there might be another, unspoken one. Her husband had just a few months earlier played a pivotal role in an embarrassing setback for China. The giant oil firm Chevron Corporation, which is based in the United States but operates in more than sixty countries, had hired Berman for assistance in a takeover battle. Chevron was trying to acquire California-based Unocal but was outbid by the Chinese oil firm CNOOC. Berman, one of several lobbyists Chevron had turned to for help, lobbied hard in Washington to block the Chinese bid, arguing that the Chinese company was unfairly benefiting from government subsidies, and that its purchase of American oil assets amounted to a national-security threat. Berman and his allies succeeded in creating a political wave that CNOOC couldn't overcome. To the chagrin of the Chinese government, CNOOC eventually withdrew its bid.

Lea Berman wondered whether that episode might be affecting her own negotiations with the Chinese over the Hu event. In any case, the CNOOC episode hung over the proceedings as one more reason for the Chinese to be prickly.

Things didn't get any easier once the visit actually began. When President Hu arrived at the White House for the opening ceremony in the Rose Garden, an American aide, as is customary, announced the two presidents' arrival over a loudspeaker. But, because of a slipup by a junior White House aide who typed up the announcer's cue cards, Hu was introduced as leader of the "Republic of China." The Chinese, to distinguish their land clearly from their rivals in the breakaway Chinese province of Taiwan, insist on being called the "People's Republic of China." As soon as the announcement was made incorrectly, a distraught State Department official rushed over to Berman, declaring that the Chinese might be so offended that they would simply leave on the spot.

They didn't. But the problems got worse when Hu moved to the microphone to make brief remarks during the opening ceremony. As he was speaking, a Chinese woman who had gotten into the ceremony by obtaining credentials as a press photographer began shouting in protest at China's treatment of the Falun Gong, a quasi-spiritual movement long suppressed by the government in Beijing. Secret Service agents had to wade into the press section to take the woman away. Later, as the two presidents walked toward the White House's West Wing, a Chinese photographer who had been sneaked into the Chinese delegation unbeknownst to American officials rushed to them to start taking pictures. Surprised Secret Service agents seized and held the photographer until the Chinese called them off.

For Berman, the complications continued while the two presidents met in private. Because the Chinese were so angry over the shouting protester at the opening ceremony—a faux pas they blamed squarely on the Americans—a handful of Chinese officials declared they would refuse to attend the lunch as a sign of their unhappiness. So Berman had to rush to the East Room to rearrange the seating chart to fill the empty seats.

While there, she was stunned to see a Chinese interpreter standing over the table where the two presidents would be sitting; the Chinese interpreter removed the name card marking the place where an American interpreter was to sit to translate conversations between the leaders, and replaced it with one carrying her name. The Chinese, in a violation of protocol for such occasions, had simply decided to impose their own interpreter and boot out the American.

Berman rushed over and told the Chinese interpreter to stop. She and the interpreter even engaged in a brief tug of war over the interpreter's chair. After winning it, Berman instructed the American interpreter to occupy the chair and stay put there for the hour remaining before the lunch began.

Little of the backstage tension was visible to the hundred or so select visitors who began arriving for the official lunch. Indeed, to the uninitiated, it would have been hard to tell the difference between this lavish meal and a real state dinner. (The most obvious difference, in fact, was that a state dinner is a black-tie affair, and guests at this lunch wore business attire.) Invitations to the event, hand-addressed by White House calligraphers, had gone out weeks ahead of time. Guests arrived by passing through one security checkpoint at the northeast gate of the White House, then walking down the boulevard that separates the White House and the Treasury Department before turning right and passing through another security station, this one complete with X-ray machines and metal detectors, finally emerging in the east driveway of the White House.

Guests entered the White House's East Wing basement and strolled past the White House library—a small and little-known jewel, filled with an intriguing and eclectic collection of valuable old volumes—and past the room where Franklin Roosevelt once pored over World War II maps. From there they headed up the grand stair-case that leads to the White House foyer, where a collection of government and business leaders mingled at a reception, serenaded by chamber music provided by a military musical ensemble. Waiters in black tie circulated with appetizers and silver trays of wine.

The guest list was set according to a well-established formula within the White House that allows various top officials to nominate a small number of guests. The vice president and White House chief of staff were allotted two couples each. The State Department, the White Hosue Press Office, the National Security Council staff, and the legislative-affairs offices also got a set number of invitations.

The largest chunk—fifteen couples—was determined by Karl Rove, the president's principal political strategist. On an individual level, that reflected Rove's immense power in the Bush White House; more broadly, it reflected the way polarization has elevated the role of political calculation on the Avenue. Muffie Cabot, the Reagan White House social secretary, says top Reagan aides and Cabinet members constantly importuned her for invitations. But none could control such a large block of invitations, since "nobody ever interfered in what Mrs. Reagan wanted."

The final guest list followed the traditional White House protocol of balancing Republican members of Congress with Democrats.[1] So Democratic Senator Daniel Inouye of Hawaii was there, along with Republican Senator Ted Stevens of Alaska; Democratic Representative Rick Larsen of Washington was included, as was Republican Representative Mark Kirk of Illinois. This makes such White House events a small antidote to the atrophy of the Avenue's bipartisan social life. "There's such resistance on both sides to being in the same room with each other," Berman says.

But the principal priority for Rove, who years earlier was a guest at the wedding of Wayne and Lea Berman, was advancing Bush's political interests by nurturing his allies. (That was not always easy. One Rove favorite, a Wall Street titan and GOP donor, once phoned Berman from New Jersey's Teterboro Airport to ask whether the Federal Aviation Administration could move up the takeoff slot for his private plane so he could make a White House event on time. She declined to pursue the request.) And on this occasion, Bush's most important allies were the nation's business elite.

Among those in the room were the chief executives of the Big Three American automakers. The chief executives of the International Paper Company, the Bristol-Myers Squibb Company, Procter & Gamble, Dow Chemical Company—all were there. Top money-managers were on hand as well: the chief executives of Goldman Sachs Group, Inc., Citicorp/Citibank, N.A., and the New York Stock Exchange.

After a bit, the military hosts and hostesses who hover over such occasions spread the word that it was time for the guests to engage in another White House ritual—getting a picture taken with the host and guests of honor. All lined up outside one of the rooms off the White House foyer to be taken, one or two at a time, to stand alongside the American and Chinese presidents and first ladies and have their official White House photos taken. It is a unique Washington ritual. Few politicians, business executives, or journalists of any stripe can resist the lure of a carefully staged picture with the president and First

Lady. And all the better if the photo also includes another world leader, to establish for everyone who later sees it on an office or den wall that the man or woman in the photo was a member of a highly select group who mingled and belonged among world-class power as offered only within the White House. The pictures arrive in the mail a few weeks later, in all their eight-by-ten glory, courtesy of a White House photo shop that puts out such photos by the thousands annually. In this case, they arrived signed by President and Mrs. Bush, and they showed Laura Bush in a neat pink and gray suit, the president in his trademark dark suit and blue tie, and the first couple of China, arms straight at their sides, staring at the camera, pleasant if somewhat stiff expressions on their faces as they went through the ritual.

From the photo line, the guests were ushered into the White House's East Room for lunch, another sign that the Chinese first couple was getting something less than full honors. A state dinner is held — not surprisingly — in the State Dining Room, which lies on the opposite end of the first floor of the White House. The East Room is slightly less formal, the place where the president holds his full-dress news conferences, where entertainers perform at the White House, where Teddy Roosevelt's rambunctious children roller-skated while living there.[2] It is a grand room, to be sure, but something less than the State Dining Room.

On this occasion, the East Room was stuffed with tables, each holding ten guests. By the president's side at the head table, animated and smiling, sat Chinese American figure-skating champion Michelle Kwan. A few seats over was John Chambers, chairman and chief executive officer of Cisco Systems, Inc., who for the occasion brought along business cards printed in English and Chinese.

At the next table sat the two first ladies, with their own interpreters, along with Henry Kissinger, still the overlord of the U.S.-Chinese relationship he helped create while working in Richard Nixon's White House. Wine flowed, and the presidents rose to offer toasts. President Hu's was long and laborious and included the usual references to the United States and China's communists aligning to fight fascism in World War II. President Bush was characteristically brief and direct, praising China's move from "isolation and stagnation to engagement and expansion." He also referred to the two leaders' conversations as "constructive and candid."[3]

That diplomatic wording reflected the fact that the Chinese had resisted American entreaties to get tougher in helping shut down the nuclear programs of Iran and North Korea, and to stop artificially holding down the value of its currency, a practice that made it more difficult for every American business represented in the East Room to sell goods to China rather than just buy from China. Then White House waiters served butter heirloom corn broth, Alaska halibut, snap peas and sweet carrots, and, for dessert, melon and warm almond cakes.

Afterward, the crowd was entertained with a bluegrass band Berman had picked, in part because she thought the fiddle music might remind the Chinese visitors of the sounds of Chinese string instruments. President Bush offered thanks, and everyone prepared to leave. If the irony of America's business elite honoring the last truly powerful communist leader in the world struck anyone in the room, it wasn't apparent.

A few weeks later, President Bush selected one of the luncheon guests, Goldman Sachs chairman and chief executive Hank Paulson, as his new Treasury secretary. One of Paulson's principal qualifications for the job was his extensive business experience in China, and the credibility he brought to the effort to fend off protectionist pressures and keep the United States–China relationship on a smooth path. That job kept getting tougher, particularly after Democrats, who generally take a tougher line on trade, took control of Congress and stepped up complaints about unfair Chinese practices. Keeping economic relations smooth got tougher still after a controversy over imports of unsafe food and toys from China.

For Lea Berman, though, the Hu visit was a success. It could have melted down into a diplomatic disaster, but didn't. The American business leaders went home satisfied. Lea Berman, having survived the toughest assignment in her career, resigned a few months later, contemplating the next step in her career, which has straddled the divide between the insiders and the outsiders along Pennsylvania Avenue.

10. THE NETROOTS WARRIOR MEETS THE ESTABLISHMENT: ELI PARISER AND KYLE McSLARROW

It was by any traditional standard a complete mismatch.

A wealthy American industry, experienced in the Pennsylvania Avenue power game, wanted something from Washington that sounded simple: the right to charge customers for the expense of investments made to improve services.

The Republican-controlled Congress and White House wanted to give the industry what it wanted.

The public was paying no attention.

But the citizens' group headed by pale, young Eli Pariser was paying attention—and wanted to stop the industry in its tracks.

That Pariser's unlikely force won the battle is a tale of how quickly power has moved outside the government offices of Pennsylvania Avenue.

When Ronald Reagan moved into 1600 Pennsylvania Avenue in January 1981, Eli Pariser was a month-old infant in Lincolnville, Maine. He was born to the sort of people Reagan launched his political revolution against: 1960s Vietnam protesters who went on to found an alternative high school. Barely into grade school, Pariser was discussing Reagan's nuclear policies with his parents.[1]

At age fifteen, Pariser was attending Simon's Rock College, a liberal-arts school in the Berkshires catering to teenagers who leave high school early. At eighteen, he joined an anti-globalization protest in Washington, during the Clinton administration. By twenty, he had graduated and moved to Boston, to provide computer services for a nonprofit firm called More Than Money.

Then 9/11 changed the trajectory of his career. Pariser created a website to promote a multilateral response to the attacks and gathered petition signatures in support of what he called "using moderation" in dealing with al-Qaeda. His venture attracted the attention of Wes Boyd, a former Silicon Valley entrepreneur who himself had ventured into politics during the Clinton impeachment drama of 1998. Boyd had co-founded the website MoveOn.org as a way of rallying liberals against the Republican effort to force Clinton from office.

Boyd tapped Pariser to help run MoveOn's political efforts just as the movement toward political networking on the Internet began to take off. In the 2004 elections, activists at the "netroots" (political activism organized online, through blogs and other means) became a major force in Democratic politics. They helped fuel the early rise of presidential candidate Howard Dean, who stunned fellow Democrats with record-breaking fund-raising totals.

In an extraordinary display of financial and organizational prowess, MoveOn raised $60 million for political activity in the 2004 election and by early 2005 had amassed a membership list of 2.7 million members. Pariser became its head. But in the end, the Democratic Party, with which MoveOn sided, lost every contest on the Avenue— for president, the House, and the Senate.

In that 2004 election, Kyle McSlarrow's side won. McSlarrow wasn't just a top official in George W. Bush's Energy Department. He was a quintessential product of the Republican rise on Pennsylvania Avenue.

McSlarrow's earliest political frame of reference—like Pariser's, but from the opposite point on the ideological spectrum—was national security. His family moved around to accommodate his father's career as an army captain. Along the way, McSlarrow figured out that, when it came to supporting the military, Republicans were "our team" and Democrats "the other team." As an ROTC student (and soccer player) at Cornell when President Jimmy Carter was facing a stiff re-election challenge, McSlarrow distributed literature for Ronald Reagan's campaign.

He delved further into conservative politics during law school at the University of Virginia. McSlarrow read Russell Kirk's influential volume *The Conservative Mind,* and was one of a handful of students who helped found a chapter of the national conservative legal group the Federalist Society.

He became steeped in Republican politics soon after law school. He began as a lawyer at the Pentagon during the Reagan administration; by 1989, when the first President Bush appointed Dick Cheney as defense secretary, he was helping to vet potential appointees alongside the likes of David Addington, who would later play a prominent role in George W. Bush's administration as an aide to Vice President Cheney.

McSlarrow tried life at a private Virginia law firm, but the high pay didn't compensate for the absence of stimulation that political life brings. "Politics was now in my blood," he recalls. By 1992, he had decided to challenge northern-Virginia Representative Jim Moran, a Democrat who had voted against the first Iraq war. With help from the National Republican Congressional Committee—then co-chaired by Spencer Abraham, with future Representative Tom Cole as chief of staff—McSlarrow raised $400,000 for the effort. Hammering Moran's war vote and the issue of Democratic corruption in the wake of the House bank scandal, McSlarrow got a respectable 43 percent of the vote but lost.

Two years later, he tried again, joining Newt Gingrich on the steps of the Capitol and signing the so-called Contract with America. "I wanted to be part of the revolution," he said. As it turned out, he lost his own election but joined the revolution anyway, signing on to the staff of Senate Majority Leader Bob Dole. After Dole lost his effort to unseat President Clinton in 1996, McSlarrow remained on Capitol Hill for a time. Later, he moved his family to Phoenix, when he was recruited to manage the 2000 presidential campaign of former Vice President Dan Quayle.

The fizzling of Quayle's effort sent McSlarrow briefly back into private life. He sought to ride the high-tech economy's dot-com boom with former Clinton White House Press Secretary Mike McCurry. They joined forces at Grassroots.com, a political-networking site. But at that time "it was a dial-up world" of slow Internet-connection speeds, he lamented—not the rapid broadband connections that would later allow the likes of YouTube.com to prosper. Grassroots.com never took off.

In December 2000, McSlarrow received a phone call from Spencer Abraham, who had helped with McSlarrow's 1992 congressional race. Abraham had just been informed by Andy Card, a top aide to President-Elect George W. Bush, that he'd been selected as energy secretary. McSlarrow agreed to join Abraham as the Energy Department chief of staff.

It proved rewarding work, especially after the 9/11 attacks invested energy issues with heightened relevance for a nation facing mortal threats from the oil-rich Middle East: "You just felt like you were doing something important every day." But by the end of Bush's first term, McSlarrow was receptive when an executive recruiter from Korn/Ferry International asked if he'd be interested in a job running the National Cable and Telecommunications Association, the cable industry's Washington lobbying arm. McSlarrow waited to see if he'd be tapped to succeed Abraham, whom the White House had decided to replace for the second Bush term. Deputy Secretary Sam Bodman got the job instead. At the request of White House Chief of Staff Card, McSlarrow delayed his decision further while the administration tried to find another suitable post for him. But eventually he tired of waiting and joined the NCTA.

The cable-television industry had matured in the pre-Reagan era, when Democrats still clung to the belief that they were the country's majority party. The NCTA's president for most of the Clinton presidency, Decker Anstrom, had been a technology official in Jimmy Carter's White House, when Democrats controlled both ends of Pennsylvania Avenue. His successor, Robert Sachs, was a veteran of both the Carter White House and the staff of then–Representative Tim Wirth of Colorado, the Democrat who chaired a key telecommunications subcommittee.

Other industries tilted their Pennsylvania Avenue giving heavily toward Republicans after the Gingrich revolution of 1994. But the NCTA didn't, dividing contributions from its robust political-action committee nearly evenly. There was good reason for that sort of balance: Half of the organization's board consists of cable-company operators, the sort of business executives who tend to lean toward the Republicans. The other half are cable-programming executives, the sort of creative types who lean toward Democrats.

But by the end of 2004, after President Bush was re-elected with augmented majorities on Capitol Hill, and Sachs had announced he'd leave his $1-million-a-year job, the NCTA decided it was time for Republican leadership.

When the 109th Congress convened, in January 2005, the NCTA was well positioned for the planned debate over telecommunications reform. Though Republicans held narrow control of Congress, the NCTA's political contributions continued to split nearly evenly between both parties. The NCTA's PAC donated to virtually every member of the House Energy and Commerce Committee, Democrat and Republican alike. That meant $10,000 for the chairman—Joe Barton of Texas, a Republican—and $10,000 for ranking Democrat John Dingell of Michigan.

Among those eyeing Pennsylvania Avenue from the outside, McSlarrow says, the influence of money "is overrated." Rather than buying favors, he explains, it's about avoiding trouble. "It's important, but not in the way people think of it. By and large, you are giving to people you have relationships with. If you're not participating when people think you have the means to, they notice."

The NCTA indeed managed to avoid trouble in the initial phase of the telecommunications debate, which aimed at the first broad rewrite of telecommunications legislation since a 1996 law that was signed by President Clinton. The initial House version granted telephone companies a "national video franchise," allowing them to compete with cable programming. But it also allowed cable companies to bypass local authorities for their own video-franchising rights.

A Senate version was even more generous to cable companies. And neither chamber's bill barred Internet service companies from providing faster access to websites willing to pay extra fees in return. The ability to provide such "premium service" had grown important to the cable industry and other broadband providers because it offered a potential revenue stream for upgrading the capacity of the Internet as it faced overload from the proliferation of massive video files.

But that was also the provision that brought McSlarrow into collision with Eli Pariser's Internet army.

MoveOn had been monitoring the issue of "net neutrality"—the shorthand term for preventing special charges for faster Internet access—ever since a federal-court decision was interpreted to mean that such neutrality was not required under law. For "net neutrality" to be preserved, Congress would have to protect it affirmatively.

But Congress plainly was not eager to do so. Late in the evening on April 4, 2006, MoveOn staffer Adam Green received an e-mailed "net neutrality alert" from Ben Scott, an ally in an ad-hoc coalition that had been helping monitor the issue. Scott warned that Barton, the Energy and Commerce chairman, was preparing to move a telecommunications bill through committee the next day on a party-line vote; it didn't protect net neutrality.

"It's a truly odious bill," Scott wrote. "Congress will recess on Friday for the 2 week Easter break. When they return, the bill will go before the full committee for a vote. Our challenge is to strike hard and fast throughout the 2 weeks, using the Subcommittee vote as evidence that we have a red alert attack on the Internet in the Congress.

If we can scare the crap out of Members while they're at home in their districts, we have a strong chance of derailing the bill."[2]

That was the beginning of something called the Save the Internet coalition. MoveOn's task was a familiar one for citizen activists: Shine a public spotlight on an issue that otherwise would be settled in near-complete obscurity in the Capitol. Quiet decisions made in the shadows are where Pennsylvania Avenue's influence industry has always wielded the greatest power. But the tools available to activists are much more powerful than those of an earlier generation, when mass-dissemination news coverage was mostly limited to major newspapers and broadcast networks.

First the coalition used the Internet to galvanize opposition, rallying not only MoveOn's own members but those of hundreds of other groups—from liberal stalwarts like Common Cause and U.S. PIRG, to conservative voices such as Gun Owners of America and the Christian Coalition, all of whom supported net neutrality because of the way it affected their own use of the Internet. Some thirty-three thousand people alone registered their support on the social-networking sites MySpace and Facebook. A popular musician posted a video on YouTube backing net neutrality.

The establishment politicians backing McSlarrow's position weren't sure how to respond. Alaska Senator Ted Stevens, the NCTA-backed Senate Commerce Committee chairman, dismissed net neutrality as a phony issue. In one fateful public soliloquy immediately circulated on the Internet, he described the Internet as "a series of tubes."[3]

That awkward phrasing, surprisingly enough, provided the breakthrough that net neutrality backers needed to elevate their debate to new prominence. A friendly blogger took an audiotape of the eighty-two-year-old senator's speech and made a "techno remix" depicting him as a doddering fool who didn't understand technology. On Comedy Central's *Daily Show*, host Jon Stewart, whose satiric faux-newscasts have become a key source of political information as well as entertainment for millions of voters under thirty, lampooned the same Stevens remarks on two different shows.

"The Jon Stewart moment was a key validator and milestone that helped raise it even higher above the radar and put the wind at our backs," Green recalled after the battle was over.

The corporate giants on the other side didn't give up. It was a rare instance in which the rival players in telecommunications—phone and cable companies—were in agreement. AT&T hired McSlarrow's old partner at Grassroots.com, Clinton White House Press Secretary Mike McCurry, to bolster its case. McCurry argued that the issue wasn't equality of access, but how to finance an improvement in the Internet's capacity to handle increasing amounts of traffic. Some Internet giants, such as Google, were backing net neutrality in hopes of avoiding parts of that tab, he noted.

Senate Commerce Committee Chairman Stevens plowed ahead with his legislation, hoping to obtain the sixty votes needed to overcome a potential Democratic filibuster. But MoveOn and its allies delivered the coup de grâce during the Senate's summer recess. Net-neutrality activists delivered thousands of petitions to wavering Democrats, such as Senators Charles Schumer of New York, Ted Kennedy of Massachusetts, Tom Harkin of Iowa, and Blanche Lincoln of Arkansas.

All of them eventually sided with the net-neutrality forces, denying Stevens the possibility of getting sixty votes for the bill. Kennedy posted a statement on YouTube backing net neutrality. Unbowed, Stevens vowed to bring the issue back at the lame-duck session of Congress, after the election. But the Democratic victory eliminated that possibility.

In the face of MoveOn's pressure, "the Democrats said, 'I don't want to vote against this,'" McSlarrow said with a shrug when it was over. "'We must be with the team.'"

The Internet activists' clout doesn't simply come from YouTube videos and riffs on comedy shows. As Howard Dean's 2004 campaign had earlier demonstrated, the netroots now can marshal the capacity to put substantial sums of its own money on the table. During the 2006 elections, MoveOn raised and spent $27 million in support of liberal causes and candidates.

That's a mixed blessing for Democratic politicians on the Avenue. On the one hand, the netroots provide a valuable counterweight to some of the business interests Democrats would like to challenge. On the other, the netroots breed the sort of political zealotry that can make compromise difficult, and push Democrats toward positions at odds with broader mainstream opinion. The best example of that phenomenon was the Iraq-war debate, as Internet activists pressed congressional liberals to confront President Bush so vigorously that Democratic pragmatists feared a public backlash.

Pariser insists that the netroots movement, after years of assailing conservative power, is in the process of adjusting to the new contours of the Avenue. "We're transitioning into a period where Democrats are in a position to start governing," Pariser said. "People are starting to understand that new reality."

McSlarrow isn't sure. Today, "both parties are more agenda-driven"; religious conservatives drive Republicans to the far end of the political spectrum, just as the netroots drive Democrats there. Even under a Republican president, McSlarrow now faces a major political problem on the right: The Bush-appointed chairman of the Federal Communications Commission, Kevin Martin, is pressing a change in cable-programming rules under the rubric of making it easier for families to avoid risqué programming. The NCTA insists that changing to "à la carte" programming would ruin the business model of cable-television delivery itself.

The ferocity on both sides isn't easy to manage. "Nineteen ninety-four changed something," McSlarrow says. "Democrats were really bitter, and Republicans wanted revenge" for perceived past abuses of power. That cycle of recrimination has never been broken. "We're so finely balanced. Everything seems to matter, and affects that calculation. It raises the stakes for everything."

Instead of backing off, Pariser is pressing to explore the new uses of technology to expand the activism and clout of the left. In 2006, MoveOn generated some seven million volunteer phone calls through its Call for Change program, which involved gathering activists with cellphones for a virtual phone bank to urge others to vote.

In early 2007, after Bush implemented his troop surge to augment U.S. forces in Iraq, MoveOn experimented with using text messaging as an organizing tool. Pariser sees even greater power in the use of online video.

"The basic fact of the Internet developing into one of our primary mass-media outlets greatly increases the potential for any given citizen to affect the political landscape," Pariser told *Mother Jones* magazine in June 2007.

> I am very excited about . . . the popularization of video, because it's the language people speak in these days. . . .
>
> When our members report back from events, they send photos to Flickr, and when we make ads, we put them on YouTube. The next few years, and especially this next presidential cycle, are going to be about separating the wheat from the chaff. There are clearly very important and exciting ideas floating around with MySpace and YouTube and all the rest of it. We're interested in what's actually going to change minds and change votes. It's going to be an exciting couple of years, because we are going to find out what is hype and what changes things.[4]

11. THE LOBBYIST: ED ROGERS

ED ROGERS HAS NEVER BEEN among the subtler figures on Pennsylvania Avenue.

Within a month of leaving his job inside the first Bush White House, he struck a $600,000 deal to represent a Saudi sheikh under federal investigation in a bank scandal. President George H. W. Bush was so offended that he told White House reporters bluntly: "Ask this man what sort of representation he is providing this sheikh. . . . I don't know what he's selling."[1]

Rogers dropped that contract with the Saudi sheikh under pressure, but he's barely slowed down since. With partners Haley Barbour and Lanny Griffith, he built one of the most lucrative lobbying firms in Washington. He describes the regular distribution of profit, in his Alabama twang, as "slicing the hog." It's a big hog, with estimated 2006 lobbying revenue of $21.6 million.[2]

Behind his desk are panels with oversized pictures of his children; to the left is a massive picture window looking out over the White House. When he has driven across the Potomac River to his home in McLean, Virginia, he pulls into the six-car garage of the seventeen-thousand-square-foot home on six acres that he has named just like a nineteenth-century plantation, Surry Hill. The design of the house, the Alabama native confesses, "brings out all of our redneck insecurities." Its massive red brick edifice, with columns flanking the door, is designed to resemble a building on the campus of the University of Alabama, which Ed and his wife, Edwina, both attended.

The house contains nine mantelpieces, and glass-encased museum displays for the artifacts Rogers has collected in travels around the world. One wall is designed with steel beams to support twelve-hundred-pound stone tablets from a Taoist temple in Taiwan (the Taiwanese government's 2006 fees to Barbour Griffith & Rogers: $1.5 million). Elsewhere in the house are doors from a castle in India (the Indian government's 2006 fees: $700,000).

The home contains an art gallery with removable rods, "so we can change our paintings just like a regular art gallery," Edwina Rogers once explained to *Washington Home & Garden* magazine.[3] In addition to private quarters for their children's nanny, with its own laundry and kitchen facilities, Edwina said, "We wanted a guest suite the equivalent to one at the Ritz-Carlton." That includes antique armoires equipped with pocket doors to accommodate TV sets. Heating and cooling vents include "reproductions that look like they're out of turn of the century grand hotels." Surry Hill is appraised for tax purposes at $5.1 million, but Rogers says it would sell for "much more."

What has made this self-styled "redneck" wealthy is a mix of hustle, savvy, political connections, and visibility. Few people better illustrate the rise in number, prominence, and power of lobbyists along Pennsylvania Avenue.

A native Alabaman, Rogers moved into the Washington inner circle by becoming an aide-de-camp to Lee Atwater, the Southern political genius who did as much as anyone to see in the late 1970s, and then execute in the 1980s and 1990s, a plan to bring Republicans to power.

Working with Atwater brought Rogers into the world of the first President Bush. He was one of Bush's first real campaign aides preparing for the 1988 presidential race. Rogers was a fixture at campaign headquarters and on the candidate's plane; but to outsiders, he seemed to occupy a position of no great importance. He was as likely to be tending to the needs of traveling reporters or the anxieties of local politicos as conferring with the candidate. But when candidate Bush become the first President Bush, Ed Rogers moved to the White

House staff as chief assistant, fixer, and errand-runner for White House Chief of Staff John Sununu. Reporters sometimes ridiculed Rogers as a coat-holder for the famously abrasive and sometimes imperious Sununu, but they missed the larger point: Ed Rogers was becoming known and credentialed as a young man firmly inside the power structure.

Rogers cashed in on that status when he left the White House in 1991. He teamed with two other Republican movers from the South, former Republican National Chairman Haley Barbour and veteran operative Lanny Griffith, to form a lobbying firm. Because all three partners knew every Republican worth knowing, the firm became very successful.

By 2000, the rush of clients domestic and foreign, from the Middle East to Asia, had swelled the firm's lobbying billings to $10 million. In a nod to the importance of the global economy to Washington, the group later hired former Ambassador Robert Blackwill, once the American envoy to India and a Russia expert, who attracted clients eager for help in, among other things, navigating the regulatory and political thickets of both countries.

Another element of the equation was maintaining a high public profile. Rogers's website boasts of 150 media appearances backing President Bush's 2004 re-election; on the day in March 2007 when we interviewed him, his next appointment was an afternoon appearance on MSNBC's *Hardball* program. Along the way, the firm followed a familiar pattern of Washington public-affairs firms: It was bought out by an international public-relations conglomerate.

Rogers is not a particular favorite of George W. Bush; memories still linger of his departure from George H. W. Bush's White House. But that hasn't stopped Rogers from replenishing his supply of political capital by hiring associates from the current Bush White House. After the president ordered the invasion of Iraq, for example, Rogers sought business in Iraq in partnership with Bush's 2000 campaign manager, former Federal Emergency Management Agency Director Joe Allbaugh. The firm has mined House and Senate leadership offices and federal agencies that generate lucrative regulatory work, including the Health and Human Services Department, the Food and Drug Administration, and the Department of Energy.

Rogers says information, not raw favor-trading, drives the process. "I haven't taken five members of Congress to dinner," he explains. "You can't take Tom Bevill [a onetime Alabama congressman] to the Palm and get your deal done anymore."

His firm and others like it on the Avenue acquire the expertise and fresh connections of young congressional and administration staffers by doubling their government pay, which at top levels can reach $150,000 a year. But Rogers says he sometimes urges job-seekers from Capitol Hill to "get your postgraduate degree" by rounding out their résumés with an administration agency job; that can help them dramatically hike the pay they can command when they enter the private sector, sometimes to $600,000 or more. A stint at the Federal Communications Commission, for instance, might substantially increase the value of a House staffer with several years' experience on telecommunications legislation.

The firm's gold-plated client list ranges from the pharmaceutical industry (Bristol-Myers Squibb) to aerospace (Lockheed Martin) to high technology (IBM) to cities and universities.

Its approach to solving a problem for a client, Rogers says, tends to follow a familiar pattern of diagnosis and action. It begins with this question: "Is there a wolf at the door?" in the form of a legislator or regulator bent on assailing the client or its interests. The next task is finding advocates to speak up for the client. "Find me some champions quick," as Rogers puts it. Then "Who are the bad guys?" Identifying rival interests can provide a useful foil in arguments over potential government action. And finally, "What's our horror story?"—a description of the most outlandish consequence a potential policy change might produce.

The information-driven reality of high-stakes lobbying, Rogers says, stands in stark contrast to what has become the caricature of the Washington influence industry: disgraced influence-peddler Jack

Abramoff, in his black hat and trench coat. "I have never been asked for a bribe," Rogers says. "I have never witnessed graft."

But long after Roger's 1991 misstep with the Saudi sheikh, his firm has continued to find controversy. In 2007, Barbour Griffith & Rogers faced an unflattering *Business Week* story about its $580,000 representation of Alfa Bank, a Russian financial company. The magazine reported that Diligence LLP, a firm that shared offices with Barbour Griffith & Rogers, used deception to persuade a Bahamian accountant into surrendering secret details of an auditing firm's audit of an Alfa competitor, by making the accountant believe the information was needed for British national security. The Alfa competitor, IPOC, sued Diligence and Barbour Griffith & Rogers.[4]

And in a sign of the change the 2006 election brought to Pennsylvania Avenue, the article drew a reaction from Congress. Representative Henry Waxman, Democrat of California, who chairs the House Government Reform Committee, wrote a lawyer for IPOC seeking documents pertaining to allegations of "corporate espionage." Waxman later withdrew that request.[5]

It's a moment that might call into question the wisdom of Barbour Griffith & Rogers's decision to build its business solely around Republicans, in contrast to other firms on the Avenue that have hedged by employing lobbyists on both sides of the partisan aisle.

But Rogers voices no regrets about his strategy. When Barbour Griffith needs Democrats to help make its case, he says, the firm simply contracts with a Democratic firm.

At one end of Pennsylvania Avenue, Republicans still hold the White House; at the other, Democrats have a majority, but the forty-nine votes Republicans control remain nine more than the GOP needs to sustain filibusters of Democratic initiatives. If Republicans ever fell below that level, he concedes with a grin, "we may have to have a meeting to decide what to do about that."

12. THE INDUSTRY MAN: BILLY TAUZIN

BILLY TAUZIN IS the pharmaceutical industry's man in Washington. How he came to hold that job—which has become one of the city's most important, as health care has come to consume ever-bigger slices of the American economic pie—is a case study in how power and politics have changed on Pennsylvania Avenue.

Tauzin is a charming, gregarious Louisianan who worked his way through college at Nicholls State University and law school at Louisiana State University. He was interested in politics and, like virtually everybody in Louisiana who wanted to play on the political stage in the 1960s and 1970s, he was a Democrat.[1] Democrats dominated the entire South in those days, and they surely dominated Louisiana, where the late Huey Long had established a Democratic dominance that paralleled the Democratic dominance his contemporary, Franklin Roosevelt, had established nationally.

Tauzin became a state legislator, and by the time he was ready to run for Congress, signs of partisan turmoil were apparent. Louisianans have a wide conservative streak that increasingly seemed out of sync with the more liberal national Democratic Party. The congressional seat Tauzin sought had been occupied by David Treen, the first Republican in the Louisiana congressional delegation since Reconstruction. Treen had just become Louisiana's governor, which was a shock to the state's system.

Treen, in fact, pressed Tauzin to switch to the Republican Party to run for his seat. Tauzin refused. Instead, he ran as a Democrat and played up the fact that he had stayed loyal to his party. His campaign supporters, playing off an old cigarette commercial, wore black patches under their eyes, so it appeared they had black eyes, and carried signs saying "I'd rather fight than switch." It didn't hurt Tauzin that his campaign was advised by a brilliant, young, and then-unknown political consultant named James Carville.

Still, the strains between the national Democratic Party and its conservative Southern chapter were apparent. Tauzin's Republican opponent mocked him in that first race by telling voters that, although he and Tauzin would probably agree on most issues, the big difference between them was that Tauzin's first official act in Washington would be to cast a vote to elect a Massachusetts liberal, Tip O'Neill, as the Democratic Speaker of the House. "It was the vanguard of the effort to dislodge the Democratic Party by using Tip O'Neill as a symbol," Tauzin recalls. "And I think it was, by and large, the end of comity in the House, that use of O'Neill. It led to this terrible politics of personal attack we have today."

Tauzin persevered as a conservative Democrat through the 1980s, in large part by crossing party lines to back Reagan initiatives. He became one of the Boll Weevils and cast one of the deciding votes for Reagan's first budget. He later became a member of the Blue Dogs, another group of conservative Democrats, largely from the South, who banded together to try to exert some influence on the party.

Tauzin was popular in his district and easily won when he ran for re-election every two years. But his views on taxes and federal spending were increasingly out of step with those of his Democratic colleagues. In some ways, the strains actually increased when a fellow Democrat, Bill Clinton, was elected president, and his party had more freedom to try to advance its agenda.

For example, Tauzin and his fellow Southern conservatives in the House were angered over the handling of a big crime bill Clinton was pushing through. The bill contained a whole series of steps to toughen crime laws and to enact new measures, such as funding inner-city basketball leagues, to help head off youth crimes. The package also included some new gun-control measures. Tauzin and other Southern conservatives supported most of the bill, but didn't want to vote for more gun control, which was hugely unpopular in their districts. They asked that the two parts of the bill—both of which seemed assured of passage in any case—be separated, so they could vote against gun controls while still backing Clinton on the broader crime legislation. The House's Democratic leadership refused. Tauzin felt the leaders' view was "You have to be with us on everything." Strains between the national Democratic Party and the Southern conservatives, who once made up one of the party's pillars, deepened.

Then came the Gingrich revolution and the 1994 Republican takeover of the House. The Republicans gained power in large measure by finally expelling Democrats, largely in the South, who were hanging on in conservative districts where the voters were increasingly drifting to the Republicans. Tauzin, still widely popular back home, was one who hung on. But he immediately came under pressure to switch parties and join the newly empowered Republicans in the majority, to increase his clout on behalf of his district. He held a town-hall meeting to let constituents speak out on the question of switching parties, thought about it overnight, then decided to stay a Democrat. But he warned that if he felt muzzled by his party he would switch.

It didn't take long for him to feel exactly that way. The precipitating event was a bill on securities litigation. When Democrats were still in power, Tauzin had written a bill designed, among other things, to reduce corporations' exposure to costly class-action lawsuits. The bill was despised by trial lawyers, who thrive on such lawsuits, and who make up a strong activist group within the Democratic Party. "I couldn't even get a hearing on it in the Democratic-controlled House," Tauzin says. When the GOP took over, California Republican Christopher Cox took up the same bill and pushed it through the House, and a version passed the Senate. After that, a conference committee of selected House and Senate members was needed, to work out differences between the two chambers' versions of the securities legislation. Tauzin wanted to be on the conference committee; he was, after all, the father of the bill in question. Democratic leaders refused to appoint him.

That was the last straw: "I couldn't even be on the conference committee on a bill I wrote." Tauzin concluded that the Democrats' reaction to losing power wasn't to move toward the center in order to win back some of those lost Republican votes but, rather, to regroup by consolidating around their reliable liberal base. When Tauzin entered Congress in 1980, he estimates, there were about sixty identifiable Democratic conservatives in the House. By 1995, that number had dwindled to about twelve. Tauzin decided he didn't want to be one any longer. He let it be known he was considering switching parties.

At one point, he was asked to speak to the full Democratic Caucus to explain why he was considering leaving. The House's full contingent of Democrats gathered on the House floor. Tauzin told of his family's long Democratic history, and of his own affiliation with the civil-rights movement and the integration of colleges in the South. The reason he had joined the Democratic Party, he told his colleagues, was that he loved its tolerance for a variety of different Americans. "I have a confession to make," he remembers saying. "I now feel I'm working among some of the most intolerant people I know." A gasp went up in the room. As he left the chamber, Tauzin recalls, he was approached by Representative Henry Waxman, a liberal and a friend, who asked whether he really felt he couldn't speak for the Democratic Party any longer. Tauzin said that was the case. Tauzin says Waxman replied: "Then you have to leave."

So Tauzin left. In the summer of 1995 he changed party affiliation to become a Republican. As a new member of the Republican majority, he eventually became chairman of a subcommittee handling telecommunications legislation, and then chairman of the powerful Energy and Commerce Committee. At one point, Gingrich asked

Tauzin what advice he, as a former member of the Democratic majority, would offer leaders of the new Republican majority. "Cherish your dissidents," Tauzin advised.

Tauzin came to feel that Gingrich's successors were ignoring that advice, repeating the former Democratic leaders' mistakes of demanding lock-step loyalty and marginalizing dissidents. Those dissidents, Tauzin says, make party leaders uncomfortable, but often give important warning signs when the party is veering away from the mainstream and into political trouble.

Tauzin himself soon faced a problem far more personal in nature: He contracted an unusual form of cancer—one that, his doctors told him later, left him with a 5 percent chance of survival. He licked it.

By 2005, a respected senior member of his new Republican Party, he decided to leave Congress and move northwest along Pennsylvania Avenue to take one of Washington's plum jobs as head of PhRMA, the pharmaceutical industry's lobbying arm in Washington. In it, Tauzin tries to steer PhRMA away from the very deep partisan divide he felt had overtaken the House he left.

Looking back at his former colleagues, he muses: "They see each other as enemies. They don't travel with each other. They don't socialize with each other." Upon taking over PhRMA, Tauzin felt the pharmaceutical lobby, long considered largely a friend of the Republicans, had fallen into the polarization trap. It was perceived as an ally of the Republican Party and an enemy of the Democrats. To Tauzin, it seemed to be fighting its opponents rather than trying to win them over. He set out to change that.

Still, Tauzin can hardly escape partisan warfare. One of his principal jobs is to maintain support in Congress for a new prescription-drug benefit for senior citizens on Medicare, which passed when Republicans controlled Congress, with only grudging Democratic support. In the 2006 congressional campaign, the drug benefit became a prime target of attack by Democrats, who assailed it as too generous to drug companies, too stingy for seniors and, in the words of Pennsylvania Senate candidate Bob Casey, "a giveaway to big

PhRMA,"[2] because the law that launched the program doesn't allow the government to negotiate lower drug prices directly with drug companies.

In response, Tauzin and the drug industry threw a lot of support to Republicans in the campaign—the drug companies through their political-action committees, and PhRMA through both its own PAC and its support for a Chamber of Commerce ad campaign backing the Republicans' version of the drug benefit.

Pennsylvania's Republican Senator Rick Santorum, running against Casey, became one of the biggest recipients of drug-company money in his re-election race. Overall, PhRMA's own political-action committee gave 78 percent of its contributions to Republicans in the 2006 election cycle, according to the Center for Responsive Politics.[3] Tauzin says the efforts on behalf of Republicans didn't reflect a PhRMA preference for them so much as a desire to stay true to those who had been allies of the drug industry, as Santorum had been.

But Santorum lost his race, and Republicans lost control of Congress. So, once the election was over, Tauzin and his organization needed to pivot to adjust to the new political reality. As a Republican who used to be a Democrat, Tauzin is one of a shrinking minority of Washington's leaders with genuine friends in both parties, which meant he was in a better position than most lobbyists and industry representatives to make the adjustment.

He sped up a change in PhRMA's legislative-relations staff that he had already begun, to make it more bipartisan. New staff members who had worked for Democrats were brought in, and the PhRMA congressional-relations team was reorganized, with one Democratic vice president and one Republican vice president, each serving under the head of the operation. "We couldn't be defined in a partisan fashion as we had [been] in the past," Tauzin says. "We have a direct relationship with both parties now, which we didn't have when I got here."

Tauzin himself tried to "rekindle" his personal ties with Democrats with whom he once served in the House. The effort got off to a rough start when the new House, as part of a "first hundred hours" blitz of legislation pushed by the new Democratic majority, passed a bill requiring the government to negotiate with the drug companies over new, lower prices on Medicare prescription drugs. That effort died in the Senate, though, meaning the Medicare debate would continue.

Tauzin settled in to deal with the new Washington of closely divided power. He had a long list of issues to hash out with the new Democratic majority in the House: Would the United States allow cheaper drugs to be imported from abroad to compete with drugs made at home, or would Congress listen to PhRMA's cries that such imports aren't safe? What kind of rules would be put in place to regulate biologically engineered drugs? What would the government eventually decide to do to keep down the cost of Mediare prescription drugs?

PhRMA had become a punching bag for many Democrats, who found it politically useful to rail against "the big drug companies" and their hefty profits. Tauzin is well aware of that. But he also has the kind of perspective that can be found only in a man who has been in Washington over a quarter-century, who has been a leader in both parties, and who has survived a serious cancer scare by using drugs produced by the very companies he now represents.

"I served twenty-five years," he says. "I've heard a lot of campaign rhetoric. But I also know a lot of House and Senate members. And the one thing that is true is that when the election is over they also have to represent the people who didn't vote for them. That sense of responsibility descends pretty rapidly on your shoulders." He accepts that PhRMA is and will remain a political target, but says his job is to get past old grievances: "There are some people who want to punish the organization over old wounds. But they won't want to punish patients."

IV. ROLES REDEFINED

IN LATE NOVEMBER 2002, while Washington was growing feverish with speculation that President George W. Bush might soon order an attack on Iraq to oust Saddam Hussein, the president's father embarked on a quiet journey of his own. Former President George H. W. Bush boarded a plane in Dallas and flew off to the Middle East for some private conversations with old friends he knew from his own considerable experience in the region.

Just before Thanksgiving, he arrived in the Red Sea resort city of Sharm El Sheikh, where Egyptian President Hosni Mubarak spent time when he wanted to escape the smog, noise, and chaos of Cairo. The two men had much in common. They came from the same generation of world leaders; on the November day they met, the elder Bush was seventy-eight, Mubarak seventy-four. They had known each other for a long time. Both had had the experience of being vice president to a charismatic leader—Mubarak to Anwar Sadat, and Bush to Ronald Reagan. Bush, in fact, was America's vice president when Sadat was assassinated, and Mubarak rose from vice president to president.

More than that, they had consulted each other over the years on all manner of crises: the Iran-Iraq war, the Palestinian intifada, Iraq's invasion of Kuwait, the first Persian Gulf War. Mubarak speaks good English, so their conversations over the years could be direct and personal.

Thus, they were two old friends sitting down that day in Sharm El Sheikh. Mubarak, of course, was well aware that Bush's son, the current American president, was seriously pondering an invasion of Iraq as part of his post-9/11 quest to rid the Middle East of terrorists, radical elements, and weapons that might be turned against the United States.

Mubarak thought attacking Iraq was a bad idea, and he let the father of the president know it. According to a memo of that conversation that was transmitted back to Washington afterward, Mubarak predicted great fallout harmful to America if the Iraq invasion went forward. Mubarak said that he didn't want to presume to tell the United States what to do. But he warned that Iraq, like much of the eastern Persian Gulf region, had a large number of Shiites sympathetic to Iran, and he fretted that an invasion that toppled Saddam would unleash them. That, Mubarak warned, would lead to a major destabilization of the region, according to the officials familiar with the memo.

Mubarak actually agreed with the U.S. assessment that Saddam probably possessed chemical and biological weapons, but he thought America should be seeking a solution other than war to deal with that problem. The two men launched into a long discussion of the new U.S. push to bring democracy to the region, and Mubarak warned that the push would essentially pave the way for the region's extremists to come to power. Views of the United States were very negative in the region, Mubarak explained, and votes for new leaders in the region would be translated into votes against America. In Iraq, the exiled Iraqi figures being counted on to move back home and run the country after Saddam was gone would be seen as traitors by many Iraqis who had endured Saddam's rule, and would find it hard to get popular support.

Mubarak had his own reasons for making such arguments, of course. He himself was hardly a popularly elected leader, having maintained power over the years by holding a series of essentially phony elections in which he was the only real candidate for president. And if there was instability in the region, he would have as much to fear as any leader in the Arab world.

Still, the forecast that Mubarak laid out in private that day proved over time to be eerily accurate. He had foreseen the consequences of an invasion of Iraq with great clarity, and directly warned the man who had the most intimate connection to the American president. The elder Bush took it all in, then boarded his plane and flew home. He landed in Waco, Texas, and proceeded to his son's ranch in Crawford to spend the Thanksgiving holiday weekend. There, the White House would tell reporters, the two men shared a family meal and spent some time fishing together.[1]

There is little sign, though, that Mubarak's warning made much difference. Within four months, the second President Bush ordered an invasion of Iraq.

Few scenes capture the way philosophical and generational changes have swept over the American system of government than the conversation of those elder statesmen. Bush senior and Mubarak are products of an old school of international thinking. They are realists more than idealists. For them, particularly in the Middle East, the paramount goal of America and its friends had always been stability. Stability reduced the risks of unpleasant surprises.

In a stable environment, extremists could be more easily contained, and secure oil supplies ensured. Yes, that sometimes meant supporting unsavory regimes as they cracked down internally, or keeping a lid on debate and dissent within troubled countries, but the alternatives appeared much more damaging to America's interests. In the eyes of many who hold such a worldview, containing Saddam Hussein was preferable to unleashing the shock waves that would result from toppling him.

That simply wasn't the view of Bush the younger and the new foreign-policy thinkers he represented and empowered. They are more idealists than realists. In their view, the quest for short-term stability had only turned the Middle East into an incubator for long-term problems and extremism that exploded with the terrorist attacks on September 11, 2001.

Just as old thinking gave way to new on national security, and as old leaders stepped aside for younger, so it has gone in Washington more broadly. Pennsylvania Avenue isn't static, but, rather, a living, breathing, evolving environment, where roles and attitudes are constantly changing. In the last decade or so, new enemies have emerged, a new global economy has evolved, and new technologies have burst onto the scene. Washington adapts, and its players operate differently as a result. What follows is a look at some of those changed roles.

13. THE POLICY ADVISER: ELLIOTT ABRAMS

IN THE SUMMER OF 2007, Elliott Abrams found himself in Prague, in the Czech Republic, pursuing an unusual mission: He was a veteran dissident, trying to help new dissidents from around the globe change the world.

Abrams was a senior member of President George W. Bush's National Security Council staff, holding down a job that had never existed before in the American foreign-policy machinery. His assignment was to find ways to spread democracy around the world.

Abrams is an intense sandy-haired intellectual with a college professor's love of debate and a street fighter's appreciation for the thrust and parry of policy battles. He has lived through a generation's worth of change and controversy in American foreign policy. As a charter member of the neoconservatives, the onetime Democrats whose hawkish views carried them out of the Democratic Party in the 1970s and into the center of the Republican Party, Abrams had in his own time railed against the foreign-policy establishment and bucked the status quo.

Now his job, in essence, was to help others do the same. After President Bush came to power, he declared that a central goal of American foreign policy henceforth would be to promote democratic change around the globe. He launched the Global Democracy Strategy, which holds that democracy has the power to move the Middle East—and, indeed, the world—away from despotism and Islamic extremism and toward more stable systems embracing more liberal Western values.

The idea was as revolutionary and controversial as it was simple, and represented perhaps the most important change in American foreign-policy thinking in a generation. It meant the United States would, implicitly or explicitly, be pushing to change governments, or at least the way governments behaved, and not just among adversaries, such as North Korea, Cuba, and Belarus, but also among friends, such as Egypt and Saudi Arabia.

This new philosophy meant that when President Bush invaded Iraq, his goal wasn't simply to overthrow Saddam Hussein and replace him with a different Iraqi strongman, but, rather, to try to create a representative democracy among the country's fractious Sunnis, Shiites, and Kurds. The philosophy meant that the United States would be cheering on some of the internal agitators that other governments around the world found most annoying. And it meant that the United States would, at least rhetorically, be rallying dissidents in Russia and China, even while seeking the help of those world powers in solving other problems around the globe.

Bush created an office in the White House specifically to advance his goal. Abrams, working out of the grand Eisenhower Executive Office Building, next to the White House, was picked to take charge of it.

All of which explains why Elliott Abrams found himself accompanying President Bush to Prague in June 2007. By that time, with the war in Iraq turning into a quagmire that summoned the inevitable Vietnam comparisons, and Bush's job-approval ratings plunging to Nixon-like lows, cynics doubted that the president really cared that much any longer about his democracy crusade.

President Bush was trying to prove the cynics wrong; he flew to Prague to speak at a meeting of dissidents and democracy crusaders from countries around the world. The appearance was hardly the result of a casual or spur-of-the-moment decision. The seeds were planted about six months earlier, when Bush sat down in the Oval Office for a chat with Natan Sharansky, an old Abrams friend and soulmate. Sharansky, a Russian Jew who immigrated to Israel and became a Cabinet minister, had written a book a few years earlier proclaiming that democracy has the power to eliminate tyranny and terror. Early in the president's term, one of Bush's college classmates sent the book to the president, who read it and found it inspirational and an affirmation of his belief that promoting democracy should be at the center of American foreign policy.

Not long afterward, Sharansky visited Washington, and Abrams ushered him into the Oval Office for a chat with the president. A friendship was struck, and subsequently Sharansky was invited to come by for a meeting with the president whenever he was in town. On one of those visits, Sharansky told Bush that he and former Czech leader Václav Havel, who crusaded for democratic reform in Eastern Europe after the fall of the Soviet Union, were putting together a global conference for dissidents to give them a boost as they pursued similar crusades in their home countries. Sharansky told Bush, in essence: Havel and I are the old guys among democracy crusaders. We want to give the new generation a shot in the arm. Would you be willing to come to the conference?

The president checked his schedule, saw that he was going to be in Europe for a summit meeting of the Group of Eight industrialized nations at roughly the same time, so he said he would be there.

By simply showing up, of course, the president would be speaking volumes about his support of dissidents. The next question, though, was what he would say in his speech to the group.

Within the White House staff, the president has his own small stable of speechwriters, whose job is to craft the actual words their boss utters in any formal speech. But the substantive message conveyed by those words is shaped as much by the experts from across the government on the subject the president is to address—and in this case that meant Abrams. A presidential speech is what Abrams calls an "action-causing device"—that is, it compels the administration to decide what it really believes, forces feuding advisers to settle debates and ar-

guments about what its policies ought to be, and drives the bureaucracy to follow through on what the president says. A major speech,
in short, isn't just a set of words, but a policy event.

In this case, the most obvious goal of the speech was to address
doubters at home and abroad who thought promoting democracy
had slipped off the Bush radar screen. "The first thing to do," Abrams
says, "was to restate that this was at the heart of not just his foreign policy but America's foreign policy." The second goal was to address the
critics who thought there was little the United States could actually
be or do to energize democracy movements.

To accomplish the second goal, Abrams and his colleagues within
the White House decided that the president should declare that he
was ordering Secretary of State Condoleezza Rice to send a cable to
every American ambassador in an "unfree nation" stating that part of
the ambassador's job was to meet with dissidents and democracy advocates, get to know them, and encourage them. The president
would say as much in his speech. He also would note that, though it
had attracted little attention, the U.S. government had recently set up
a financial fund to help dissidents by, for example, paying their legal
fees and supporting their families if the dissidents were thrown in jail
for their political activities.

A principal goal of the speech, in short, was to have the president
of the United States declare on the world stage that he still cared pas-
sionately about promoting democratic change, and that he could do
something about it.

The trickiest part of preparing the speech was deciding how specific to be in citing countries where democracy crusaders were being
suppressed. "One of the things we said to ourselves was 'You have to
name names,'" Abrams says. "The president fully agreed that had to
be in the speech. He was willing to take what flak would be coming
for doing so. There was never any debate on that." Inevitably, that task
would lead the Bush administration into a diplomatic minefield. The
speech's credibility would be undermined if the only countries cited
as standing in the way of democracy were proven American enemies

Ken Duberstein speaks on NBC's *Meet the Press.* The premier Washington wise man laments that TV guests often are expected to say something outrageous.

GETTY IMAGES FOR *MEET THE PRESS*

Deputy Treasury Secretary Robert Kimmitt was a standup guy in the furor over Dubai Ports World, but he paid a public-relations price, in a quintessential example of how Washington doesn't work. COURTESY OF THE DEPARTMENT OF THE TREASURY

President Bush's position on the Dubai Ports World deal—that the sale of port operations to a foreign firm should be allowed to go through—matched the private sentiments of top Democrats and Republicans alike. But it was undermined by his threat to veto any legislation blocking the deal, issued during this February 2006 interview with White House reporters on Air Force One.
WHITE HOUSE PHOTO BY ERIC DRAPER

After the grind of the Carter White House, David Rubenstein helped create a worldwide financial powerhouse that changed Pennsylvania Avenue and made him a billionaire. COURTESY OF
THE CARLYLE GROUP

Brash and cocksure, Rahm Emanuel commanded the political guerrilla war that ousted Republicans from control of the House in 2006 but didn't change its crippling partisanship. U.S. HOUSE OF REPRESENTATIVES

Chris Van Hollen displays a genial style with his constituents in Washington's good-government suburbs, saving his competitive aggression for the fight to maintain Democratic control of the House. VAN HOLLEN FOR CONGRESS PHOTO

The unhappy twilight of the Bush years will test the smile of Tom Cole, a onetime football player trying to help his party fight back from adversity.

COLE FOR CONGRESS PHOTO BY MIKE CALCOTTE

Young enough to be Speaker Nancy Pelosi's daughter, Representative Debbie Wasserman Schultz (left) has rapidly parlayed a safe district and ferocious drive into a place within the House power structure.

JONATHAN BEETON, OFFICE OF REPRESENTATIVE DEBBIE WASSERMAN SCHULTZ

Karl Rove helped modernize the conservative movement for the demands of America's polarized political environment; in George W. Bush he found a candidate who could capitalize. It was a bond of mutual dependence and deep emotion, as displayed when they appeared together in August 2007 to announce Rove's departure from the White House. WHITE HOUSE PHOTO BY JOYCE N. BOGHOSIAN

Republicans looking to purge Pennsylvania Avenue's lucrative lobbying community of Democratic influence gave "a pass" to Hilary Rosen and Jack Valenti, who spoke, respectively, for the music and movie industries in the capital. GETTY IMAGES

Lea Berman, pictured here with White House chef Chris Comerford, had the title of "social secretary," but it was a job that had become enmeshed in the business of politics far more than a generation before.
WHITE HOUSE PHOTO

The smiles of President Bush and Chinese leader Hu Jintao masked
deep tensions within the two countries' relationship, which burst into
view even at this Rose Garden meeting in April 2006.

WHITE HOUSE PHOTO BY ERIC DRAPER

With astonishing speed, Eli Pariser and MoveOn.org have marshaled the power of the left-leaning "netroots" to wield influence in policy debates on Pennsylvania Avenue as well as election campaigns.

COURTESY OF MOVEON.ORG

Kyle McSlarrow brought experience at the highest levels of Congress and the Bush administration to his work for the well-heeled National Cable and Telecommunications Association. But on the issue of regulating the Internet, he met his match in the power of the liberal "netroots."

OSCAR EINZIG PHOTOGRAPHY

After leaving the first Bush White House, Ed Rogers built a $30 million lobbying business—and "sliced the hog" profitably enough to build a suburban mansion with a six-car garage, an art gallery, and a guest room modeled after a suite at the Ritz-Carlton. LEPOLDPHOTOGRAPHY.COM

Billy Tauzin's defection from the Democratic Party reflected the GOP's Southern rise, and his move to head the drug industry's lobbying behemoth tracked the rise of health care as a dominant issue on Pennsylvania Avenue. COURTESY OF PHRMA

Elliott Abrams's path to the top ranks of Republican foreign-policy thinkers and onto George W. Bush's foreign-policy team began three decades earlier—in an unhappy meeting with an earlier president, Democrat Jimmy Carter. WHITE HOUSE PHOTO

President Bush speaks to a conference of pro-democracy activists from around the world in Prague in June 2007. The event both rekindled Bush's campaign for democratic reforms around the globe and illustrated the power of a presidential speech to focus his administration's agenda.
WHITE HOUSE PHOTO BY CHRIS GREENBERG

As communications director for House Speaker Nancy Pelosi, Brendan Daly faces an unprecedented and unpredictable array of news outlets, from traditional newspapers and broadcast networks to cable TV and the blogosphere. HOUSE SPEAKER'S OFFICE PHOTO BY CINDY JIMENEZ

In his work, be it for presidential candidates or labor unions assailing Wal-Mart, Democratic operative-for-hire Jim Jordan carries all the tools of his trade: laptop, BlackBerry, cellphone, and coffee. TAYLOR WEST

Following the triumph of the 2004 Bush re-election campaign, Republican operative Terry Nelson faced turbulence on a series of fronts: in defending Wal-Mart, trying to protect the GOP's Senate majority, and briefly managing the rocky presidential bid of Senator John McCain.

ASSOCIATED PRESS

Though he faltered as a Republican presidential candidate, Senator Sam Brownback of Kansas helped shape a new and more nuanced message for religious conservatives along Pennsylvania Avenue.

COURTESY OF SENATOR
SAM BROWNBACK

Pete Wehner, a former White House speechwriter and onetime aide to Bush political mastermind Karl Rove, is at the vanguard of a new wave of Christian conservatives: He's concerned about issues such as poverty as well as traditional evangelical concerns such as abortion, and he's somewhat leery of those who too overtly use religion for political gain.
DUPONT PHOTOGRAPHERS, INC.

Of all the freshman Democratic senators who arrived on Pennsylvania Avenue in early 2007, Jim Webb may have been the most remarkable by virtue of the red state that elected him (Virginia) and the Republican he defeated (presidential hopeful George Allen). CAROLYN WASLER

Mara Vanderslice's attempts to infuse the Democratic Party's agenda with religious themes and values was embraced by John Kerry—but not by all parts of his campaign or by the liberal establishment.

COURTESY OF MARA VANDERSLICE

The unconventional advocacy of Andrew Stern (right) led him to split from the traditional labor movement and seek common ground on health care with one of the leading targets of the Democratic left, Wal-Mart CEO Lee Scott (left). (Center: Bill Clinton's former White House chief of staff John Podesta.) COPYRIGHT © 2007 KRIS PRICE

Bernadette Budde, one of the business community's leading political strategists, sees a solution to Pennsylvania Avenue's gridlock in coalitions of "the lions and the lambs."

COURTESY OF BIPAC

Democratic Representative Charles Rangel of New York (left) was a match in affability for a Republican president but was frustrated by the gulf preventing partisans on both sides from reaching consensus on tax issues. WHITE HOUSE PHOTO BY ERIC DRAPER

President Bush greets Representative Jim McCrery and other Republican House members at a reception.

The career of onetime Democratic National Chairman Robert Strauss (left) tracked the erosion of bipartisan cooperation; his law partner, Ken Mehlman (right), was the chairman of the Republican Party as partisan polarization peaked—and left Americans away from Pennsylvania Avenue yearning for change.

such as North Korea, Belarus, and Syria. The president's credibility would be enhanced by showing that he was willing to chide even friends, but that risked a diplomatic backlash from allies needed in Iraq and the war on terror.

Similarly, the president was to meet shortly after the speech with Russian President Vladimir Putin, with whom relations were already on a downhill slide. How much worse might the relationship get if Bush used the speech to criticize the Russian leader for quashing dissidents just before their get-together? Bush decided to take the risk and specifically cite problems in Russia, China, and Egypt, among other nations.

In the end, Bush appeared at the conference before dissidents and democratic activists from seventeen countries on five continents. He told them: "The policy of tolerating tyranny is a moral and strategic failure. It is a mistake the world must not repeat in the twenty-first century."[1] Then he made a more personal statement by striding out into the conference to meet the dissidents in attendance, one by one.

Afterward, the reaction was mixed. The Russians, surprisingly, didn't complain. The Egyptians, America's strongest allies in the Arab world, were outraged that they had been cited for blocking democracy. The Egyptian ambassador in Washington visited both the White House and the State Department to complain. The Chinese complained vociferously that the president had cited by name Rebiya Kadeer—an exiled Chinese Muslim dissident—and then met with her at the conference.

To Abrams, though, the most annoying reaction came from within the U.S. government itself. The State Department, never eager to make the kinds of diplomatic waves the president was seeking to create in countries where American diplomats are generally trying to foster good relations, delayed for weeks in sending out the cable President Bush had announced would be dispatched, ordering ambassadors to meet with dissidents. The speech was, as Abrams said, an action-causing event, though the action didn't come quite as quickly as he had hoped.

• • •

Pushing the foreign-policy bureaucracy into new and uncomfortable directions was hardly a new experience for Abrams. Such efforts were, in fact, the hallmark of his career, one marked by controversy and an enormous rethinking of America's role in the world. Abrams has found himself in the midst of that upheaval over and over again, and he has the scars to show for it.

Abrams was born in New York and became fully credentialed as a foreign-policy intellectual at an exceptionally early age. He got undergraduate and law degrees at Harvard and a master's degree in international relations at the London School of Economics.[2] In his political life, as in the political lives of many of those Abrams would come to consider his comrades-in-arms, he began as a liberal Democrat and then moved rightward. As a young man, he went to work in the Senate for two of the intellectual giants of the Democratic Party, Washington Senator Henry "Scoop" Jackson and New York Senator Daniel Patrick Moynihan.

Abrams came onto the Washington scene as a young man precisely as a long bipartisan consensus about America's role in the world was crumbling. For almost four decades after World War II, there was a genuine foreign-policy establishment in Washington that created and nurtured that consensus. Wise men—and it was almost all men in those days—from both parties generally agreed on a policy of containing the Soviet Union, which produced a rough bipartisan agreement about the great contours of America's role in the world. By the 1970s, in the aftermath of the Vietnam War, that consensus was falling apart.

Abrams's first mentor, Scoop Jackson, broke away from the Democratic mainstream on the giant issue of the time: the threat from the Soviet Union. He didn't share the relatively benign view of the Soviets common among many liberal Democrats; he was, instead, a proud Cold Warrior. Moynihan, in turn, was unconventional in every sense and difficult to pigeonhole ideologically. He crossed party lines to work in Richard Nixon's Republican White House. On social policy, he was deeply concerned about poverty, as many Democrats are, but was also deeply concerned that the welfare system Democrats had constructed to deal with it was seriously flawed. Moynihan shared Jackson's dire view of the Soviet system. On that score, they made common cause with another Democratic heavyweight, AFL-CIO President George Meany. Those three men—Jackson, Moynihan, and Meany, all hard-liners on foreign policy, none in step with the prevailing views of their own party—formed the core of an alternative Democratic view of the world.

They became like magnets, attracting brilliant young thinkers who either shared or came to share their fierce anticommunist views. Richard Perle, Jeane Kirkpatrick, Norman Podhoretz, Midge Decter, Elliott Abrams—all were foreign-policy intellectuals who became part of a kind of Moynihan-Jackson-Meany circle. They would form the core of what became known as the neoconservatives—literally, the "new conservatives."

The neocons had a different view of the world from that of either the Democratic Party's liberals, who hated the Vietnam War, or realists in the Republican Party, who saw the Cold War as a struggle that needed, above all, to be managed so its tensions wouldn't break into the open. They were comfortable with neither George McGovern on the left nor Henry Kissinger on the right. Instead, they saw the Cold War as a part of a global struggle between personal liberty and freedom on the one hand, and governments that would restrict liberty and freedom on the other. The U.S. role in the world, they believed, was to lead the fight for liberty and personal freedom in all cases. Communism then (like radical Islam later) was the ideology that most threatened these ideals. "We didn't view the Cold War as a clash of superpowers," summarizes Douglas Feith, a neoconservative who became a senior Pentagon official under the second President Bush. "We viewed the Cold War as a fight between totalitarianism and liberal democracy."

They saw many Republicans—particularly those from the traditional Ford-Kissinger wing of the party—as indifferent to people's yearning for freedom and liberty around the globe, and they saw many Democrats as indifferent to the threat that communism posed to American values. But they were Democrats nonetheless, and considered themselves to be under the party's broad tent.

Until 1976, that is. In that year, the neocons dreamed that Scoop Jackson would be the Democratic nominee for president and sweep into the White House on the heels of the Watergate scandal that had laid low the Nixon and Ford administrations. Instead, a very different kind of Democrat, surrounded by very different foreign-policy thinkers, was nominated. Jimmy Carter became the beneficiary of Nixon's failings, and he was the Democrat who used them to ride the party to power.

Jimmy Carter had little use for the neocons. He tended to share liberal Democrats' antipathy toward the Vietnam War and their embrace of détente with the Soviets. A president most effectively demonstrates his views and his intentions through the kinds of people he appoints to top jobs around him, and on that front Carter delivered a loud and clear message to the Jackson wing of the party: By and large, he shut them out of top jobs. Abrams and his intellectual fellow travelers remained on the outside of the administration, looking in. The rupture eventually caused an irreparable split in the Democratic Party's national-security community. More than that, the split was the surest sign that the anti-Soviet glue that had held together a bipartisan foreign-policy establishment after World War II had finally dried up and begun to crack.

Carter's emphasis on human rights rather than fighting communism affirmed the neocon view that he didn't understand the lethal nature of the global conflict with the Soviet empire. The idea that the Carter administration was more interested in criticizing the internal policies of allies than in bucking up anti-Soviet leaders within those allied nations grated on the Jackson wing of the party. When the Soviets invaded Afghanistan, the neocons felt that their view of Carter— that his softness invited Soviet aggression—was vindicated.

Yet they were still Democrats, and there was one last attempt to hold the party together and bridge the national-security gaps. Abrams keeps on the wall of his office a black-and-white picture commemorating the occasion. Taken in April 1980, it shows Abrams and his fellow Democratic hawks sitting around a table in the White House, meeting with Carter. The Carter camp was alarmed that the neocons were drifting toward support of Ronald Reagan in the 1980 presidential campaign, so Carter's aides invited them to meet with the president to try to repair the breach and keep them in the party fold.

It didn't work. In fact, it was a disaster. As Abrams recalls the meeting, the hawks complained that Carter foreign policy had drifted leftward, and away from the traditional Democratic mainstream. Carter responded, Abrams recalls, by saying, essentially: There has been no change in my foreign policy; I don't know what you're talking about. The neocons walked out of that meeting and away from the party in the 1980 campaign. Eventually, every one of them pictured in that meeting with Carter became a Republican.

For his part, Abrams was adopted by the Republican Party, where he soon found a comfortable home. When Reagan beat Carter in that 1980 election, the Republicans who came into power pointedly invited the prominent neocons rejected by Carter into important policy jobs, their way of finally and forever taking over that wing of the Democratic Party. Abrams, seen as brilliant, brash, and aggressive, was given some of the most hot-button assignments of all. He went to the State Department, where he was put in charge first of international organizations (where he could act on neocons' doubts about the usefulness of the United Nations), then human-rights policy (where he could put into practice their view that a misguided Carter policy on human rights was harder on America's right-wing friends abroad than on its left-wing enemies).

Ultimately, Abrams became the assistant secretary of state in charge of Latin American affairs, which put him on the front lines of a premier ideological struggle of the 1980s: the argument over whether the United States should be helping right-wing governments and movements in Central America because of their staunch anti-communist views, or opposing those same governments and movements because of their shoddy records on human rights. The Reagan view was that you stood with those who were with America in opposing communism, and you tried to improve their behavior along the way.

For Abrams, trying to navigate Central American policy was a bracing lesson in just how divided Pennsylvania Avenue had become on foreign affairs. The political formula was simple: Virtually all Republicans backed Reagan's efforts to support rightist elements in Central America, and most of the Democrats who then controlled the House opposed them. In the middle stood some forty-five Democrats who wavered between the two camps. If Abrams could convince all forty-five of those Democrats to vote for an administration initiative, he could get the initiative through Congress. If his Democratic support in the House fell to forty or below, he was sure to lose. The issue was that close, that divided. "It was a draw between the two parties," Abrams recalls.

That struggle led Abrams into the middle of the biggest foreign-policy controversy of the time, the Iran-Contra scandal. Under a scheme devised by White House aide Oliver North, the administration secretly sold military equipment to Iran, then used the proceeds to help Nicaragua's Contra rebels, who were trying to overthrow their country's left-wing government. The idea was a clever way around a ban Congress had imposed on aiding the Contras.

When the Iran-Contra affair became known, an independent counsel, Lawrence Walsh, was appointed to investigate whether the administration had broken the law by aiding the Contras. He went after Abrams for concealing the administration's maneuvers from Congress, and Abrams pleaded guilty to misdemeanor counts of withholding information.

Reagan was succeeded by the first President Bush, who pardoned Abrams and other Iran-Contra figures but generally had much less use for them and their brand of aggressive and confrontational foreign policy. The first President Bush was more drawn to the realist school of foreign policy.

So neocons were, in essence, out again—out of favor with the first Bush White House, and certainly out of favor when Bill Clinton's Democrats took over for the next eight years.

Abrams retreated to Washington's parallel universe for out-of-power policy-makers, the constellation of think tanks that surround Pennsylvania Avenue's decision-makers. He became president of the Ethics and Public Policy Center, which was established in 1976 and describes itself as an institution that is "dedicated to applying the Judeo-Christian moral tradition to critical issues of social policy."[3]

It served as a kind of intellectual counterweight first to the realists of the Bush administration, and then, more so, to the Democrats running Clinton foreign policy. In essence, the center pressed American policy-makers not to sacrifice religious and moral values in pursuit of a foreign policy intent on establishing and maintaining stability at all costs. Thus, one of the center's scholars once gave a lecture equating "appeasers" of fascists before World War II with those who would appease radical Islam in the twenty-first century.[4]

In such settings, Abrams and other neocons planted and nurtured the ideas that would become the backbone of the foreign policy of President George W. Bush. A common complaint voiced by Abrams and other neocons—with considerable justification—is that there is now widespread misunderstanding and distortion of what neocons actually stand for. There is, in fact, a tendency among critics simply to point to anything they don't like in Bush foreign policy, particularly the Iraq war, and blame it on the neocons.

Neocons aren't nearly so monolithic in their thinking as is commonly assumed. It's true that they supported the overthrow of Saddam Hussein, but they often disagreed among themselves about what should have happened after that: Some favored the American occupation and wholesale remaking of the Iraqi government that unfolded, but others advocated a quick turnover of power to Iraqis and a rapid exit.

The common denominator for neocons is their belief that the United States should aggressively and unabashedly promote freedom around the world, and be willing to shake up friend and foe alike, and occasionally break some crockery, in doing so. Neocons oppose making concessions to tyrannical systems—communism in the old days, radical Islam now. Freedom, they argue, is the best tonic for tyranny and, ultimately, the best antidote for anti-Americanism. America loses its way, they believe, only when it loses sight of that truly idealistic goal.

To the surprise of many inside the world of foreign-policy thought, the younger Bush proved himself drawn not to the realist thinking of his father's administration, but, rather, to the more idealistic approach of the neocons. That was signaled early on in his 2000 presidential campaign when Paul Wolfowitz, a neocon in good standing, became one of the principal drivers of his campaign's foreign-policy team. Once Bush won, the neocons came back into power, Abrams chief among them.

Abrams was named a senior adviser on the National Security Council staff. As the Bush term took off, Abrams began to accumulate more assignments and power, overseeing U.S. relations with the United Nations, the initial humanitarian relief effort for Iraq after the U.S. invasion, and the strategy for seeking an elusive peace agreement between Israelis and Arabs.

Eventually, Abrams was put in charge of two "directorates," or staffs, within the larger National Security Council staff. One oversees Middle East policy outside of Iraq. The second was the directorate created by Bush to push his new Global Democracy Strategy.

Abrams was lucky enough not to have responsibility for Iraq policy, though the mess in Iraq had made his job plenty hard enough anyway. In a sign of how reality intrudes even on the idealists, the Middle East came to occupy far more of Abrams's time by the latter stages of the Bush presidency. To smooth waters in the Arab world roiled by the American occupation of Iraq, the administration decided it had at least to try to make progress on the other issue that obsessed Arabs, the Palestinians' unresolved fight with Israel.

For the Bush team, the Palestinian problem became the classic example of one style of foreign-policy decision-making, which might be called the small-circle style. The key question was how to revive Palestinian-Israeli peace negotiations, and on that question the large bureaucracies at the State Department and the Pentagon were largely cut out. The important strategizing was done by just four American officials: Secretary of State Rice; National Security Adviser Stephen Hadley; Assistant Secretary of State David Welch, a career Foreign Service officer who has been living and working in the Arab world since he was a young man; and Abrams. Often, decision-making involved a meeting among those four officials, in Hadley's or Rice's office, followed by a trip to the Middle East by Rice, accompanied by Abrams.

The problem of Iran's growing influence in the region and its expanding nuclear program became the other major Abrams headache. Iran, unlike the Palestinian issue, was a policy problem tackled in the more traditional way: lots of big meetings of second-tier officials from across the national-security system, including the State Department, the Pentagon, the Central Intelligence Agency, and the National Security Council staff, hashing out options and churning out memos for the president and his inner circle. The logical result of this process came in late 2007, when the administration produced a "National Intelligence Estimate," a consensus of all intelligence analysts, that shocked Washington by concluding that Iran had suspended its nuclear weapons program.

In fact, the press of such immediate problems creates for Abrams, as for other top government insiders, an avalanche of electronic information and paperwork. Each day, Abrams slogs through messages he gets from three different e-mail systems: an NSC classified e-mail system, an interagency classified system connecting him to other government offices, and the regular Internet.

Those channels pour into his office more material than he could ever read. In fact, he has an assistant whose job is to plow through diplomatic cables and forward to him the ones she thinks he needs to see. Even that help isn't enough; he is in his office virtually every Sunday, the day he sets aside for reading hard copies of lengthy reports, such as classified CIA analyses of Middle East issues.

For Abrams, the twin problems of Iran and the Palestinians meant over time that he was devoting more time and energy to those questions, and less to the idealistic pursuit of freedom and democracy around the world that drives neocons like him. The sheer press of the world's affairs can sometimes overwhelm everything in its path.

Which is why the president's trip to Prague and his speech to the dissidents' conference came as a welcome opportunity to pull democracy back to the center of the Bush agenda. Not long afterward, Abrams was huddling with National Security Adviser Hadley to discuss ways to advance the crusade. A seemingly simple speech, Abrams says, "requires you to figure out what you're going to say, but also what you're going to do."

14. THE SPINNER: BRENDAN DALY

CLIMB A WINDING STAIRCASE from the Capitol Rotunda to the third floor, above the House and Senate chambers. There, perched above the center of American democracy, sit the offices of House Speaker Nancy Pelosi in all their nineteenth-century splendor. In Room H-331, Communications Director Brendan Daly directs a staff of ten charged with a twenty-first-century task: advancing Pelosi's agenda, and deflecting attacks from opponents in a world of nonstop Internet-driven message wars.

"You're engaged in a battle every day," says Daly, a genial veteran of the Clinton administration, where he handled press relations for the U.S. trade representative and the Peace Corps. The cast of antagonists he faces changes by the day. Sometimes it's the office of House Republican Leader John Boehner, sometimes the House Republican Campaign Committee, sometimes the Bush White House, sometimes conservative media voices from the Fox News Channel and the Drudge Report website.

Daly's background as a newspaper reporter—he worked for *The Patriot Ledger* in Massachusetts after graduating from Duke in 1984—prepared him for dealing with his media audience to some extent. But that audience has been transformed within the span of his career in political communications.

Consider the range of interlocutors Daly may encounter on any given day. Much of his core audience still resembles what MSNBC talk-show host Chris Matthews faced two decades earlier, when he handled communications for an earlier Democratic Speaker, Tip

O'Neill: reporters for national newspapers such as *The New York Times, The Washington Post,* and *The Wall Street Journal;* for broadcast television networks and major weekly newsmagazines; and for the traditional narrow-gauge magazines for readers inside the Beltway, *Congressional Quarterly* and *National Journal.*

But now that's only the start. Instead of the daily or weekly deadlines of those organizations, Daly faces the hour-by-hour deadline demands of their websites and of cable-television stations from CNN to MSNBC to Fox News Channel. There's also the clamor from a wide range of additional competitors for news and analysis: two tabloid newspapers devoted solely to Congress, *The Hill* and *Roll Call; The Politico,* which publishes a print edition but is best known for its website, politico.com; blogs such as Daily Kos, MyDD, and Firedoglake, which have become important elements in the daily communications chain; Pelosi's own website (speaker.gov/blog) and video portal on YouTube (youtube.com/SpeakerPelosi). In addition, Daly communicates regularly with Democratic insiders to keep them informed of Pelosi's agenda (and limit intraparty criticism). He also provides material for Democratic "talkers" who appear on political talk shows such as Matthews's own *Hardball,* a political venue that didn't exist when Matthews served O'Neill.

For Daly and his staff, the skirmishing started well before Pelosi took the gavel as Speaker. Shortly after the Democratic triumph at the polls in the fall of 2006, the Speaker-elect was buffeted by press criticism of her decision to support Pennsylvania Representative John Murtha for the job of majority leader—the second-ranking Democratic post in the House. Murtha was the party's highest-profile opponent of the Iraq war; Pelosi chose him rather than support one of her old leadership rivals, Representative Steny Hoyer of Maryland. Critics cited her decision to support the antiwar Murtha as an example of her liberal bent, which had potential for exacerbating the Democrats' traditional weakness on defense issues, and also as a sign of her shaky political instincts, because Hoyer was strongly favored to win. The criticism was all the more difficult for Pelosi aides and

House allies to rebut because many of Pelosi's friends had advised her against becoming involved in the majority-leader race in the first place.

After Hoyer triumphed as expected, Daly and his team set out to recover ground by staging a public-relations blitz surrounding Pelosi's ascension to the Speaker's chair in early January.

A decade earlier, when Newt Gingrich and his fellow Republicans took control of the House, they sought to amplify their message by catering to talk-radio hosts, then representatives of a hot new medium. Today, the hot new political force is the Internet. So, on the day Pelosi became Speaker, Daly and his team created Radio Row and Blogger Alley in homage to the strength and influence of the party's "netroots." The alley offered desk space, coffee, doughnuts, and interviews with Democratic House members for more than a dozen bloggers and liberal radio hosts, who in turn amplified the Democratic message to Internet users and radio listeners around the country. For both parties, such "viral marketing" has largely supplanted inside-the-Beltway gossip among insiders as the engine of consequential "buzz" on Pennsylvania Avenue.

"We are all having a very fine day," Taylor Marsh wrote on The Huffington Post. "I must tell you that everything is running like clockwork here."[1] Kagro X, the correspondent for Daily Kos, declared, "I had the rare privilege of watching today from inside the Capitol, where evidence of the change was visible around every corner."[2] The biggest PR bounty Daly reaped was visual. Every television network and most major newspaper front pages carried pictures of the first woman Speaker in American history assuming the gavel in the company of children—her own grandchildren and the children and grandchildren of Democratic colleagues, including Rahm Emanuel. But the echo effect of the Internet is something no twenty-first-century communicator can afford to neglect.

Daly built his résumé at a series of positions on the Democratic team: the staff of the late Representative Gerry Studds of Massachusetts, a liberal who was one of the first openly gay members of Congress; then the Clinton administration's trade office, the Peace Corps, and the Brady Campaign to Prevent Gun Violence. He came to work for then–Minority Whip Pelosi in 2002.

The job's luster increased exponentially after Democrats recaptured the House. So did the pressure. During the Democrats' hundred-hour opening legislative blitz, Daly faced questions about whether Democrats' methods of parliamentary control, in quickly pushing through their initial list of top priorities, were mimicking practices Democrats once cited as Republican abuses of power. Daly insisted those early tactics were different, because the initial agenda items were "things we said we would do." The challenge reflected one unshakable fact of the new Pennsylvania Avenue: Controlling the political agenda is critical in order for parties to succeed, and all strategies and tactics flow from the imperative of achieving that goal of control.

Soon Daly faced another reality of the Avenue: A well-placed attack on some personal foible or extravagance can sometimes break through the political clutter more effectively than any policy debate. During the 1990s, the Clinton White House would undercut Republican Speaker Newt Gingrich by portraying him as having thrown a tantrum over his seating on Air Force One. Now Republicans were seizing on Pelosi's request for a government airplane capable of flying cross-country nonstop to her residence in San Francisco. Because that meant a larger plane than her predecessor, Dennis Hastert, used for his shorter hop to Illinois, her adversaries had ammunition to portray her as demanding taxpayer-funded excess.

Daly called the charges "ridiculous," arguing that the paramount issue was her security. One of the veteran communications aces Daly leans on to amplify Democrats' public argument, Anita Dunn, jumped to Pelosi's aid. More of the "smash-mouth politics of Washington," she told the *Los Angeles Times*.[3] "Take something that's fairly routine and make it sound as bad as possible." In the end, it wasn't such stratagems that quieted the furor. It was, rather, the luck of the news media's wheel of fortune: The death of ex–*Playboy* model

Anna Nicole Smith siphoned away interest in Pelosi's transportation arrangements from the cable-television news programs that had previously given them the most attention.

Like any political communicator, Daly is happiest when playing offense against partisan adversaries. His Internet aide, Karina Newton, frequently posts clips of Democratic members of Congress on the video-sharing website YouTube.com. One of them, of Iowa freshman Democrat Bruce Braley upbraiding General Services Administration Director Lurita Doan about a Republican political meeting on government property, drew eighty-three thousand hits—helping drive home the Democrats' pledge to hold a Republican administration accountable for misdeeds. Another prominent posting featured Murtha leading Democratic arguments against Bush's Iraq policy, blistering Republicans for failing to support benchmarks for troop performance in Iraq. The clip drew an approving post on the Daily Kos website, demonstrating again the ripple effect generated quickly by political use of technology.

Nothing tested Daly's skills like the controversy that enveloped Pelosi's spring 2007 trip to the Middle East, while the Iraq-war debate raged on Capitol Hill. Her travel was a response to the mandate Democrats claimed from the 2006 election results for a new direction on foreign policy. Democrats had embraced the recommendation of the bipartisan commission chaired by former Secretary of State James Baker and former Representative Lee Hamilton that the Bush administration start a dialogue with Syria and other countries in the region as part of a new strategy for ending the Iraq conflict. The hot-button destination on Pelosi's itinerary was Damascus, the Syrian capital.

The trip was shot through with tension from the beginning, because the Bush administration had rejected talks with Syria until that nation abandoned support for terrorists, including Hezbollah guerrillas in Lebanon. Daly and other Pelosi aides decided to keep word of the trip quiet, for security reasons. Pelosi gave Bush a personal heads-up in the Capitol Rotunda during a tribute to the Tuskegee Airmen; the president offered good wishes for safety.

But the next day, White House spokeswoman Dana Perino criticized Pelosi's trip from her briefing podium as unwise. Daly promptly countered by releasing a statement explaining that the delegation included Republicans as well as Democrats, and was acting in furtherance of the recommendations of the Iraq Study Group. Privately, Daly dashed off an irritated e-mail to Perino, with whom he was on friendly terms, complaining about the security implications of criticizing a trip he hadn't yet officially announced. Perino apologized, assuring him that no breach of security was intended. She had been told that a network-television reporter had already confirmed news of the trip. In any event, that public criticism placed Pelosi on the defensive before she'd left the United States.

The next day, at the annual white-tie Gridiron Dinner, an old-style roast attended by Washington journalists and their Pennsylvania Avenue sources, Perino approached Daly and reiterated her chagrin over the mixup. By then Pelosi had already arrived at her first destination, Tel Aviv. At the dinner, Daly used his handheld BlackBerry device to exchange e-mail messages with a colleague traveling with Pelosi, sharing information about the trip and relating spoofs involving Pelosi that were part of the entertainment at the dinner. (The Speaker herself neither carries a BlackBerry nor regularly uses a computer.)

Israel, by protocol the first stop of American politicians visiting the region, was intended to be the easy part of the trip. Pelosi had special reason to reiterate her staunch support for American's foremost Middle Eastern ally. During intramural jockeying for the chairmanship of the House Intelligence Committee, major Jewish American campaign donors had lobbied Pelosi to select fellow Californian Jane Harman. But Pelosi bypassed Harman to select Representative Silvestre Reyes of Texas. A stop in Israel was one way to ease any lingering problems with the Jewish community.

At first, her Tel Aviv foray appeared successful. At a dinner in her honor, Israel's acting president ignored White House criticism to praise Pelosi's trip, saying she'd be carrying a message to Syria concerning prospects for peace. But even that seemingly noncontroversial gesture soon turned into a club for Pelosi's adversaries—and thus a communications headache for Daly.

When Pelosi met with Syrian President Bashir Assad the next day, she told reporters she had delivered the message: Israel was ready for peace talks. The problem came when Israeli Prime Minister Ehud Olmert then issued a written "clarification" asserting that Israel had not changed its policy that Syria must first end support for terrorism. That clarification, suggesting that Pelosi had fumbled the message, fueled further Republican attacks. And the White House amplified its criticism of Pelosi's suggestion that "the road to Damascus is a road to peace." National Security Council spokesman Gordon Johndroe, a veteran of both Bush presidential campaigns and of the First Lady's staff, noted acidly that the road to Damascus is littered with victims of terrorism.

Daly's communications challenge reached critical mass the next morning, when he awoke to a *Washington Post* editorial headlined "Pratfall in Damascus."[4] The *Post* editorial, further emboldening her antagonists on the right, slammed Pelosi's trip as "not only counterproductive, it is foolish." On Fox News, conservative talk-radio host Mark Williams attacked Pelosi for "lip-locking" with a terrorist leader.[5] An organization filled with GOP luminaries called the Republican Jewish Coalition—board members included former Bush campaign manager Ken Mehlman and White House spokesman Ari Fleischer—prepared television and newspaper ads attacking Pelosi's trip.

Daly's first step in hitting back was to send print and broadcast reporters for major news organizations a statement, issued in his name, denouncing the *Post* editorial as "poisonous" and wrong. His second was to call Democratic "talkers" to supply information for their planned appearances on cable-television talk shows. His third was to dash off material to friendly websites. Less than an hour after the Williams remarks were posted on the liberal website Think Progress, the site featured a rebuttal from Daly under the headline "If Pelosi Endangered National Security, Prove It."

That hardly quelled the controversy. So, the following day, Daly arranged for Pelosi, stopping in Portugal on her way back, to conduct interviews with three media outlets, defending her trip. The three were selected with different and specific purposes in mind: the Associated Press because its wire service would spread her message to all media; *The New York Times* because it carried considerable clout with America's foreign-policy opinion elites; and National Public Radio because that ensured she could be heard in her own voice. Daly also enlisted surrogates to help out. One of them, Representative Tom Lantos of California, traveled with Pelosi on the trip. As a Holocaust survivor, Lantos, who died in early 2008, had impeccable credentials as a supporter of Israel. Lantos wrote an op-ed defense of Pelosi in *USA Today*, which also criticized Pelosi for having "crossed a line" on the trip.[6]

When Pelosi finally returned to the United States, Daly decided to play one more card to put the matter to rest: a full press conference to address the criticisms. His chosen time, 2 p.m. San Francisco time, riled East Coast reporters pushed up against early-evening deadlines. Fox News carried part of the news conference live but cast the press conference as a blunder that extended the controversy rather than ending it.

"What's the point of bringing it up again in such a prominent way?" asked Fox anchor John Gibson. Fox's on-air Democrat at the time echoed Gibson's point. "From [the point of view of] a communications strategy," said Kirsten Powers, like Daly a veteran of the Clinton trade representative's office, "I don't know what they're thinking."[7]

Things got worse from there. At the press conference, Lantos was not only unapologetic about the trip but indicated he might also want to go to Iran—part of what Bush had once called "the axis of evil." Pelosi hardly wanted to associate herself with that idea, but chose not to dispute her colleague publicly.

The result: a *San Francisco Chronicle* headline the next morning indicating "Pelosi Is Open to Iran Trip."[8] That story became fodder for the right when it was featured on the site of Internet gossip Matt Drudge, a favorite conduit for news, tips, and rumors for conservatives since the Monica Lewinsky scandal rocked the Clinton White House. Perino fired off another criticism from the White House, saying it would be "unproductive and unhelpful" for lawmakers to travel to Tehran.[9]

Those fresh arrows extended the controversy for another news cycle. "If there's something on Drudge, I get a call within five minutes," Daly says. But this time Daly decided on a lower-profile approach to knocking it down. Instead of distributing a mass press release, which might bring the controversy to the attention of some news outlets that hadn't noticed it, Daly sent a posting under his own name to the Speaker's weblog, The Gavel. The posting, which Daly also sent to liberal websites, sought to erase any doubt by declaring unequivocally that Pelosi would not visit Iran. The story soon fizzled—helped in part by a new cable-TV sensation, the controversy over racial remarks by radio shock jock Don Imus.

Daly's work in quelling the controversy, however, was not done. The following day, he flew to Los Angeles to accompany Pelosi for an appearance on *The Tonight Show with Jay Leno*. Chatting in the makeup room before the taping, Leno told Daly he might ask about the Iran issue. "She's not going to Iran," Daly assured him. "Why waste time on that?" Problem avoided: Leno didn't bring up the matter.

Flush with success, Daly climbed into an SUV with Pelosi for the ride from NBC's Burbank studios to the oceanfront Malibu home of Barbra Streisand. The legendary singer was hosting a fund-raiser for the Democratic Congressional Campaign Committee attended by couples who had raised up to $50,000. Pelosi brought along two of the party's young stars to introduce them to the Hollywood elite: Representative Chris Van Hollen of Maryland, the chairman of the Democratic

Congressional Campaign Committee, and Representative Debbie Wasserman Schultz of Florida, a chief deputy whip and chair of an appropriations subcommittee.

As guests mingled and listened to the entertainment by singer Melissa Etheridge (Josh Groban was there, but skipped his scheduled singing gig because of illness), Daly's BlackBerry buzzed. A colleague had sent a favorable story about Pelosi's visit from *The Jerusalem Post*; Daly forwarded the message to others as part of his defense of her trip.

It is a wearying business. But Daly had a feeling of vindication after his return to Pennsylvania Avenue. A reporter for washingtonpost.com called, seeking comment about the new *Post*–ABC News poll, the first major national survey after her travels. The results: Notwithstanding the avalanche of criticism, Pelosi's national favorability rating actually rose to 53 percent from 50 percent. Her unfavorable ratings climbed a hair more, to 35 percent from 31 percent. But it felt like a triumph.

"There are certainly days I feel we're getting hammered," Daly says over yogurt in a Capitol cafeteria. In this case, "I felt that we limited the hammering."

15. THE POLITICAL OPERATORS: JIM JORDAN AND TERRY NELSON

As it grew toward becoming America's largest employer over the last generation, Wal-Mart was slow to involve itself in the politics of Pennsylvania Avenue.

But when it did, the company made clear its preference for the Republican Party's market-based economic doctrine. After Republicans captured Congress in 1994, Wal-Mart joined Project Relief, a coalition of business groups pushing for deregulation that was organized by Republican Representative Tom DeLay.[1]

Three years later, Wal-Mart hired its first Washington lobbyists and established a political-action committee. The PAC, now one of the largest on Pennsylvania Avenue, established a record of lopsided giving in favor of Republican candidates. It backed President Bush in 2000 and 2004. When the president was re-elected in 2004 with enlarged Republican congressional majorities, Wal-Mart had the election outcomes it had placed its money on.

But on today's Pennsylvania Avenue, winning elections is hardly the only means of wielding power. Which is how the Wal-Mart behemoth, in the flush of Republican triumph at the polls, suddenly faced a serious threat from some of Election 2004's biggest losers: some canny political operators who held no public office at all. They were among the thousands of itinerant electioneering professionals who move from campaign to campaign or cause to cause, earning a living from their skills at harvesting votes and harnessing public sentiment.

One of those people was a fast-talking Southerner named Jim Jordan. Jordan is among the best of Washington's twenty-first-century political operatives, skilled in communications rather than policy substance, campaign combat rather than governance.

He came late to the craft. The son of a college professor and a librarian in Winston-Salem, North Carolina, Jordan grew up dreaming of becoming a major-league shortstop rather than a political professional. But as he played baseball at Hampton-Sydney College and went on to the University of North Carolina School of Law, he grew increasingly intrigued by the power game.

His first political job was press secretary for Democratic Representative David Price of North Carolina, a onetime political-science professor trying to survive the Republican rise in the South. Like so many other Dixie Democrats, Price was swamped in 1994. Jordan had impressed enough people so that he was tapped to work for one of the hottest Senate campaigns of 1996: Representative Tim Johnson's bid to oust Republican incumbent Senator Larry Pressler in South Dakota. Johnson won.

Soon Jordan was in the thick of scandal warfare between the Clinton White House and the Gingrich-led Republican Congress. His first Senate boss was Democratic Senator Bob Torricelli of New Jersey, who himself soon fell to scandal. Later, Jordan worked for the Senate Democrats who were trying to fend off allegations of dubious fund-raising practices leveled by Republicans against the Clinton White House, and still later trying to fend off the president's impeachment and removal from office.

If that was the political equivalent of a master's degree, Jordan's Ph.D. came from his management of the Democrats' Senate campaign committee in 2002. It was a bitter midterm election in which several strong Democratic candidates were ultimately swamped by President Bush's post-9/11 strength on national security, wielded on behalf of his fellow Republicans. Few races have stirred Democratic rancor more than the successful GOP effort that year to oust then–Democratic Senator Max Cleland of Georgia, a Vietnam War amputee who had headed the Veterans Administration during Jimmy Carter's presidency.

Jordan emerged from that battle to assume one of the top jobs of the 2004 campaign, as manager of Senator John Kerry's White House bid. But, just as television-network executives fire anchors for low ratings, candidates often replace campaign aides for weak polls. When Howard Dean surged in the fall of 2003, Kerry fired Jordan. Jordan wasn't out of the election battle for long. Three of the dons of Democratic politics—former Clinton White House aide Harold Ickes, Emily's List founder Ellen Malcolm, and labor strategist Steve Rosenthal—drafted Jordan to assist their massive advertising and get-out-the-vote operation.

In that operation, a precise reflection of the Democratic Party's DNA, an interlocking web of organizations was created to capitalize on a loophole in the McCain-Feingold campaign-finance law. That law banned "soft money," the term for donations to political parties, which weren't previously limited as are donations to individual candidates. The theory was that multimillion-dollar checks from wealthy donors were less party-building than party-buying.

As a result—and this was the loophole—those fat checks went instead to newly created organizations that amounted to shadow parties. Jordan created a one-man consulting firm called Thunder Road Group—named for the Bruce Springsteen rock anthem—to service America Votes, the biggest such Democratic organization. It was his only client.

In December 2004, after the Republican victory, the biggest single financier of America Votes had a new project in mind. Andrew Stern, the president of the Service Employees International Union, set out to create political change in a different way: He wanted to launch a pressure campaign against Wal-Mart Stores. Organized labor had grown as frustrated trying to establish unions at Wal-Mart as small-town retailers had been in fending off "big box" competition.

But Stern had a grander idea than merely organizing. It was based on two convictions. One was that Wal-Mart was a template for larger trends in the economy that were driving down American wages and benefits. If Wal-Mart could be pressured to act differently toward its employees, the giant company would influence the rest of the economy. The second was that the techniques of modern Pennsylvania Avenue could make a difference. That's what led Stern—and other stalwarts of the Democratic coalition, including Carl Pope of the Sierra Club—to hire political operatives such as Jordan to put political pressure on the retailer through "Wal-Mart Watch." Staked with a few million dollars in union money, Wal-Mart Watch began with Jordan as a senior adviser and Andy Grossman, Jordan's former deputy at the Democratic Senatorial Campaign Committee, as top staffer.

The organization had no illusions that it could throw open the doors of Wal-Mart to unions, or raise the wage scales or health benefits that labor complained were unfair to workers and taxpayers. Rather, it aimed to hit Wal-Mart by using the same fine-tooth targeting techniques that the Bush campaign had used to defeat Kerry to, in this case, influence shopping and investment decisions. If, say, 15 percent of potential Wal-Mart shoppers might consider the retailer's policies as a factor in deciding whether to patronize the store, "we only have to peel off 25 percent of them to put real pressure on their bottom line," Jordan said.

Within two years, Wal-Mart Watch had built a full-scale campaign war room in an office building a few blocks from the Avenue. It had a field director, a publications staff, and a clergy-outreach coordinator, many of them drawn from past campaigns and poised to leave whenever good jobs opened on 2008 campaigns. The executive director, David Nassar, was a veteran of House and gubernatorial campaigns. The communications director, Nu Wexler, had worked for a Democratic polling firm and the South Carolina Democratic Party. Their goal was to move Wal-Mart to the center of political debate by moving the story from newspapers' business pages to the front page. That involved funneling a steady stream of negative information to journalists covering Wal-Mart and to those covering political developments as well—information on the company's flat stock price, any poor sales reports, complaints about its employee benefits or discrimination claims.

"They'd do Wal-Mart stories every day if they had the content," Wexler explained. "We're able to feed that beast. I view this work as campaign work."

"We want to bring that election-campaign approach," Nassar said. "It was aggressive, it was fierce, it was smart about doing opposition research. The Wal-Mart story already existed. We wanted to make it more political."

They succeeded well enough that Wal-Mart was forced to respond with its own costly public-relations campaign. The company hired Leslie Dach, the public-relations whiz who had been handling the Wal-Mart account for the Edelman public-relations firm, and made him executive vice-president of corporate affairs and government relations. To put it more simply, the man who had been coaching Wal-Mart from the outside on how to navigate the dangerous shoals of political life would now be doing the same thing, full-time, from the inside. Wal-Mart made Dach rich as he made the jump, lavishing him with $3 million in stock and a load of options on top of that.[2]

Dach brought a particular Washington savvy to the debate. He knew, for example, that it's better to have a message of your own to promote than to respond to the other side's message. So he pushed, successfully, for Wal-Mart to institute and then widely publicize a program in which it sells some generic prescription drugs at a flat $4-a-prescription price. Dach also took advantage of his own background in environmental activism—he was a lobbyist for the National Audubon Society and Environmental Defense, and serves on the board of directors of the World Resources Institute—to help Wal-Mart craft a green image. The company touted what it called a "sustainability" program. "Our environmental goals at Wal-Mart are simple and straightforward: to be supplied 100 percent by renewable energy; to create zero waste; and to sell products that sustain our resources and our environment," declared the company's website.[3]

Wal-Mart also turned to prominent Republican political operatives. For survey research, the company hired Jan van Lohuizen, Karl Rove's favorite pollster and a veteran of the 2000 and 2004 Bush campaigns, to gauge public relations. For outreach, it enlisted Bush's 2004 political director, Terry Nelson.

Nelson learned the business on the proving grounds of his Iowa home. The Marshalltown native ran congressional campaigns for Jim Nussle, chairman of the House Budget Committee, then moved to Washington to work for the National Republican Congressional Committee in the 2000 campaign. The next year he established a media firm. In 2002 he worked for the Republican National Committee and then joined the Bush re-election team.

Bush's victory made Nelson a hot commodity. The Florida law firm of Akerman Senterfitt signed him up to help land business. Nelson maintained his partnership in a media firm that made ads for political candidates. He cashed in on his reputation for effective organizing by forming the Crosslink Strategy Group. Crosslink's mission was mobilizing coalitions—not just average Americans at the "grass roots," but opinion elites who made up the "grass tops."

For Wal-Mart, Nelson set out to implement one of the fundamental strategies of Pennsylvania Avenue: countering enemies by causing allies to stand up and be counted. That meant asking Wal-Mart suppliers to defend the company publicly. And in two test markets, Atlanta and Denver, it meant using a new organization called Working Families for Wal-Mart to showcase average families who benefited from Wal-Mart's low prices. If the tests proved effective, the company could try to expand that technique nationwide.

But just as everything went wrong for Republicans in 2006, it began to seem as if every step taken by the Wal-Mart team—from its headquarters in Bentonville, Arkansas, to Pennsylvania Avenue—was a stumble. *The New York Times* obtained and published a memo from Nelson that some interpreted as representing heavy-handed pressure on suppliers.[4] An Atlanta newspaper carried a story showing that some shoppers signing Working Families for Wal-Mart petitions were given coupons to do so and didn't know what they were signing up for. A pro–Wal-Mart website purportedly featuring happy customers was revealed to be a paid Edelman project involving a *Washington Post* photographer.[5]

Wal-Mart Watch played a part in those difficulties. The labor-backed group obtained an internal Wal-Mart memo detailing flaws in the company's health-benefit programs, and leaked it to *The New York Times* in the same way political campaigns leak negative information about adversaries to the press.[6] The story's long-term effect was even more consequential than the initial embarrassment of its disclosure. A Wal-Mart security employee subsequently obtained telephone records of the *New York Times* reporter who wrote the story. When that security employee was fired, he made the bombshell disclosure that he had bugged the meeting room where Wal-Mart directors met. Eventually, the Securities and Exchange Commission would decide to look into the surveillance program. The onetime security employee also disclosed the existence of Project Red, a secret Wal-Mart project designed to turn around the company's lagging stock price.[7]

The most vivid demonstration of Wal-Mart Watch's agility came in a controversy involving, improbably enough, former civil-rights leader Andrew Young. The former congressman and Atlanta mayor had been hired to lend his credibility to Wal-Mart's effort to break into America's urban markets. On a trip to Los Angeles for that purpose, Young gave an interview to a small-circulation African American weekly in which he spoke, with impolitic frankness, of shopkeepers who had poorly served African American customers. "I think they've ripped off our communities enough. First it was Jews, then it was Koreans, and now it's Arabs," he was quoted as saying.[8]

The comments didn't make an immediate sensation in Los Angeles or anywhere else when they were published; the weekly newspaper's circulation was modest. But back in Washington, Wexler's phone at Wal-Mart Watch rang that afternoon. A friend in Los Angeles called to alert him to the potentially incendiary implications of Young's derision of specific ethnic and religious groups.

Wexler grasped immediately that it could become "an earthquake" in his Wal-Mart campaign. "We got the word out very quickly" by forwarding it to Wal-Mart reporters at major media outlets, who in turn sought comment from the company. By the time Wexler stepped off the subway after riding home at 8 p.m., his BlackBerry buzzed with word that Young had resigned from his Wal-Mart job.

"I couldn't believe that happened in less than twenty-four hours," Wexler said. "That's when I knew the effect our campaign was having."

All the while, the Pennsylvania Avenue combatants in the Wal-Mart fight were playing dual roles in the 2006 campaign. Jordan was advising Democratic political clients, including the national trial lawyers' advocacy group. And he was working on the election bid of one of the Democrats' brightest stars: Harold Ford, Jr., scion of a prominent West Tennessee political family, fourth-term House member, and candidate to become the first African American elected to the Senate from the South since Reconstruction.

Nelson was on the other side of the same race. He was directly involved in the Republican National Committee's attempt to assist Senate candidates with TV ads to supplement their own. One of those Republican candidates—Ford's opponent, Bob Corker—was trailing Ford by roughly six percentage points in the polls during the October campaign homestretch. Nelson's team on the RNC's advertising campaign held a conference call to discuss ways to shake up the race.

With voters increasingly numb to the negative clamor of the Avenue, campaign ad-makers have turned more and more to humor as a way of grabbing their attention. Nelson's team settled on the idea of a parody ad to drive home their contention that Ford, an attractive bachelor, was not as tempered and conservative in his personal life as in his campaign rhetoric.

A few days later, a film crew shot "Call me Harold," which would become one of the iconic images of the 2006 campaign. It features a young blond woman, shoulders bare, beckoning Ford's attention after reminding him they'd met at a "Playboy party." That line referred to Ford's once having attended a large *Playboy*-magazine fête at a Super Bowl football game.

Some political analysts thought the ad broke Ford's momentum and altered the campaign dialogue in Tennessee in Corker's favor. But outside Tennessee, the ad caused a political outcry, with charges that it played on racism, and ancient fears of miscegenation.

And thus, just as with Andy Young's comments, the ad became a political problem for Wal-Mart. At Wal-Mart Watch, Wexler was at first cautious in pushing the story of Nelson's involvement in the ad, wary of amplifying a controversy that might be hurting Jordan's Senate candidate. But the ad created a five-alarm political brushfire on its own, to Wal-Mart's embarrassment.

"Jesse Jackson called on them to fire me," Nelson recalls. Republican National Committee Chairman Ken Mehlman distanced himself from the ad. On a Friday afternoon, Nelson received a phone call from Leslie Dach. "We're under a lot of pressure, constituency-group pressure," Dach said. "I hope you'll agree to resign." Nelson didn't resist. He phoned an Associated Press political reporter and put the word out publicly that he was leaving the Wal-Mart account.

Nelson insisted the ad wasn't an attempt to inflame racial fears. "We don't have racial politics in Iowa," Nelson explained. "Nobody who looked at it thought it was racial politics. The intention was very straightforward: This guy says he is a conservative. He's not a conservative." But deciding to quit working for Wal-Mart, he added, "took me out of the firefight" over the matter. Soon he had moved on to a new job that would prove even more challenging: managing John McCain's campaign for the 2008 Republican presidential nomination. (That effort would have an unhappy ending as well. Nelson resigned in mid-2007, as the campaign foundered and ran seriously short of cash.)

By early 2007, Wal-Mart Watch was ready to claim that it was affecting Wal-Mart's profitability. The company's sales growth was weak, and its stock price was flat—"dead money," in the parlance of Wall Street analysts. Bank of America invited Andrew Stern to address a conference in New York. One of its securities analysts released a report concluding that critics were hurting the company in a "meaningful" way by distracting management from its core retail strategy and forcing the expenditure of millions for public relations.[9]

In mid-April, Wal-Mart Watch staged its own conference in New York. The pressure group invited stock analysts and reporters to Manhattan's posh Waldorf Astoria Hotel to release results of a new survey documenting what it argued was the impact of its campaign on Wal-Mart's reputation.

The survey didn't claim to have turned Wal-Mart's reputation upside down. Wal-Mart Watch pollster Jeff Levine conceded that the company's overall reputation was strong, with 71 percent of Americans still holding a favorable view of the company. But it argued that that figure was down from 76 percent two years earlier. Some 27 percent of respondents reported developing a more negative opinion of Wal-Mart over the past year. One in five reported shopping less often at Wal-Mart, or spending less while there, because of controversy over the company's business practices. The survey also pointed to fallout among some target groups Wal-Mart wanted to reach, including women with family incomes above $50,000 and urban "opinion elites."

Nelson and Dach argue that Wal-Mart's bedrock constituency—the blue-collar consumers of red-state America—hadn't been shaken. But the Wal-Mart Watch campaign underscores the diffusion of modern political power, with implications from Pennsylvania Avenue to Wall Street. "We're living in a world not as dominated by the old media," Nelson says. "One of the consequences of the Internet age is it has given a lot more people means to take direct action. [Wal-Mart Watch is] trying to raise awareness of Wal-Mart shoppers to its practices. On that front they have not been very effective. . . . I think on the elite campaign with opinion-makers they have had more success."

One sign of that success was a press conference in early 2007 at which Wal-Mart CEO Lee Scott stood alongside Stern, one of his foremost tormentors. Joined by representatives of other corporations and unions, the two men called on Pennsylvania Avenue to summon the political will to press for universal health insurance. In theory, at least, the idea could provide a victory for both sides. Government action could relieve companies like Wal-Mart, struggling to compete in a global economy, of pressure to improve benefits for its workers; to the company's embarrassment, many Wal-Mart "associates" were enrolled in the Medicaid health-care system for low-income Americans.

For Stern, support from Wal-Mart's Scott added a powerful voice to his attempt to achieve a level of worker protection that traditional union organizing and advocacy had been unable to. It was a measure of rapidly rising expectations on the Avenue that some of Stern's union compatriots were furious about the press conference. They complained privately that Stern was selling out just as Wal-Mart was on the run.

V. CHANGING THE SYSTEM

IN SOME WAYS, the history of Washington represents a recurring discovery: Everything old is new again. There's precedent on Pennsylvania Avenue for every one of Washington's present-day pathologies.

Dismayed by strident values-rhetoric blaring across the wild media landscape? It happened when Thomas Jefferson, under attack for his skepticism toward organized religion, ran for president in 1800. "GOD—AND A RELIGIOUS PRESIDENT; OR JEFFERSON— AND NO GOD," shouted a headline in the *Gazette of the United States*.[1]

Disgusted by partisan acrimony and the occasional tie-pulling spat on the House floor? It's tame compared with the beating Senator Charles Sumner of Massachusetts suffered in 1856, when Representative Preston Brooks of South Carolina pummeled him unconscious with a cane on the Senate floor in a bitter feud over slavery.

Disheartened by the "culture of corruption" exemplified by now jailed lobbyist Jack Abramoff, who offered free golf trips and meals for lawmakers at his Pennsylvania Avenue restaurant, Signatures? The nineteenth-century super-lobbyist Edward Pendleton once ran a gambling house on Pennsylvania Avenue called the Palace of Fortune, featuring forgiving terms for members of Congress.[2] "To reach the heart or get the vote, the surest way is down the throat," famously declared Samuel Colt, who entertained lawmakers and their relatives while seeking a patent extension for his signature firearm.[3]

The fund-raising targets the parties set for today's lawmakers, forcing them to spend ever-increasing amounts of time raising campaign cash, have roots dating to 1913, when the Democratic National Congressional Committee requested $100 from each Democratic member of Congress for campaign expenses.[4] The ranks of Pennsylvania Avenue special interests were also exploding then, with the number of trade associations in the capital swelling to fifteen hundred by the mid-1920s.

In that decade of "normalcy" there was even a Monday Lunch Club of influentials resembling the "Wednesday Group" of conservative activists that brought Republican firebrand Grover Norquist notoriety in the 1990s.[5]

And when the Great Depression lifted Franklin Roosevelt into the White House in 1932, the utility companies he battled over legislation to regulate them practiced the same black arts of the influence game that latter-day public-relations conglomerates have since refined. From the Mayflower Hotel, "the utilities used every tactic at their disposal, ranging from disinformation to intimidation," wrote David McKean, biographer of Roosevelt aide Tommy Corcoran. "A whispering campaign began that the president was suffering from mental instability. The companies organized a massive letter-writing campaign, although the letters and telegrams turned out to be from nonexistent constituents. Congressmen were bluntly told that if they did not vote against the public utilities bill, their opponents in the next election would be provided with enough funds to ensure victory."[6]

Their efforts failed to stop FDR's plan—but just barely.

And yet Pennsylvania Avenue has not always been the way it is now.

Today's combination of ideological polarization and partisan division, of distant personal relations and intense heat from constituents, of viselike pressure from old money and new media, is historically unique. At various times, different incentives and circumstances produced a different capital city.

In the Avenue's earliest days, desolate living conditions shaped the capital culture. Sharing a nearly impassable swamp, those holding power turned the young nation's constitutional design of separate executive and legislative branches into everyday reality: Aides in the executive branch lived near the executive mansion, and lawmakers lived near the Capitol, a mile away. That limited their interactions, since a journey between the two was arduous then.

"The separation of powers became a separation of persons," wrote the prize-winning historian James Sterling Young.[7] Lawmakers identified with the institution they served more than with their party. Voting alliances were forged in the dormitory-style boarding houses where they shared living space.

In the mid-twentieth century, a dimly understood threat to national survival broke down customary political divisions. As Hitler's Nazis threatened to overrun Britain, Roosevelt pursued a politically risky "lend-lease" deal to assist Winston Churchill, and an unprecedented peacetime draft to prepare for direct involvement in the war. His Republican rival in the 1940 election, Wendell Willkie, bucked his party's isolationism and provided Roosevelt political cover at the cost of his own ambitions.

"Roosevelt could not have done it without Willkie . . . and his triumph over partisanship," author Charles Peters has written. "At the same time," Peters added, "Americans themselves managed to rise a notch or two above the usual limits of human nature. Something about the time seemed to heighten their generosity, idealism and public spirit."[8]

Following World War II, shared battles against economic depression and totalitarianism had the effect, at least for a time, of pulling politicians together. The aura of high stakes that surrounds today's political battles was largely absent; both parties accepted the legacy of dominance Roosevelt left as the only president elected more than twice. "Eisenhower was convinced that he could make no significant change in the nation's basic Democratic Party preference," political historian Michael Barone wrote in *Our Country.*[9]

Both parties were still scrambled, ideologically and geographically, embracing politicians from across the spectrum. Neil McNeil, in his postwar study of the House called *Forge of Democracy*, wrote: "There has scarcely been a partisan vote . . . that has not found Republicans supporting the Democratic position and Democrats the Republican position. Many districts had no firm political commitment to Republicans or Democrats, to conservatism or liberalism, and the Representatives from these marginal districts could be expected . . . to swing back and forth politically and avoid polarization on one side or another."[10]

The journalist William S. White described a 1950s-era Senate so at odds with today's version as to be virtually beyond recognition. "This is, oddly, not really a very partisan place . . . as partisanship is normally understood—that is, as the bitter and unending friction between two parties," White wrote in *Citadel*. "The general movement has been one of inwardness. The political center has thus greatly enlarged and the extreme wings have greatly shrunk."[11]

Inside the Capitol, the Senate historian's office offers a glimpse into that lost civilization of Pennsylvania Avenue through a series of oral-history interviews with Stanley Kimmitt. His career placed him at the center of the institution, and his unlikely rise within the chamber embodies much of what seems absent from today's Pennsylvania Avenue: moderation and bipartisan cooperation, service and shared values.

The son of Montana ranchers who fell on hard times during the Great Depression, he joined the army, manned artillery guns in Germany during World War II and later in Korea, then, afterward, was assigned to the army's legislative-affairs office as a liaison to Congress. He rose within the Senate in tandem with his onetime college professor of Asian history, Mike Mansfield, who would eventually become majority leader.

"Style, procedures, civility if you will, camaraderie, dignity were paramount," Kimmitt said. "There was a club. It was not a club of partisan Democrats or partisan Republicans, it was a bipartisan group, usually committee chairmen with a few trusted additions. That club ruled the legislation. They ruled everything."[12]

Business was lubricated by familiar personal relations; in many cases the lubricant was alcohol itself, consumed in hideaway Capitol offices at bipartisan gatherings on both sides of the Capitol. Historians record the Civil Rights Act of 1964 as a centerpiece of Democrat Lyndon Johnson's presidency, but Everett Dirksen of Illinois, the Senate Republican leader and Johnson's friend, played a pivotal role.

"There would not have been a civil-rights bill in 1964 if it hadn't been for Dirksen," Kimmitt recalled. "It was not the political thing for the Republicans. . . . But I think Lyndon Johnson finally convinced him it was the right thing to do, and it was important. So Dirksen . . . must be credited with passing the Civil Rights Act of 1964."

But by then the sun was beginning to set on that sort of cooperation. Kimmitt's patron, Mansfield, served as ambassador to Japan under presidents of both parties after retiring from the Senate. He was dismayed by what he found after returning from Tokyo for his last Washington job, as a consultant to the investment firm Goldman Sachs at its offices on Pennsylvania Avenue. "The feeling of friendliness is gone," he said. "A little hate is getting into it."[13]

The famously gentle Mansfield died in 2001; Stan Kimmitt, three years later. By then their Pennsylvania Avenue was gone, and Kimmitt's son Bob was discovering, on Dubai Ports World and a raft of other issues, how bitter and contentious the Avenue he inherited had become.

There's no road back from today's turbulent Pennsylvania Avenue to the comparatively tranquil one that Bob Kimmitt's father experienced. The pressures of media, money, ideology, partisanship, and the absence of the intimacy and familiarity that once buffered those forces, are here to stay.

"Until we move the nation's capital from Washington, D.C., to Paducah, Kentucky, or Cape Girardeau, Missouri, we're not going to be living in a small town again," says Bush's former political adviser Karl Rove, who more than any other person came to symbolize the altered character of twenty-first-century Washington. "We'll never be that way again. There is a civility that is missing from politics in Washington, and a coarseness that exists, and I don't see it getting less."

Yet there are people across the political spectrum, inside government and out, who are working to break some of the patterns that have made the modern-day Avenue so dysfunctional. Even while they reveled in the recent woes of a Republican White House, Washington's Democrats also knew the unexpected fire could consume their agenda next time. Even as serial breakdowns along Pennsylvania Avenue brightened their party's near-term electoral fortunes, some Democrats with larger ambitions worried about the causes and costs of the capital's dysfunction.

One of them was Senator Barack Obama of Illinois. In early 2007, Obama launched a campaign for the presidency by arguing that the polarized political system wasn't simply a problem, but *the* problem. Moreover, Obama offered a novel interpretation of the causes of political polarization, and of part of the solution.

The son of a black African father and a white mother from Kansas, Obama was a prototypical political leader for the generation that followed the Baby Boom. That biographical fact lay at the center of his diagnosis of the political system's ills. Obama blamed a series of divisive Baby Boom political figures—from Clinton to Gingrich to Bush—for carrying on fierce arguments, the origins of which were in the turmoil of the 1960s. "In the back-and-forth between Clinton and Gingrich, and in the elections of 2000 and 2004," he wrote, "I sometimes felt as if I were watching the psychodrama of the Baby Boom generation—a tale rooted in old grudges and revenge plots hatched on a handful of college campuses long ago—played out on the national stage."[14]

It was not a fanciful argument. Vietnam, race riots, drug abuse, and the sexual revolution—those were the formative experiences of the Baby Boomer generation that now rules Washington. Vietnam separated today's neoconservatives, who supported the war, from fellow Boomers who opposed it, for example, and the split has never been resolved. Drug use and changing sexual mores spawned arguments over values that persist in the policy and rhetorical splits between conservatives and liberals over cultural issues. The fight for equal rights for blacks led to a bitter debate over affirmative action that lives on, and helped create a two-party system in which it is simply assumed that more than 80 percent of African American voters will cast their ballots for Democrats.

Some Republicans scoff at Obama's high-sounding call to common ground in the middle, arguing that it comes from a politician whose short record shows him to be solidly on the left wing of the political spectrum. Still, Obama's arguments found a Republican echo on the West Coast. California Governor Arnold Schwarzenegger, a Republican, once a darling of his national party, was one of its few leaders who emerged from the 2006 election unscathed. After enduring bitter setbacks a year before on a series of unsuccessful referendum fights, Schwarzenegger engineered a political comeback by declaring himself in revolt against bitter infighting. It was an ironic stance for a governor who gained his office after fellow Republicans launched a midterm recall effort against Democratic incumbent Gray Davis. But then Schwarzenegger, who had survived campaign controversy over libertine behavior as a bodybuilder to go on and lead a socially conservative party, had a proven talent for reinvention.

"The people are disgusted with a mind-set that would rather get nothing done than accomplish something through compromise," he said in his inaugural address as he opened his second term as California's leader.[15] In almost open defiance of a political Zeitgeist that said the most important thing for a leader was to show that he or she had principles and would stand by them through thick or thin, Schwarzenegger said almost the opposite. His rhetoric proclaimed that results trump principles as the political order of the new day. "We don't need Republican roads or Democratic roads. We need roads,"

Schwarzenegger told Californians. "We don't need Republican health care or Democratic health care. We need health care. We don't need Republican clean air or Democratic clean air. We all breathe the same air."

A third prominent politician left both parties behind while sounding the same themes. New York City Mayor Michael Bloomberg quit the Republican Party in June 2007 and declared himself an independent, fueling talk of a Ross Perot–style third-party race for president. Any such bid would face huge practical challenges, but Bloomberg's well-publicized flirtation underscored the level of discontent with Pennsylvania Avenue gridlock.

Outside the media spotlight, scores of others on the Avenue were exploring fresh strategies at the same time. Some may prove fruitless quests; others may simply prove fruitless in the short term, in the way that Barry Goldwater's landslide defeat in 1964 helped clear the path to Ronald Reagan's conservative triumph sixteen years later. But win or lose, they are attempting in their own ways to respond to Americans' hunger for a different Pennsylvania Avenue.

16. THE NEW REPUBLICANS:
SAM BROWNBACK AND PETE WEHNER

SAM BROWNBACK AND PETE WEHNER arrived on Pennsylvania Avenue by markedly different routes. One was sent by voters in the heart of Middle America; the other traveled in on his own, propelled from the West Coast by the public-policy bug he caught during a college internship.

In some ways, both men might be viewed as part of the Republican Party's inflexibly ferocious core, charter members of party factions whose endless warfare with Democratic counterparts alienated America and left the Avenue in gridlock. After all, Brownback is a Christian conservative elected as part of the Gingrich revolution of 1994. Wehner was a top deputy to Karl Rove, the Bush strategist who came to symbolize the politics of polarization.

In fact, both represent forces that are changing their party in ways that, in the long run, could soften its hard edges and broaden its reach. Brownback, in his work on Capitol Hill and a long-shot presidential candidacy, has sought to strengthen the "compassionate conservatism" that Bush adopted as a campaign theme but often neglected in office. Wehner, having run his own tiny White House think tank, now has set out to build a durable intellectual legacy for Republican conservatives to come.

· · ·

Brownback is a native Kansan who grew up near the tiny town of Parker, on a farm still operated by his parents. His rural roots are deep; his mother was a rural mail carrier, and his Senate website carries a picture of a young Sam Brownback riding a bull in a rodeo. He has a full head of wavy black hair and a laconic speaking style that belies the strong beliefs and personal drive that lie within.

In high school, Brownback became president of the state Future Farmers of America chapter; he was elected student-body president at Kansas State University. He chose law school over the farm after graduation, moving from K-State to its archrival, the University of Kansas, to attend law school; there, he became president of his law-school class.[1] He was named the youngest agriculture secretary in Kansas history. Then, like other smart and ambitious young people from around the country, Brownback was introduced to Washington when he won a White House fellowship, a program that brings a select group of young men and women to Washington to work for a year at the top levels of the executive branch. (Among those it has introduced to Washington: former Secretary of State Colin Powell and Labor Secretary Elaine Chao.)

Brownback returned home to resume his agriculture post. When a chance arose, he ran for and won election to the House, and just two years later, in 1996, decided to seek the Senate seat vacated by Bob Dole when he ran for president.[2] After trailing by twenty-eight percentage points in the polls, Brownback roared back to win a double-digit victory. Brownback is a deeply religious man whose ruminations about faith led him to convert to Roman Catholicism while in the Senate.

He isn't shy about talking about either his faith or the kinds of policies it makes him champion, though he knows some of his positions have little or no political benefit back home in Kansas. But what is most striking about Brownback is his desire to break out of the Christian-conservative mold and expand Republican thinking about what constitutes a "values" issue—and his willingness to ruffle some feathers within his own wing of the party to do so.

Whereas traditional religious conservatives identify themselves as "pro-life"—a code word meaning they are opposed to abortion—

Brownback describes himself as "whole life." This view holds, in essence, that if a conservative values the dignity of life enough to fight abortion, he or she should feel obliged to fight for life in all its other forms as well.

For Brownback, the whole-life message means that, in addition to opposing abortion, gay marriage, and embryonic stem-cell research (because extracting stem cells requires destroying a human embryo), he also crusades against genocide in Darfur and sex trafficking in the Third World, and pushes for more aid to Africa, and prison reform in America to give those behind bars greater tools to avoid returning after release. His concern about prison reform, in fact, once led him to travel to Angola State Prison in Louisiana, home to most of that state's most hardened long-term convicts, where he spoke to eight hundred of the inmates and spent a night in solitary confinement.

Unlike many fellow conservatives, Brownback wants to pursue the possibility of a formal U.S.-government apology for its treatment of Native Americans and African Americans over the years. More jarring still to the conservative system are Brownback's questioning of the death penalty and his tolerant attitude toward immigrants.

If a religious conservative wants to protect life at all stages, Brownback believes, he or she can't easily accept a government's right to end the life of anyone, even a convicted felon, by imposing a death sentence. As a consequence, he now says of the death penalty: "I'm opposed except in cases where we can't protect society from the perpetrator"—a small subset of capital cases, given that lifetime in prison goes a long way to protect society from any perpetrator.

In sheer political terms, Brownback's views on immigration have proved the hardest sell to those in his own conservative base. Brownback, like George W. Bush, believes in a guest-worker program that would allow immigrants to qualify for legal status and protections when they come to the United States to work, both as a way to decrease the pressure for illegal immigration and to improve the treatment of immigrant workers. "I believe in immigration," Brownback says. "It would grow our party through the compassion side. . . . I go to the Christian community and say, 'These are beautiful souls, too.' "

When discussing the topic in his quiet private office down an obscure basement hallway in the Capitol one afternoon, Brownback points out: "The Biblical admonition is to take care of the widow and the orphan and the foreigner amongst you." That isn't, however, a message many of Brownback's fellow conservatives have been eager to hear. In fact, at one point in 2006, when the immigration debate was heating up, Brownback, already pondering a presidential run, simply stopped going to Iowa, because he found audiences only wanted to argue about immigration.

When he did engage skeptics, Brownback would counter that he had the same view of immigration's virtues as the one held in his time by Ronald Reagan, patron saint of Republican conservatives, but even that wouldn't change minds. Still, unlike some other Republicans, Brownback held his ground. "I believe you're shaping a generation of Hispanic voters right now," he says. A guest-worker program is "the only right thing to do, and it's the only realistic thing."

Even the abortion debate, the staple of social-conservative doctrine, isn't as simple for Brownback as it is for others. On a speaking swing through California several years ago, he met a couple who had written a book about their own experience in receiving a genetic test indicating a likelihood of Down syndrome in a baby they were expecting. They were shocked, they told Brownback, that the medical system seemed to push them at every turn simply to abort the unborn child. Now Brownback worries that advances in genetic testing, which can detect early signs of birth defects, have led to what he calls "the genocide we have taking place in this country against Down-syndrome children." Sometimes those diagnoses of Down syndrome are wrong, Brownback says, and even children who are born with Down syndrome can lead happy and productive lives.

Within Congress, the most visible and practical sign of Brownback's emergence as a leader on the values front is his role as head of the Values Action Team, a little-known and loosely organized collection of more than 125 groups interested in pushing a conservative social agenda. Every Tuesday afternoon, in strict privacy, Brownback sits down with representatives of some of those groups, as well as representatives from the White House and Senate offices, to discuss how to push issues of importance on the religious right. For Brownback, it's a way both to show his leadership and to pursue his goal of broadening the agenda.

When AIDS funding for Africa came up for consideration in the Senate, for example, Brownback persuaded the group to get behind a push for the money and to pressure lawmakers to vote for it. He has lobbied the group not only to exert pressure to keep restrictions on abortion in federal funding bills, but also to join him in pushing the United States to fight harder against sex trafficking abroad.

All told, Brownback's is a different Senate career from the one pursued by the man who held Brownback's seat before him. Bob Dole was the pre-eminent Senate Republican of the post–World War II generation, nominated twenty years apart in losing national campaigns as the vice-presidential candidate in 1976 and the presidential candidate in 1996. Despite his role as party standard-bearer, over time he displayed a penchant for cross-party cooperation with the likes of liberal Democratic Senator George McGovern on issues such as food stamps. Indeed, the mutual fondness that developed between Dole and McGovern, who seemed to be ideological polar opposites, was so great that Dole confided to a guest at a gala in his honor in Washington in early 2007 that he was proudest that McGovern had spoken at a political think tank Dole established at the University of Kansas. He looked forward to returning the favor by speaking when McGovern set up an institute to house his personal papers.

If Dole's political persona was shaped by wounds sustained on a World War II battlefield, Brownback's was molded by the teachings of his church. But although Brownback is gentle in demeanor, he is dogged in pursuing his beliefs.

He was among those driving the Senate to intervene in the Terri Schiavo case to try to stop her husband from taking her off life support. That intervention proved to be a political disaster for Republicans. Yet for Brownback, his belief in protecting life from conception to natural death left no other choice. The thread running through

Brownback's politics is clear: Ideology outranks pragmatism, and being true to your ideals is more important than being popular.

Still, that hasn't stopped Brownback from working with Democrats on some issues. Whereas Dole tended in his day to reach across the partisan divide on economic issues, Brownback has begun to look for common ground on values issues. Thus, he has worked with Democratic Connecticut Senator Joseph Lieberman on steps to reduce religious persecution in Sudan and liberal Democratic Representative John Lewis of Georgia on the construction of an African American Museum on the Washington Mall. He conferred with Democratic Senator Joseph Biden of Delaware on ways to end the feuding of Iraq's religious sects and with Senator Paul Wellstone of Minnesota on a 2000 law to fight sex trafficking. Other and older religious conservatives wouldn't put such items high on their agenda, or be so willing to work with liberals on them. Brownback isn't merely willing to do so, but looks for the chance. He even talks, somewhat wistfully, of cooperating with liberals to reduce the incidence of abortion, even while disagreeing with them on its legality.

Brownback's most ambitious quest—some would say his most unrealistic one—was his decision to run for the Republican presidential nomination in 2008. He announced his candidacy on the eve of the massive annual pro-life rally in Washington to protest the 1973 *Roe* v. *Wade* Supreme Court decision legalizing abortion.

On the one hand, Brownback's move made sense: The party that had become home to millions of social-conservative voters had no obvious presidential candidate to speak for, and to, those voters. Some well-heeled Republicans were looking for someone to carry that banner; among Brownback's early key supporters was Tom Monaghan, the exceedingly wealthy founder of Domino's Pizza who now uses his riches to further conservative Catholic causes. As Dole's successor, Brownback hoped to inherit some fragments of the Dole presidential-campaign network in nearby Iowa, where it would help in the nation's first caucuses.

The early returns were not promising. Brownback was little-known outside his home state and his core audience of social conservatives.

In the first three quarters of 2007, he raised only about $4 million—roughly one-tenth the amount collected by Republican rival Mitt Romney.[3] Citing his financial disadvantage, Brownback withdrew from the race in October 2007.

But the Brownback message that there is a new generation of Christian conservative thinking, and a new set of leaders to carry it forward, wasn't lost to the presidential campaign. Instead, it was picked up by another new-style Christian activist, former Arkansas Governor Mike Huckabee, a Baptist minister and former president of the Arkansas Baptist State Convention. Almost none of the traditional leaders of the Christian conservative movement endorsed his long-shot candidacy, yet the foot soldiers in the movement made him the early sensation in the 2008 Republican race anyway. Against long odds, Huckabee won the Iowa caucuses by drawing in a surge of Christian conservatives: Six in ten of those who voted in the Republican caucuses identified themselves as evangelical or born-again Christians, and almost half of them voted for Huckabee. Like Brownback, Huckabee ranged well beyond the traditional issues of abortion and gay rights, stressing economic fairness as much as anything, and talking openly about how Christian compassion had affected decisions he'd made as governor. His unlikely rise illustrated that Christian conservatives had changed but hadn't faded as a force in Republican politics.

For Brownback, the 2008 campaign isn't likely to prove the measure of his influence. Rather, that measure will likely be his ability to press his "whole life" message on others within the party. The modern Republican Party cannot compete nationally without vigorous support from Christian conservatives. But it also needs to expand the ranks of those who could be attracted alongside those voters.

That message "doesn't offend anyone in our base, and it's the best way to attract people to the pro-life message," says Brownback, who now is considering running for governor of Kansas. "Our base is shrinking. This is one of the key ways to expand the base."

• • •

If Brownback has symbolized the new religious right on the political front, Pete Wehner has symbolized its rise within Washington's intellectual community, and within the Bush White House. Jerry Falwell or Pat Robertson he's not.

For Wehner, values and politics are intermingled in a complex, sometimes uneasy mix. There was little in his background that seemed to push him toward the role he now plays. Wehner was born in Dallas but moved to Washington State when he was six years old.[4] There, his father did biomedical research while his son began cultivating an intense interest in politics. Pete Wehner came to realize that he was, instinctively, more conservative than many of his classmates, and more conservative than many of his teachers. When he participated in a grade-school debate during the 1972 presidential campaign, he spoke in favor of Richard Nixon, and squared off against a classmate who spoke on behalf of George McGovern.

But he also harbored some liberal sentiments—sentiments that would help him and others of his generation start to mold a new way of mixing values and politics. After he moved on to the University of Washington, he indulged in what has become a standing fascination with two slain Democratic icons, John and Robert Kennedy. Wehner was especially taken with the high-minded idealism and soaring style of Kennedy rhetoric. As a student, he would retire to the university's library and listen to hours of Kennedy speeches. In them, he found sentiments he admired: "I like those terms 'common good,' 'social concern,' 'compassion,'" he says.

Wehner was making a parallel discovery about himself. Though his family isn't especially religious, he found himself dwelling on deep questions of faith and life's meaning. Even before college, he discussed them with an older sister who had experienced a religious awakening. He and a friend formed a Bible-study group. At the university, he became close to a campus minister, who ultimately married Wehner and his wife. "Faith wasn't easy for me," he says. "The faith smoothed out for me after a few years. I don't know how. But the cross of Christ became central for me."

Thus, politics and faith coexisted as Pete Wehner ventured out into the world. He got an internship in the Washington State Legislature, and then, in the spring of 1983, moved to Washington, D.C., to become an intern at the Center for Strategic and International Studies, a right-of-center think tank. After working briefly on a State Department commission, he became a full-time analyst at CSIS, specializing in Latin American affairs.

From there, he hooked up with a group of like-minded conservatives at the Ethics and Public Policy Center, a think tank devoted to bringing religious values into politics and public policy. At that point, like so many bright young people in Washington, Wehner found a kind of mentor and godfather. He began playing in a regular touch-football game also frequented by William Bennett, the social conservative who was then serving as secretary of education (and who later would become famous and wealthy by writing *The Book of Virtues*, a wildly best-selling collection of stories and writings with moral messages). Bennett was familiar with articles Wehner had written for *The Washington Post* about the relationship between faith and politics.

But Wehner made his real impression on Bennett one day on the football field, when their team was playing a squad that included several former pro football players. Wehner went up for a pass, throwing his body in the path of a couple of muscled-up opponents, got knocked to the ground, and came up with a bloody lip. His determination made an impression: "That's when Bill decided he wanted to hire me," Wehner recalls.

He wrote speeches for Bennett at the Education Department, then followed him to Empower America, an organization Bennett had set up with former Housing Secretary Jack Kemp, to advance conservative policy ideas. Empower America was a small incubator for smart young policy wonks, especially those interested in Kemp's gospel of tax cuts and Bennett's gospel of social policies illuminated by values and religious beliefs. There, Wehner struck up a friendship with Michael Gerson, a like-minded young conservative who was working for Indiana Senator Dan Coats.

Wehner and Gerson represented a different brand of conservative thinkers. Breaking with the Republican faction that blended budget cutting with libertarian zeal, they argued for a brand of policy embracing limited government, but also using some of those limited government powers to advance new and innovative programs to help the poor, the ailing, and the homeless. For most of the 1980s and 1990s, Republican conservatives became known mostly as people who were *against* things—abortion, gay marriage, pornography. Compassionate conservatism meant being *for* things: for using government funds to support faith-based groups that ran programs to support and train the poor to lift them out of poverty, for example. Being a compassionate conservative meant being not simply against abortion but for government assistance for groups that helped unwed mothers.

Practicing compassionate conservatism meant not simply opposing illegal immigration but helping Hispanic immigrants enter the mainstream of America. It meant not simply battling communism and Islamic extremism, but actively favoring aid to Christians being persecuted in sub-Saharan Africa.

For a born-again governor of Texas named George W. Bush, a politician deeply influenced by the religious beliefs he embraced relatively late in life, the message had great appeal. Bush was interested in courting the religious right but also in broadening his message beyond that particular subset of the Republican Party. Compassionate conservatism seemed the ticket to do that. Bush became an adherent, and he carried the message of compassionate conservatism all the way into the White House. He hired Gerson as his chief speechwriter, and Wehner came along as well, first as a speechwriter and later as a political adviser working under Karl Rove.

Placed at the helm of the White House Office of Strategic Initiatives, Wehner became the White House's link to intellectuals on the outside, engaging policy wonks of the left, center, and right in high-minded debates about the virtues and vices of Bush policies. Wehner developed the habit of blasting out e-mail missives on all manner of questions, sometimes giving his own explanation of a Bush decision, sometimes taking exception to columnists and op-ed writers who disagreed with the Bush team, sometimes circulating articles he found especially helpful and persuasive.

He entered the Bush White House on friendly terms with many journalists. But the searing disputes of the Bush era, most powerfully over the Iraq war, took a toll on some of those relationships. He privately lamented mistakes in the administration's handling of postwar Iraq. But Wehner maintained his core belief that the war to oust Saddam Hussein was justified and the cause of spreading freedom in the Middle East remained worth pursuing—even as so many others turned bitterly against those notions.

"The temptation we all face—those of us in politics and those outside of politics—is to simply surround ourselves with like-minded people," he said at the University of Pennsylvania in 2005. "It then becomes easy to caricature and ridicule those with whom we disagree. You and your colleagues can safely agree that you are all-wise and your critics are all foolish. And before long, you can find yourself in an intellectual cul-de-sac. And that's a dangerous place to be."[5]

Wehner, like other young conservatives of faith, is hardly a Christian who simply uses his faith or a Scripture passage to justify every political position. He was, after all, a conservative before he became religious. "My hunch is I would be conservative even if I weren't religious," he says. So, for example, Wehner would be a natural supporter of the Bush foreign-policy goal of advancing freedom and democracy around the globe in any case, but his faith makes him a stronger supporter. Making people free is a way to bestow on them the dignity that Christianity says they deserve, Wehner argues. Besides, people's religious beliefs are more likely to flourish when they are free than when they are living under tyranny, so a religious person interested in spreading the faith should naturally want policies that advance freedom around the globe.

On the other hand, "when you get to specific policies on taxes and spending, I get really wary" of using religion to justify a position. "You can pull out Scriptures for anything you want." He once explained, in a piece written for *The Washington Post*, his own discomfort with the combination of religion and politics: "Consider, too, how the political arena undermines traditional Christian virtues such as love, humility, forgiveness, forbearance, kindness, mercy and gentleness," he wrote. "These virtues are not the coin of the political realm—including the Christian political realm. Often when Christians organize politically, the rules that are supposed to govern their behavior individually seem not to apply to them collectively. And so we find that the fuel driving much of modern-day Christian activism is anger, bitterness, resentment."[6] He was more personal in the University of Pennsylvania speech in discussing the collision between his professional and spiritual lives. "There is a tension between Christianity and politics," he said, "that I have not been able to escape."[7]

Within the Bush White House, Wehner found others who shared his combination of religion and politics—for example, a loosely organized group of aides called the "Thursday Group," named for the day of the week when they meet for a Bible-study session. Wehner attended occasionally, but wasn't a regular. And he says that, though he and Gerson frequently discussed the values embedded in a policy decision, he can't recall any occasions when religious points were specifically used to advance an argument during staff deliberations.

Now Wehner has left the White House, and continues his exploration of the role of faith in politics at the Ethics and Public Policy Center. He sees the world of religious conservatives undergoing a significant transformation. "There's a huge change going on among Christian conservatives, especially those in their twenties and thirties, away from issues like abortion and toward social issues—social justice and aid to Africa, for example." The cutting-edge college for political conservatives no longer is Jerry Falwell's Liberty University but, rather, Wheaton College, a small, Christian liberal-arts college near Chicago, he says. Young Christian activists are likely to think that preserving the environment of the earth God created is a moral issue, just as is fighting for the unborn life God created. The role model for young Christian conservatives is no longer Pat Robertson, Wehner says, but rock star Bono, the crusader for aid to Africa's poor.

17. THE NEW DEMOCRATS:
MARA VANDERSLICE AND JIM WEBB

BILL CLINTON'S SKILLS temporarily concealed a double-barreled political problem for Democrats. Clinton had the style and idiom of a Southern Baptist preacher, and thrived in churches with black and white congregations alike. By contrast, though, most national Democratic politicians struggled with religious themes. As Clinton's former Press Secretary Mike McCurry put it, "Our operatives aren't likely to be in church on Sunday. They're more likely to be watching Tim Russert on NBC-TV's *Meet the Press.*" It's a party with a secular soul.

At the same time, Democrats, despite their roots as representatives of the working class, have become more a party of comfortable incomes and lifestyles. One little-noticed electoral trend, in fact, has been the Democrats' increasing success in winning the allegiance of upscale voters, who sometimes display Republican-like friendliness toward trade and globalization.

On those two fronts, Mara Vanderslice and Jim Webb are pushing back.

Mara Vanderslice hails from a "progressive" Democratic family in Colorado. She attended Earlham College, a Quaker school in Indiana, and became an evangelical Christian while in college, but her seminal political experience was a stint living and traveling in Latin

America. "To live in and see that poverty was very formative for me, as it has been for many others," she says.

Vanderslice decided to become an anti-poverty crusader. She went to work for Sojourners, a liberal religious organization dedicated to fighting poverty and promoting social justice, then Jubilee 2000, an international campaign that crusaded to convince First World nations to forgive crushing Third World debts. She also embarked on a mission to Africa.

She soon came to see politics as crucial to the social work she was doing. She says she was appalled, for instance, when President Bush made a splashy promise to spend billions of new dollars to fight AIDS around the world but his aides then did little or nothing to persuade Congress actually to appropriate the money. "It's very hard to spend much time in Washington without seeing how important those guys who sit in the big chairs are," she says. "We lobby people all day long, but sometimes you have to change who sits there. For me, if I wanted to make a change in the issues I care about, I had to get involved in politics."

So she did. She naturally did so on the Democratic side, because Democrats tended to be more sympathetic to calls for government aid for the poor and the Third World. Yet she also came to believe Democrats actually weren't fighting all that hard for the poor and had no real connection with people who cared about religion.

Consequently, Vanderslice set out on what was virtually a one-woman crusade to change the party. With the 2004 presidential campaign getting under way, she moved to Iowa, rented an old car, enlisted a student from the University of Iowa to help, and embarked on an effort to get every Democratic presidential candidate passing through the state to sign a promise to double Bush's pledge of funds to fight global AIDS. She tried to attend, or have some ally attend, every campaign event in the state leading up to the quadrennial caucuses. Vanderslice herself often walked up to candidates or their top staffers to solicit the candidates' signatures on the pledge.

The effort worked. As the Iowa caucuses approached, Vanderslice had secured a signature from every candidate except the front-runner at the time, Howard Dean. Ironically, Dean was the candidate who most appealed to Vanderslice, because she shared his staunch opposition to the war in Iraq. But his campaign was oddly resistant to signing the AIDS-funding pledge. Finally, Vanderslice scheduled an event in Davenport to announce the results of the campaign—an event that three Iowa television stations planned to cover. She called a Dean campaign leader as she headed to the event, saying, "I'm going to have to stand up in front of three TV stations and say, 'Dean is the only candidate who hasn't signed the pledge.' " The campaign got the message and responded instantly. A pledge signed by Dean was faxed to Vanderslice just before the event began.

The effort impressed the Dean campaign enough to hire Vanderslice. Soon enough, though, she found the campaign staff uncomfortable or resistant to the idea of reaching out to religious leaders and voters. Dean himself was busy taking potshots at evangelicals and their influence on the Republican Party; that didn't exactly invite outreach to evangelicals or religious voters. For Vanderslice, the attitude was crystallized at a Dean staff meeting at which senior advisers went around the table so newer and younger staffers could say who they were and what they did. When Vanderslice's turn came, she said she was working on outreach to religious groups. As she recalls the scene, one senior Dean aide instantly looked at her and replied, "How the f— did you get hired?"

Dean eventually imploded, John Kerry got the Democratic nomination, and his campaign hired Vanderslice to handle its outreach to religious voters. She believes that made her the first full-time staffer ever hired by a Democratic campaign to handle relations with religious voters. Still, she didn't find the attitude within the campaign much different from the one she had encountered in Dean's ill-fated effort: "People were either hostile or ignorant." After a conservative Catholic group attacked Vanderslice personally for her previous work with liberal causes, the Kerry campaign barred her from speaking publicly. She continued to try to organize religious leaders behind the scenes, but most of her energy was devoted to pushing within the campaign for Kerry to give a defining "values" speech to serve as his marquee statement of how religious and moral views affected his life and his views. It seemed a good idea. Kerry, a lifelong Catholic, was being attacked at the time by Catholic leaders for his support for abortion, and much media attention was focusing on the contention by some bishops that Kerry should be refused Holy Communion because of his views.

Vanderslice wanted a big speech in which Kerry would declare what personal faith and beliefs meant to him. But she couldn't get the campaign to schedule such an event, even though she convinced some Catholic leaders in the crucial swing state of Ohio to provide a forum. Finally, McCurry, who was acting as a part-time outside adviser to the Kerry campaign, accompanied the candidate and his aides on a trip and persuaded them to do the speech. But it was a shadow of what Vanderslice wanted. She had hoped for a speech early in the campaign; it came in October. Instead of the Catholic event in Ohio she had wanted, it was made at an event in Florida.

In the latter stages of the campaign, Vanderslice did find one Kerry state campaign leader, in Michigan, sympathetic to her call for outreach to religious voters. She organized dozens of volunteers, and Kerry did fifteen percentage points better among active Catholics in Michigan than he did among such voters nationwide. Ultimately, of course, Kerry lost the presidential race, and lost the Catholic vote, and did miserably among evangelical voters.

The outcome did have a bracing effect on party strategists, though. Vanderslice was hired by the Democratic National Committee to continue her work. But McCurry and Doug Sosnik, the onetime White House political director for President Clinton, convinced her that if she wanted to make a real difference she needed to break away and set up her own firm to show the political value of religious outreach to Democrats. So, in July 2005, she did exactly that. She recruited another young Democrat of similar views, Eric Sapp, a former congressional aide, and they started a political-consulting firm called Common Good Strategies, which they describe as "a political strategy firm dedicated to helping Democrats reclaim the debate on faith and values." Their first test came in the 2006 congressional elec-

tions. They worked for seven Democratic candidates in six states, trying to help them connect with religious voters.

In part, their work involved highlighting issues on which some religious voters might share their views—poverty, AIDS, the environment, and the Iraq war, for instance. On the unavoidable question of
abortion, she urged candidates to talk about efforts to reduce the
number of abortions—an area where all sides of the abortion debate
could in theory come together—rather than engage in the typical debate about whether the courts could or should overturn the *Roe* v.
Wade Supreme Court decision legalizing abortion.

But much of the effort was aimed simply at making Democrats
more comfortable in talking about their faith to voters who want im-
plicit or explicit assurance that a candidate is a person with moral values. Vanderslice would start her work for a campaign by conducting
an interview with the candidate, almost as a journalist would, to get
them to start talking about what religion and faith mean to them. The
process, she says, helps candidates become more comfortable talking
publicly about faith, and helps them form a message that they can use
when the opportunity arises.

A centerpiece of the effort in each campaign is to do for a congressional candidate what Vanderslice tried to do for Kerry: schedule and
craft a high-profile speech on values. When Ted Strickland, running
for governor of Ohio, gave such a speech, his campaign printed book-
lets with the text for distribution later. They proved so popular that
a second printing was required. Ultimately, ten thousand were
distributed—and Strickland beat Republican Kenneth Blackwell,
who had spent years courting the religious right. Vanderslice also
worked for Kansas Democratic Governor Kathleen Sebelius, who won
re-election in Sam Brownback's backyard, and Bob Casey of Pennsylvania, who came to Catholic University in Washington to make his
centerpiece values speech, and who made waves by winning a Senate
seat as a Democrat who opposes abortion rights. Vanderslice also
worked for Heath Shuler of North Carolina, the former Washington
Redskins quarterback who wavered for a time between running as a

Republican or a Democrat, and who won a seat in the House as a Democrat with conservative cultural values.

In the end, all seven of the Common Good Strategies candidates won, and exit polls indicated that each of them did from ten to twenty percentage points better among religiously active voters—white Protestants who attend church regularly, active Catholics, and white evangelicals—than did Democratic candidates overall.

Vanderslice moved ahead after the election to, among other things, push legislation sponsored by a pro-life Democrat, Representative Tim Ryan of Ohio, and a pro-choice Democrat, Representative Rosa DeLauro of Connecticut, that is designed to reduce abortions. Called the "Reducing the Need for Abortions and Supporting Parents Act," the bill would try to prevent abortions by increasing support for family-planning programs, and by increasing assistance for women who choose to keep their babies. It now appears that Vanderslice has gone from being an aberration within the Democratic Party to being in the vanguard of a movement of young like-minded activists who are starting to reshape the values debate. "There is a kind of informal network of about twenty of us, all about the same age, trying to find our voice on these issues," she says.

The early phase of the 2008 campaign offered evidence that their efforts are working. In June 2007, the three leading Democratic candidates for president gathered to discuss their faith at a forum in Washington sponsored by the liberal evangelical group Sojourners. Former Senator John Edwards of North Carolina allowed that he sinned every day. Senator Hillary Rodham Clinton of New York called herself a "praying person" who relied on her Christian faith to survive personal and political turmoil. Senator Barack Obama of Illinois quoted the Bible in asserting, "I am my brother's keeper."[1]

The anodyne character of their comments wasn't the important part of the event. It was the fact that all three party front-runners decided the faith-based event was important enough to command their presence.

• • •

If the source of Mara Vanderslice's inspiration is spiritual, the source of Jim Webb's is visceral. When Webb describes the working-class culture he comes from, he sounds more like the leader of an uprising than a national political figure. "Who are we?" he asks—and then answers in uncompromising terms. "We are the molten core at the very center of the unbridled, raw, rebellious spirit of America. We helped build this nation, from the bottom up. We face the world on our feet and not on our knees. We were born fighting. And if the cause is right, we will never retreat."[2]

That pugnacious description, from a book Webb wrote to describe his Scots-Irish background, helps explain why Jim Webb of Virginia—boxer, war hero, proud descendant of America's working classes—is such an intriguing new voice in Pennsylvania Avenue's argument over values.

War is what first brought Webb to Pennsylvania Avenue. The son of a military man, he graduated from the U.S. Naval Academy and won medals for valor in Vietnam. He came home and wrote a critically acclaimed war novel, *Fields of Fire*. His political views were shaped by the country's fault lines over Vietnam—specifically, the disdain for the military he saw among left-leaning professors and classmates at Georgetown University Law Center. In 1984, Webb joined Ronald Reagan's Republican administration as assistant secretary of defense and later as navy secretary. After his administration service, Webb made his living as a novelist and filmmaker.

But over time he became disaffected enough to return to the Avenue again—and to seek to redefine its values debate. As President Bush and John Kerry battled it out in the 2004 presidential election, Webb published a history of his Scots-Irish forebears, who settled the American South and Midwest and became unheralded mainstays of America's military as well as its blue-collar workforce. Republicans and Democrats had turned into a "hybrid royalty" offering "grand useless speeches . . . on issues such as flag-burning, homosexual marriage and abortion," Webb wrote in *Born Fighting*. What was needed instead, he declared, was a debate about fundamental questions of educational and economic opportunity, for working-class whites as well as for blacks.

If that sounded like a blast at Republicans, it didn't fit easily into Democratic theology, either. "My people," as Webb put it, "don't go for group identity politics any more than they like to join a labor union."[3] He criticized affirmative action and decried the slurs working-class whites had routinely endured: "rednecks," "trailer-park trash," "racists," "cannon fodder."[4] Webb concluded: "I am determined to reclaim the dignity of these people."[5] While he was researching his seventh book, President Bush was moving toward what Webb considered a fundamental foreign-policy blunder. In September 2002, Webb offered a stark warning about the administration's preparation for war to oust Saddam Hussein. By invading Iraq, Webb wrote in *The Washington Post*, Bush would commit the United States to a decades-long troop presence in the Middle East, turn U.S. soldiers into targets for terrorists, and fuel the hostility of Muslims elsewhere.[6]

By the spring of 2006, that warning was looking prescient—and Jim Webb was a Democratic candidate for the U.S. Senate. His effort was awkward at first. At once brash and diffident, Webb was no one's idea of a back-slapping pol. He bridled at pressure from Democratic leaders to devote more time to soliciting campaign donations. His past critiques of affirmative action and women soldiers' suitability for combat roles provided fodder for primary opponent Harris Miller, a wealthy technology executive, who attacked him as being out of the Democratic Party's liberal mainstream. Only after a last-minute boost from the Democratic Senatorial Campaign Committee—whose chairman, Senator Chuck Schumer of New York, considered Webb, as he did Bob Casey in Pennsylvania, a strong general-election candidate— did Webb capture the party's nomination. In the general election, the defining moment came when Republican incumbent George Allen made a famous gaffe by referring to a Webb aide of Indian descent as "macaca."

But Webb couldn't have taken advantage of that opening without his intimate connection to the values that had shaped Virginia's political culture. In his own earlier successful race for governor, wealthy Democrat Mark Warner had studiously cultivated Virginia's small towns and rural areas by sponsoring a NASCAR team. Webb made an even more dramatic cultural statement by wearing the combat boots of his son, like him a soldier, and one who was stationed in Iraq.

"We walked Mark Warner through the culture," Democratic consultant Dave "Mudcat" Saunders told Webb. "You *are* the culture." Webb, in fact, placed values at the center of his attack on Republican-dominated Washington. "They speak to you of values but know nothing other than political expediency and blind loyalty to a money-drenched political machine," he wrote. His desire to connect with voters of modest means was sometimes discomfiting to some of the upscale Democrats fueling the political money machine of the left. At a summer summit of candidates and Democratic luminaries on Nantucket, Webb rebutted one participant's observation that Democrats had failed to attract more working-class votes because they weren't "optimistic" enough. Countered Webb: "They don't vote for you because they don't think you like them."

He embraced Virginian values on issues far beyond populist economics. "I have possessed a concealed-carry permit for many years, and shoot regularly," Webb wrote to Virginia gun owners during the campaign. "I have made no secret during this campaign of the fact that I carry."[7] Republicans tried an unusual "values" rejoinder as Election Day approached. Pointing to sex scenes in Webb's novels, they attacked him from the left for portraying women as "promiscuous" and from the right as a purveyor of licentious prose.[8] But the eleventh-hour attack failed. Webb won a narrow three-thousand-vote victory, over a Republican conservative once considered Republican presidential material, a victory that instantly turned Webb into a Democratic star.

Republicans on the Avenue didn't miss an opportunity to bruise him, though. Webb brought to politics the reputation of a hothead.

For all his bravery in combat, author Robert Timberg wrote in his chronicle of prominent Naval Academy graduates, *The Nightingale's Song*, Webb also could be "mean, vindictive . . . and overbearing."[9] In late November, word leaked to the press of a brusque encounter at a White House social event, at which Webb declined to engage President Bush in small talk about Webb's son's deployment to Iraq. Conservative columnist George Will slammed Webb in print as "a boor."[10]

In the polarized politics of the Avenue, such attacks only enhanced Webb's reputation among Democratic activists. But what really elevated the freshman senator was the national spotlight he received after being selected to deliver the Democratic response to Bush's State of the Union Address in 2007. Displaying a picture of his father in his air-force uniform, Webb excoriated Bush with unusual intensity and passion for "recklessly" launching the Iraq war. "We are now, as a nation, held hostage to the predictable — and predicted — disarray that has followed,"[11] he said. At the same time, his populist economic message was a challenge of sorts to moderates within his own party who had supported President Clinton's free-trade policies in the 1990s. "The middle class in this country, our historic backbone and our best hope for a strong society in the future, is losing its place at the table," he declared. "We're working to get the right things done, for the right people and for the right reasons."

Webb's goal is no less audacious than reshaping the Democratic electorate — in effect, rolling back the Reagan tide that capitalized on cultural values to suck working-class voters into the GOP. "What should be the makeup of the Democratic Party if you get back to Jacksonian principles?" he asks while sitting in his spare Senate office, his belongings only partly moved in, months after his arrival. "It's time for the Reagan Democrats to come home. The Democrats have forgotten that this culture even exists. Karl Rove has studied it so much he knows how to manipulate it." Webb is realistic about his attempt to buck the twenty-first-century trends on Pennsylvania Avenue: "I'm never going to change what I believe for a [campaign] contribution," he says. "If they don't like it, I'll go write a book in Bangkok."

Given his simultaneous opposition to gun control and to a gay-marriage ban during the campaign, Webb had quipped, "I'm going to get the gay hunters' vote." Still, none of that quite prepared Pennsylvania Avenue for the bracing news that broke a few weeks after Webb's State of the Union response. A Webb aide, Philip Thompson, was arrested for trying to bring a gun belonging to Webb into a Senate office building. It was, to say the least, not typical behavior for the office of a Democratic senator. "I want to thank Senator Webb for providing security," Bush joked a few days later at the Radio-TV Correspondents Dinner, one of the Avenue's annual rituals of forced conviviality between reporters and their sources.

But Webb, who was in the audience, may have gotten the last laugh in the reaction of the Democratic activists who had applauded his nationally televised speech. Notwithstanding the party's reputation for weak knees, some Democrats thrilled at the masculine spectacle of a firearms arrest. "Yeah, he had a gun," Kagro X blogged on Daily Kos, daring Republican "sissies" to make it an issue. "Best possible way to get arrested, I say."[12] By springtime, Webb had become one of the Democratic Senatorial Campaign Committee's biggest fund-raising draws. To advance his unlikely values agenda, Webb also formed his own leadership PAC. He gave it the same name as his book about the beleaguered, oft-ignored Scots-Irish: Born Fighting.

18. THE DEAL-MAKERS:
BERNADETTE BUDDE AND ANDY STERN

THE PENNSYLVANIA AVENUE of the early twenty-first century has brought Americans together in at least one way: disdain for its self-seeking, divisiveness, and inability to solve national problems. In June 2007, a *Wall Street Journal*–NBC News survey showed that seven in ten Americans believed the country was headed in the wrong direction. It was the poll's bleakest measurement of the nation's mood in fifteen years.

What might surprise some of those disillusioned voters is that those wielding power on the Avenue are in many cases just as dispirited. Through the Republican ascendance of the Bush presidency, strategists for corporate America have grown increasingly frustrated at Washington's failure to move ahead on energy policy, immigration, entitlements, and the environment. Nor has the Democratic revival in the midterm elections of 2006 inspired much hope at the opposite end of the spectrum, within the labor movement, which has traditionally served as the most powerful adversary to corporate America's goals.

That's why Bernadette Budde and Andy Stern are both searching for new ways of doing business.

Bernadette Budde is as far removed from the caricature of a corporate power-broker lobbyist as it is possible to be. The senior vice president for political analysis at the influential Business-Industry Political Action Committee does not own a car. She lives in the same apartment in Washington's Foggy Bottom neighborhood that she has rented for the past three decades. Most days, she walks the twenty-minute commute from her apartment to BIPAC's offices, a block from the White House. On Sunday morning, she greets fellow parishioners at St. Stephen Martyr Catholic Church, eight blocks west of the White House, on Pennsylvania Avenue.

"It's hard not to be repelled" by Washington's money culture, Budde says. That culture, she says, plays a significant role in deterring resolution of policy problems. "The people are fighting more about the spoils and rewards of power than to get things done. . . . Maybe the Bible is right about greed being at the root of all evil."

She'd be less repelled if Pennsylvania Avenue were producing results. But it isn't. And so, she says, "We have to rethink the whole model of how things get done in this town. Somebody's going to have to create a new way."

Budde has earned her disillusionment. She was raised on a farm in Wisconsin, where as a child she fed the chickens. Educated at Catholic schools and at Marquette University in Milwaukee, she came to the Washington area in 1969 to get a master's at the University of Maryland, when liberal politics still reigned. When she landed a job at BIPAC, it was "the only game in town" speaking broadly for the business community.

The influence of the business lobby has grown steadily ever since. During the Reagan years, there were victories on slashing tax rates. After Gingrich Republicans seized control of the House, the K Street Project to put Republicans atop lobbying firms tightened connections between lawmakers and their private-sector benefactors, who in turn benefited from legislative favors and regulatory breaks.

Budde and her colleagues at BIPAC became intellectual leaders of corporate political strategy. BIPAC used its relatively modest level of donations in highly targeted fashion, eschewing "habit giving" to safe incumbents in favor of writing checks for promising but underfunded pro-business challengers. Other business donors in turn used BIPAC's endorsements as guideposts for their own decision-making.

BIPAC also became a leader in business uses of political technology. As labor redoubled its efforts at internal communications—seeking to spur turnout through direct contact between unions and their members—BIPAC developed high-tech tools for corporations to do the same through its Prosperity Project.

With surveys showing that most workers invest high credibility in guidance from employers, businesses rapidly adopted BIPAC's tools. By 2004, more than nine hundred companies were participating, delivering some forty million messages to voters and providing voter forms for some 1.6 million voters. BIPAC was in the vanguard in promoting the use of "early voting" programs, as states increasingly gave time-pressed residents broader opportunities to cast ballots long before Election Day.

So BIPAC had good reason for optimism after the 2004 elections handed Bush a second term with expanded House and Senate majorities. It was "the ideal set of conditions for the old way of doing things," Budde says wistfully. The two ends of Pennsylvania Avenue did, indeed, notch a few early accomplishments, enacting legislation making it harder for consumers to declare bankruptcy and harder for class-action lawyers to pursue suits against corporations in federal court.

But progress stalled after that; even after losing the 2004 election, Democrats and their allies retained the clout to stymie Bush's most ambitious initiatives. And their clout grew in the run-up to the 2006 elections, as Bush's power ebbed from the blows inflicted by his Social Security misfire, the Schiavo case, the Iraq war, and the Katrina fiasco. Republicans on Capitol Hill became mired in scandal in the wake of revelations about the mutually beneficial relationship between Jack Abramoff and his congressional allies; details of the bribes from a defense contractor that would send Representative Randy "Duke" Cunningham of California to prison were even more sensational.

By the summer of 2006, when most prognosticators were still expecting Republicans to hold one or both houses of Congress, Budde was bracing BIPAC's members for the likelihood of a Democratic sweep of the midterm elections. That her prediction proved accurate only deepened her conviction that business lobbyists can't count on conventional political processes that have grown damaged and incapable of action.

"We've learned that power isn't predictable," she says. "Party control can change." In business and politics alike, the communications revolution has flattened hierarchies. "Everybody matters," for good or ill, on Capitol Hill.

That mirrors the changes coursing through BIPAC's own membership. American firms are at once drawn outward into the international marketplace and confronted with activism at home from new and nontraditional kinds of shareholders as stock ownership proliferates.

"Whatever we thought the investor class used to be," she notes, it now includes substantial representation from workers through their individual holdings or those of union pension funds. "Our internal audience has changed." A rapidly changing, customer-driven business landscape has made corporate managers themselves less secure—and less patient to wait for results from Washington.

Budde finds encouragement from the fact that so many experienced politicians have risen to the helm of key trade groups along the Avenue. They include former Representatives Billy Tauzin at the drug industry's lobbying organization and Dan Mica at the Credit Union National Association; former Governors Frank Keating of Oklahoma at the American Council of Life Insurers, Marc Racicot of Montana at the American Insurance Association, John Engler of Michigan at the National Association of Manufacturers.

But it will take innovation and pragmatism, not partisanship, to overcome gridlock on unresolved policy fights. "We think they will get unstuck," Budde says. But "I don't think party's going to be what drives the resolution."

As it happens, by early 2007 Pennsylvania Avenue was becoming rife with examples of what she was talking about. General Electric,

Duke Power, and other corporate titans staged a press conference with leading environmentalists to call for action against global warming—a national "cap and trade" system to limit carbon emissions. The Bush administration, business's traditional ally, was resisting that step. But pressure from outside the government from the likes of former Vice President Al Gore was drawing responses from Governor Arnold Schwarzenegger of California, among others. Former GE Chairman Jack Welch said it only made good business sense for leading corporations to join the parade.

In similar fashion, the new tycoons of private equity displayed their own agility at linking political compromise with the bottom line. In its record-setting $45-billion leveraged buyout of the TXU Corporation energy concern, private-equity firm Kohlberg Kravis Roberts anticipated and defused environmentalists' opposition in advance. KKR pledged to shut down several high-polluting coal-fired TXU power plants, and in turn the environmentalists agreed not to foment political opposition to the deal.[1]

"The ability to work and play well with others matters," Budde says. And that means the business lobby on Pennsylvania Avenue will need the flexibility to create unconventional, ad hoc coalitions on targeted issues—sometimes making common cause with their traditional labor-union antagonists.

"The time is going to come when they are less the adversary than they are a potential partner," Budde says. The twenty-first-century campaigns that succeed on the Avenue, she concludes, will join "the lions and the lambs."

Andy Stern is nobody's idea of a lamb. Rivals in the labor movement call him arrogant, egocentric, and power-hungry. They blame him for dividing the movement and diminishing its clout in the process.

But Stern has reached the same conclusion Budde has: Pennsylvania Avenue needs to devise a new path to success. And this path, if it has any chance at all, must turn old enemies into allies.

Stern's political journey has been a process of coping with declining expectations. He graduated from the University of Pennsylvania and became a social-service worker when memories of Lyndon Johnson's Great Society were still fresh. But Richard Nixon had won the White House by then, and American business was beginning to gravitate toward the nonunion Sunbelt, gradually eroding labor's presence in the workforce and thus its power on Pennsylvania Avenue.

President Reagan's success in breaking PATCO, the air-traffic controllers' union, punctuated that decline. By 2006, as Stern served as president of the Service Employees International Union, labor's share of the workforce had fallen to 12 percent, down by two-thirds from its post–World War II high.[2]

A combination of political and personal crisis spurred Stern to take the steps that would change the face of labor on Pennsylvania Avenue. As he battled inside the AFL-CIO for a more aggressive stance toward union-organizing efforts, Stern lost his fourteen-year-old daughter, Cassie, to complications from spinal surgery. Initially paralyzed by grief, Stern eventually threw himself into work with fresh energy—and led SEIU and several other major unions to split off from the AFL-CIO and form the Change to Win Coalition. At the same time, his search for new strategies led him to the attempt to confront the world's largest retailer through Wal-Mart Watch.

Once Democrats recaptured Capitol Hill in the 2006 elections, some liberal constituencies sensed a tidal shift that would continue through the 2008 presidential race and break Pennsylvania Avenue's gridlock. Stern doesn't believe it. He figures Republicans will retain sufficient strength to stymie a Democratic president's agenda just as Democrats stymied much of Bush's after winning control of Congress in 2006.

"It's going to be a long time before one-party action is going to be a successful strategy," Stern says. "Someone has to help provide a better framework."

Improbable as it sounds, one of Stern's partners in that effort is Lee Scott, the president and CEO of Wal-Mart. In early 2007, a Bank of America analysts' report concluded that attacks from antagonists such as Wal-Mart Watch had cost the world's largest retailer as much as $16 billion in market capitalization through its slumping share price; those efforts almost certainly also heightened the danger that Scott would be forced from his job. But they didn't stop Stern and Scott from striding together into a luncheon meeting of Democratic senators in early May, promoting their partnership in advocating government action to expand access to health-insurance coverage.

"It's odd and at times uncomfortable for us both," Stern says. "We each appreciate that we've compartmentalized our lives." But both had found, in ways that have lately eluded Pennsylvania Avenue officeholders, a way to find mutually beneficial common ground. For companies such as Wal-Mart, government action to help expand health-insurance coverage could alleviate competitive pressure against low-cost rivals abroad; for unions, it would provide a way to deliver benefits to low-wage workers even at companies where their organizing efforts have failed. "If the health-care issue will be solved, it will be solved because business and labor come together," Stern says.

The question is how to align the political forces so that government can do anything at all. The traditional Pennsylvania Avenue legislative process has been largely discredited by recent misfires. As an alternative, Stern envisions Congress handing policy-making duties to a commission embracing business, labor, and other interests that could offer recommendations for up or down votes by Congress.

"We'll get it done," Stern says with characteristic confidence. "There's a greater sense of common purpose outside the political system than there is inside the political system. The question becomes, can it permeate the body politic? Everywhere in America people are ready to solve the health-care problem but in Congress and the White House."

Stern has already notched some successes with this strategy of treating elected officials as the means of facilitating solutions reached by interested parties, rather than as the source of solutions. One example is his odd-bedfellows partnership with Beverly Health and Rehabilitation Services, a leading nursing-home chain. The company, relying on an uncertain revenue stream from the government's Medicaid program, had resisted union-organizing attempts. SEIU and Beverly eventually struck a deal: The company allowed the union entrée, in return for the union's wielding its clout with several state legislatures to obtain increases in government reimbursements. Beverly Health's chief operating officer, Dave Devereaux, called Stern "a standup guy."[3]

That kind of bold joint action, rather than an unlikely return to the cozy, clubby Pennsylvania Avenue of yesteryear, may hold the most promise for changing political outcomes. "When you get to trust somebody, when they take a risk for you, it's different than when you can work with someone because they're good dinner partners," Stern says.

It's the same impulse that lies behind Representative Barney Frank's pursuit of a "grand bargain" on trade in which labor would support trade expansion in return for business's backing better wages and benefits. Yet Stern fears partisan venom has so poisoned Pennsylvania Avenue that lawmakers may be of little use. "Have we lost the art of deal-making in our system? Where are the deal-makers?"

One place he sees them is at 1001 Pennsylvania Avenue, at the offices of David Rubenstein and the Carlyle Group. Not only do Carlyle and its rivals make their own deals to buy companies, they often join together in "club deals" in which they share risks and profits. "The private-equity guys have huge egos" and clashing agendas, Stern marvels. But they still manage to cooperate in a way Democratic and Republican politicians ought to, but cannot, seem to emulate.

So Stern is pursuing his own deals with the private-equity dealmakers. SEIU has identified the burgeoning sector as a fresh target for political pressure on the model of the Wal-Mart Watch campaign. In its report on private equity called "Beyond the Buyouts," SEIU criticized some of the industry's money-making techniques, singling out

Carlyle's profitable "quick flip" of the Hertz Corporation at the cost of added debt and job losses for the company.

In its published report, SEIU proposed that private-equity firms adhere to "principles" that would allow workers greater ability to achieve security and share profits amid the financiers' dizzying deal-making. Privately, Stern in early 2007 was holding dinner meetings with top private-equity executives in hopes of winning concessions.

The private-equity executives wield immense financial power, but Stern wields the power to embarrass them with scrutiny at a time of swelling public discontent over the gap between rich and poor.

The tools of new media make that balance of power more even than ever, ripening conditions for the sort of lions-lambs bargain that Bernadette Budde envisions. Stern was pursuing the same strategy in his bid to press the pharmaceutical industry—a rising target of Americans' ire—to allow increased union organizing.

In the early phase of the 2008 campaign, Stern saw an increased appetite for bargaining, even on the politically ascendant left. The core appeal that launched Obama's primary campaign was achieving change by surmounting partisan bickering. Senator Hillary Clinton touted the hard-won Washington experience that could allow her to achieve results. Privately, elected officials in both parties welcomed Stern's work with Lee Scott on health care.

"Usually, what people say is 'I'm getting torn apart by the special interests,' " Stern explained, referring to a familiar private lament of elected officials. "It's a different situation when the special interests are clearing the way forward.

"We need a culture of success more than a culture of partisanship. It's the question of how you balance ideology with success. We've valued ideology way above success. We need to rebalance."

19. THE TAX MEN:
CHARLIE RANGEL AND JIM McCRERY

FEW ROLES are more prized and powerful on Pennsylvania Avenue than the chairmanship of the House Ways and Means Committee. The panel writes tax legislation, which under the Constitution can originate only in the House. That places the politician wielding its gavel at the center of events on Capitol Hill and within the vast American economy.

Because of the midterm elections of 2006, Charlie Rangel realized his long-standing dream of holding that gavel. Jim McCrery watched his dream slip away. And yet both men, the garrulous African American Democrat from Harlem and the proper white Republican from Louisiana, have reached the same conclusion: Even the best jobs along the Avenue aren't worth doing in the way Washington became accustomed to by the dawn of the twenty-first century.

And so, in early 2007, they set out, in modest but real ways, to do something about it—together.

Rangel, the voice of Harlem on Pennsylvania Avenue, has spent most of his nearly four decades in Congress on the Ways and Means Committee. It was a heady perch when his fellow Democrats controlled the House, an empty privilege after Republicans took charge in 1994.

For Rangel, the years that followed brought unremitting rancor. He and Representative Bill Archer, the Texas Republican who became chairman after the 1994 elections, weren't on speaking terms. They interacted only in public committee hearings.

Things went from bad to worse when Archer retired and was succeeded by Representative Bill Thomas of California, a gruff and eccentric lawmaker. Thomas once called Capitol police to roust Rangel and other Democratic members from a Capitol meeting room after they walked out of a Ways and Means hearing, complaining that they hadn't had the chance to review a piece of legislation.

Most problematic for Rangel, Thomas assiduously followed the paramount new rule of the Avenue: The majority party relies as little as possible on support from the minority. "He never asked me for a vote," Rangel says. To the contrary, he complains, Thomas would insert "poison pill" provisions in tax legislation to ensure that Democrats would *not* support them. When asked about his relationship with Thomas, Rangel says flatly, "I never cared enough about Bill Thomas to have feelings one way or the other."

Because he won his seat in 1970, Rangel had served long enough to see lawmakers of an earlier generation enjoying easier and more productive working relations. The committee's chairman from 1981 to 1994, Dan Rostenkowski of Illinois, was a man whose "word is good," as ranking Republican member Barber Conable of New York once put it. Conable was "the kind of guy who had to strain to be partisan," a Democratic colleague declared in tribute when President Reagan tapped Conable to head the World Bank.[1]

Rangel knows that sort of clubbiness won't likely return. As damaged as Washington's reputation with the rest of America has become, partisan divisions along the Avenue are actually deeper than many outsiders recognize.

President Bush's hard-charging Treasury Secretary Hank Paulson, who three decades earlier had served in the Nixon administration, returned to Washington in 2006 with high hopes of surmounting red-blue divisions with the same forcefulness he brought to the chairmanship of the Wall Street investment firm Goldman Sachs. He was taken aback by the breadth of those divisions, which quickly dashed his hopes for compromise to shore up the solvency of the massive Social Security and Medicare entitlement programs for the elderly, which threaten to bankrupt the government and damage the economy as Baby Boomers retire. Initial talks on solutions—which inevitably require some combination of structural change, tax increases, and benefit cuts—went nowhere, for fear that warring political tribes would exploit any such proposals for political advantage.

"Nobody wants to talk about pain because of lack of trust," Rangel says.

But Rangel began in small ways to try to rebuild some of that trust. As chairman beginning in 2007, he began holding private meetings with Republicans to build bridges of cooperation. His most important interlocutor was the ranking Republican on Ways and Means, Representative Jim McCrery of Louisiana.

"When people ask about my relationship with McCrery, I say I hardly know the guy," Rangel explains. Though they'd served together on Ways and Means for close to two decades, their relationship for most of that time was limited to courtesy greetings on the way in and out of committee meeting rooms.

Given the constraints of today's Pennsylvania Avenue, Rangel tried to keep expectations low. "We haven't become friends," Rangel said of McCrery in the spring of 2007, "but we're going down that road."

Jim McCrery concluded that he might travel that road with Rangel a few days after Democrats took control of Congress. McCrery objected to an element of the Democrats' hundred-hour legislative blitz that affected the tax-writing committee, and sent Rangel a letter that said so. Rangel surprised the Louisiana Republican by calling and requesting a meeting.

Rangel walked over to McCrery's office and said he shared the Republican's irritation. He pledged to resist such infringements in the future. McCrery believed him and offered a peculiarly Southern gesture of gratitude. "I made him some turtle soup," he said. Thus began their effort to work together.

McCrery in turn sought to demonstrate good faith in handling legislation raising the minimum wage. Republicans had long since abandoned the idea of blocking an increase, as they had succeeded in doing when they controlled the congressional agenda. To obtain that acquiescence, Democrats had conceded the inclusion of some tax breaks for business to offset the burden of higher wages. Since Democrats had committed themselves to avoiding legislation that increased the federal budget deficit, those tax cuts had to be "paid for" by various minor increases in government revenue. Instead of trying to slow the legislation down by objecting to "tax increases," McCrery adopted a low-key approach that allowed the bill to move through quickly.

That kind of accommodation is rare on today's Pennsylvania Avenue — to the chagrin of many who served in an earlier era. "Congress was always political, but now it's mean," says former Senator Bob Packwood of Oregon. During the Reagan presidency, he worked together with Rostenkowski to write a tax-reform bill that eventually drew more than ninety votes in the Senate. No major legislative initiative has passed with a comparable level of bipartisan support since. Packwood worries that the fund-raising chase has distracted members' attention and distorted their priorities at the expense of legislative prowess.

In his time, Packwood recalls, members' campaign fund-raising revolved around their own re-elections, not kicking into the kitties of colleagues and party leaders. The "leadership PACs" now commonplace for advancing congressional careers didn't exist. "If that's the system you have," Packwood says, "inevitably you are going to pass over talent" for getting things done.

McCrery decidedly does not long for that time. He hasn't forgotten which party was in control then. "Dan Rostenkowski ran that committee with an iron fist," he says. By his lights, Republicans under Archer and Thomas were only returning the favor after the Gingrich revolution. In an era of close party divisions, when losing a few House seats can tilt control of the chamber, there's no alternative to fierce fighting.

McCrery happily beats the fund-raising bushes to help his party; it was one of the factors that elevated his chances for the top Ways and Means Republican slot over those of Representative Clay Shaw of Florida, who had more seniority on the panel but was less adept at the money game. "You have to do more than be a legislator," says McCrery, who proved it by chairing the GOP's President's Dinner in 2006. "You've got to go the extra mile to help the team."

Yet McCrery believes that the system has gone too far for the good of a nation seeking answers from the Avenue. "There are members in both parties who think the most important thing is to regain the majority," he says. "If you take that too far, it's damaging to the institution and to public policy." Among the drivers of that all-or-nothing partisanship, in his view, is the same factor auto industry representative and congressional spouse Debbie Dingell points to. More often than not, members relate to one another as virtual strangers.

For the first fourteen years of his service in Congress, McCrery, a former lawyer and paper-company executive, commuted regularly to Washington from his home district. His wife remained in Louisiana to work as a college professor, and his children attended local schools. It was a wearying weekly grind, since there are no nonstop flights between Washington and Shreveport. As he approached the 2004 campaign, he confronted the prospect of finally achieving the chairmanship of Ways and Means; because of the Republican Party's term limits on committee chairmen, Thomas had decided to retire.

McCrery was conflicted. The Ways and Means chairmanship is one of the most coveted perches on the Avenue—the crossroads of power on everything from taxes to health care to retirement policy. But McCrery realized that the demands of the chairmanship would force him to spend more time in Washington, and away from his family. He decided he wouldn't seek re-election, shrugging off the pleas of President Bush and House Speaker Hastert.

Then, one summer weekday, as McCrery was driving from his apartment in Virginia across the 14th Street Bridge to work at the Capitol, his cellphone rang. It was his wife in tears, informing him that, after praying over the issue, she had decided the chairmanship was too important for him to pass up. She would quit her job in Shreveport and move the family to Washington.

McCrery changed his mind and won re-election—enduring attacks along the way for having "gone Washington" by moving his family north from Louisiana. But the move changed the political calculus for McCrery in another way, too. The family bought a house in McLean, Virginia, and placed the kids in public schools there. As it happened, they ended up in the same neighborhood as a Democratic congressman whom McCrery had served with for a decade but barely knew: Representative Chet Edwards of Texas. Their sons joined the same Boy Scout troop—and changed the two lawmakers' political relationship.

"When you get to know somebody as a neighbor, or your kids play together on the soccer team, it's harder for you to go on the floor and call them names," McCrery says. It also makes it harder to work for the person's defeat at the polls. In 2004, McCrery had sent $10,000 from his leadership PAC to the campaign treasury of Edwards's Republican opponent. Though the Republican team once again targeted Edwards in 2006, McCrery decided he wasn't going after his neighbor's job. "This last election, I told the leadership, I'm not contributing to Chet's opponent."

One of the first issues Rangel and McCrery sought to cooperate on was one of the most divisive. Trade expansion is an ideological lodestar for free-market Republicans, and a top priority for American business. Yet the issue spurs intense rancor within the Democratic coalition, not to mention between Democrats and Republicans.

Pro-trade Democratic centrists, such as Will Marshall at the Democratic Leadership Council, complained of "globaphobia" among the party's anti-trade wing. Ascendant Democratic populists, such as Robert Borosage of the labor-backed Campaign for America's Future, aimed to "curb corporate power" after watching politicians on the Avenue enact deals such as the North American Free Trade Agreement, "written in the headquarters of multinational corporations."

That's why Barney Frank was realistic about the prospect for achieving the "grand bargain" he offered for business and labor. "An interesting fact of life in American politics today is how angry it has gotten," Frank explained in early 2007. "Both sides that I have approached in terms of the bargain think it's a bad idea, because I am going to sell out to the other one. The degree of confidence Americans have today is pretty low."

Rangel and McCrery were aiming far lower. They merely sought a measure under which the House might be able to pass trade agreements with four countries: Peru, Panama, Colombia, and South Korea. In private meetings through the winter and spring, they joined with the Bush administration's trade representative, Susan Schwab, to try to meet liberals' concerns that such trade deals result in environmental degradation and a "race to the bottom" in which cheap labor in developing countries shifts American jobs overseas and drives down wages of U.S. workers.

By May 10, they had a deal: labor and environmental protections strong enough for the Democratic chairman, but not so restrictive of the market as to devalue the trade deal itself in the view of his Republican counterpart and the administration.

The ultimate fate of that rare cross-party cooperation wasn't immediately clear. Some on the Democratic left attacked it as a sellout to business; the Republican right doubted that a Democratic Congress would pass trade deals under any circumstances.

But it was a start that Rangel and McCrery decided to keep building on. A month later, legislation emerged in the Senate that would have the effect of increasing taxes on the Blackstone Group, a private-equity giant that was seeking to reap fresh billions through an initial public stock offering. The Avenue's ideological warriors quickly took to their familiar battle stations, with Republican conservatives condemning a "war on wealth" and Democratic liberals affirming their eagerness to target the twenty-first-century robber barons of American capitalism.

Rangel and McCrery took a more measured approach. Rangel praised the Senate's bill but withheld offering one of his own; McCrery affirmed his openness to holding hearings on the issue.

It was the kind of issue certain to generate more intense pressures— ideological, partisan, and financial—the more deeply Congress waded into it. In such fights, Rangel and McCrery can hardly act alone; each must account for the needs of the "team," as directed by House Speaker Nancy Pelosi, Minority Leader John Boehner, and the election campaign committees of both parties.

But Rangel figures his four decades of experience entitle him to some maneuvering room to work with McCrery to get things done. "Our leadership can't deny us the opportunity to bring some prestige back to the House," he says.

Whether they succeed or fail in their own efforts, Rangel says in an interview, he has no doubt that a shift toward pragmatism is coming. The night before, he had dined with Microsoft Corporation chairman Bill Gates. Like other business leaders, Gates fears that American competitiveness is eroding while Washington is gridlocked—over education improvements, immigration reform, tax policy, and a host of other issues.

"There's something that's going to happen in the next couple of years that's going to break down this Republican-Democratic stuff," Rangel predicts. "The private sector thinks their base is weak." Crafting a response to meet that concern, he concludes, "may be my reason for being chairman."

Any progress he makes will come without McCrery, however. Facing long odds against claiming the chairman's gavel anytime soon, the Louisiana Republican announced in late 2007 that he would retire.

20. THE CHAIRMEN:
ROBERT STRAUSS AND KEN MEHLMAN

IN A BRIGHT, AIRY OFFICE in downtown Washington sit two men, one old, one young, representing the opposites in the capital over the last generation. The first, Robert Strauss, was the Democratic Party's national chairman in the 1970s. The other, Ken Mehlman, was the Republican Party's chairman in the era of George W. Bush. Now they work together as partners at the giant law firm that Strauss helped found, Akin Gump Strauss Hauer & Feld, their offices are down the hall from each other, and their friendship spans the generational and partisan divisions that might be expected to keep them apart.

And on this day they sit in Strauss's office and wonder: If the two of us can come together, is there some way the rest of Washington can do so, too?

In his prime, Strauss was the man to see in Washington. He ran presidential campaigns, served as Middle East envoy and U.S. trade representative, raised huge amounts of money for his party, yet was widely enough respected that a president of the opposite party named him the first American ambassador to Russia after the fall of the Soviet Union. Along the way, he built a wildly successful law firm; one testimonial to his stature lies in the fact that the gleaming office building in which he sits is named for him. He, better than perhaps anyone in town, has seen Pennsylvania Avenue evolve.

And he doesn't like a lot of what he has seen. "I think Washington has definitely changed. It's changed since I came, a great deal," he says. "If you went to Paul Young's restaurant"—an old political hang-out, now defunct—"you'd see Democrats and Republicans. Now, they weren't all running around together. But they'd come over to each other's table, and they'd gossip, and that was my kind of life."

These days? "In this town now it's very difficult for people to mix and mingle, so to speak. I have always blamed a lot of that on the fact of money. People who hold office have to go home every weekend to raise money, so they work two days or three at the most on the Hill, and then they're back home. . . . They can't stay here and meet each other and have their wives meet and have a social life on weekends, because they're out raising that damn money."

To be sure, the Democratic Party Strauss used to lead has been transformed. Its conservative wing, personified by former Washington Senator Henry Jackson and filled out by Texas native Strauss and fellow Southerners, has evaporated. "That Democratic Party doesn't exist anymore," Strauss says. Many of the bridges between the ideologues of the left and right are down, and haven't yet been replaced.

That has helped produce the polarized climate in which Strauss's partner Ken Mehlman ran his national party. Mehlman is a graduate of Franklin & Marshall College—the same school that produced Ken Duberstein, Strauss's successor as the Washington man to see—and Harvard Law School. He did a stint as a lawyer at Akin Gump before throwing himself into Republican politics, eventually becoming political director of the Bush White House, chairman of the 2004 Bush-Cheney re-election campaign, and ultimately party chairman after that 2004 victory. He came of age on a Pennsylvania Avenue wholly different from the one Strauss knew in his younger years, an Avenue of Republican dominance, vastly diminished bipartisanship, and a shriveled political center.

"Part of why there is the polarization that exists is that both parties, having accomplished the big things that they set out to do, fight over the small things," Mehlman contends. In the twentieth century, he argues, Democrats struggled for a New Deal set of social-welfare programs, civil rights, women's rights, and a solid set of environmental protections, all of which were achieved. Republicans wanted most of all to defeat the Soviet Union and the communist threat, lower tax rates, and effect welfare reform and a reduction in crime rates. All of those things have been achieved as well.

"Ironically, part of why today our politics is about small things is because, on the big things, it's worked very well for the last generation," Mehlman says. Now, he says, the agenda may be changing in character again, and that in turn may usher back in an era of greater cooperation across partisan and ideological lines:

"If you look at the challenges we face today, those challenges are once again big things—the war on terror; the need to expand access and reduce the cost of health care; whether you come at it from an environmental perspective or a national-security perspective, the need for energy independence. Those are three huge issues, all of which I think are very amenable to bipartisan solutions. . . . At a moment when we have big issues, hopefully we can come together."

Much as World War II brought together conservatives and socialists to fight fascism, Mehlman says, radical Islam is the kind of threat that actually should unite Americans across the spectrum. "Islamic fascists are the most anti-Semitic, sexist, homophobic, religiously intolerant force in the world. There is a coalition of the threatened that typically leans left in politics. So a robust response to that ought to be something that appeals across the ideological spectrum."

Mehlman and Strauss—one spry, the other now in a wheelchair—point to themselves and their firm as evidence that bipartisanship and cooperation across ideologies is possible. Mehlman rose from a place that often breeds liberals—middle-class Baltimore—to become chairman of the Republican Party. Strauss rose from a place that often breeds conservatives—small-town Texas—to become chairman of the Democratic Party. The law firm that Strauss has built houses not only the two former chairmen of the Republican and Democratic parties, but also former Representative Bill Paxon, once the chairman of the National Republican Congressional Committee, and former Representative Vic Fazio, once the chairman of the Democratic

Congressional Campaign Committee. "There isn't an elected official in America that one of us didn't help get elected," Mehlman quips.

Adds Strauss: "Most of the good things that I've done have been by fluke. But that ability to bridge all these different people is something I grew up with. My father, I guess, taught us that, because we were the only Jewish family in town. You had to get along."

In one sign of the way people can build bridges across ideological and even generational divisions if they choose to do so, Mehlman, the Republican, happens to have been a law-school classmate of Barack Obama, the Democratic Party's rising new star. And it was Mehlman who brought in Obama for lunch one day to introduce him to Strauss, the Democratic Party's wise man.

Mehlman also endorses an Obama theory, that political cooperation will become easier once a younger generation slowly takes over from the Baby Boomers who now dominate Pennsylvania Avenue: "I think that people who were raised and came of age during the sixties tend to focus more on where you come from philosophically than their older brothers and sisters did, or their younger children do. I look at my generation, people in their forties, having not gone through that period, who were too young to have political consciousness then—I think we're less polarized and ideological. You have a bunch of people who would see Clinton and say, 'Man, that guy is slippery, look at how smooth he talks, I don't like him.' And you have a bunch of guys who would look at Bush and say, 'Man, he's not articulate at all, I don't like him.' Whereas I think people who are older and younger don't judge someone on the same qualities that the Baby Boomer generation judges people."

Strauss, the elder statesman, offers a simpler view. He expects a return, slowly and over time, to a climate with more of the comity and bipartisanship he once knew, simply because that is a more natural state. "I think we'll go back to it because it makes sense," Strauss says. "People are not as foolish as sometimes they act."

ACKNOWLEDGMENTS

Writing a book can be an intimidating task—but less intimidating when we remember it's a collective enterprise that taps skills and insights far beyond those of the authors alone.

In our case, we were blessed with a particularly talented group of colleagues and friends. Chief among them is Kate Medina, our editor, muse, and confidante at Random House. She played a large role in shaping this project, drawing upon her earlier experience in editing Hedrick Smith's hugely successful *The Power Game* nearly two decades earlier. Kate has a wonderful sense of a good story, a marvelous curiosity about the way our world in Washington really works, and an unerring feel for the construct and flow of a book. This work would not exist without her. We'd also like to thank her team at Random House, Frankie Jones, Robin Rolewicz, and Abby Plesser. They are all remarkably able, good-humored, and efficient, beyond what we had a right to expect.

We owe a debt of gratitude to our agent, Rafe Sagalyn, a keen observer of both Washington and the publishing world. He thought we might be able to realize this vision as first-time authors, guided us out of port, and shrewdly helped map out our eventual destination.

We also are indebted to *The Wall Street Journal* and our colleagues there. The *Journal* has given to both of us the ultimate contribution: the freedom over the years to travel the country and the world, to meet and get to know the kinds of interesting people who populate this book, and to write expansively about big events and big ideas. The *Journal* brought the two of us together, made us partners, and allowed a satisfying friendship to grow. In many ways, this book represents the cumulative knowledge we developed through the in-depth reporting and writing the *Journal* allows and appreciates.

Within the *Journal*, we owe particular thanks to Paul Steiger, our longtime managing editor, who has been unduly kind to us over the years, and who blessed this undertaking. We're also grateful to David Wessel, Nik Deogun,

Jacob Schlesinger, and Mary Lu Carnevale, who provided the kind of flexible support that allowed us to pursue this project while holding down demanding day jobs (and who tend to share our propensity for 6 a.m. e-mails). Other gifted *Journal* colleagues produce stories every day that shed light on the way our world works, and we've drawn on many of them here. In particular, we're grateful for insights from Neil King, Jr., Jess Bravin, Greg Hitt, Jonathan Karp, and Jackie Calmes, stellar reporters and good friends all.

The CNBC television network has been terrifically helpful and understanding as well. Since March 2006, just as our project was really getting off the ground, John has spent most of his working days at CNBC. While spreading himself thin on the book, maintaining *Journal* responsibilities, and learning the new field of television journalism, John benefited from the generosity of CNBC bosses and colleagues Jonathan Wald, Tyler Mathisen, Matt Cuddy, and Joanne Fuchs.

The bulk of the material in this book came from extended interviews with the Washington figures portrayed here, and we're grateful to all of them for their willingness to offer their time, stories, and insights. Within that group, some have been especially generous during the preparation of this book and, more generally, over the years we have known them; in this regard, we'd single out Ken Duberstein, Bob Kimmitt, Pete Wehner, Rahm Emanuel, and Sam Brownback.

Finally, we thank our families. John can never repay his debts to his mother, Beatrice Harwood, and his late father, Richard Harwood, who taught him about life and journalism on Pennsylvania Avenue and everywhere else. Jerry was blessed to have parents, Richard and Annette Seib, who both put a little printer's ink in his blood and fostered an interest in how the world works. Our shared experiences as journalists pale beside our shared luck in finding smart, accomplished, sophisticated, and sympathetic women to fill our lives in Barb Rosewicz and Frankie Blackburn. They and our children—Jerry's three boys and John's three girls—have been wonderfully forgiving of the demands and distractions of this book over the past two years. It is for our kids—Luke, Jake, Joseph, Avery, Leigh, and Mary Jeanne—that we most hope Pennsylvania Avenue can find better ways of solving the problems of the nation and world.

JERRY SEIB *and* JOHN HARWOOD
Washington, D.C., November 2007

The bulk of the material in this book came from a series of on-the-record interviews the authors conducted with the subjects from late 2005 until late 2007. In addition to that material, these sources were used:

I. WASHINGTON WRIT LARGE
1. GRIDLOCK ON AMERICA'S MAIN STREET

1. *Wall Street Journal,* Oct. 31, 2005, p. A2.
2. Letter to Stewart A. Baker, assistant secretary for policy, planning, and international affairs, U.S. Department of Homeland Security, Jan. 6, 2006.
3. "UAE Company Poised to Oversee Six U.S. Ports," Associated Press, Feb. 11, 2006.
4. *Wall Street Journal,* March 10, 2006, p. A1.
5. *Washington Times,* Feb. 14, 2006, p. A18.
6. "Frist Calls for Halt to U.S. Ports Deal," Associated Press, Feb. 22, 2006.
7. *Wall Street Journal,* March 17, 2007, p. B5.
8. Nielsen Media Research, Full Season Average, Sept. 2004–Sept. 2005.
9. "A Time When Partisanship Didn't Mean Enmity," National Public Radio, Jan. 26, 2007.
10. *Washington Post,* June 22, 2005, p. 1.

2. THE FIXER: KEN DUBERSTEIN

1. *Wall Street Journal,* May 15, 2006, p. A1.
2. Ibid., Aug. 2, 2006, p. A6.
3. Ibid., Sept. 22, 2006, p. A8.
4. *Chicago Sun-Times,* Sept. 14, 2006, p. 33.

5. Ibid., March 8, 2007, p. 29.
6. *The Hill*, March 30, 2006.

3. THE BUSINESSMAN: DAVID RUBENSTEIN

1. "Firm Profile," thecarlylegroup.com.
2. Ibid.
3. Factiva search, "The Washington Post."
4. "Big Deals," *Washingtonian*, June 2006, pp. 56–61, 130–41.
5. "Carlyle Team," thecarlylegroup.com.
6. *Wall Street Journal*, June 13, 2007, p. A1.
7. "Private Equity Council Is Formed to Provide Research and Information," press release, Dec. 26, 2006.

II. WORKING THE SYSTEM

1. Paul C. Light, "The New True Size of Government," Robert F. Wagner Graduate School of Public Service, August 2006.
2. Bureau of Economic Analysis, U.S. Department of Commerce.
3. "Demographics," capitolfile-magazine.com.

4. THE DEMOCRATIC STRATEGIST: RAHM EMANUEL

1. *Chicago Tribune*, Nov. 9, 2003, p. 1.
2. Center for Responsive Politics, 2004 and 2006 reports for congressional campaign committees, opensecrets.org.
3. Jackie Koszczuk and Martha Angle, *CQ's Politics in America* 2008 (CQ Press, 2007), pp. 599, 1038.
4. "Text of the Democratic Resolution," Associated Press, Feb. 14, 2007.

5. THE PARTY CAPTAINS FOR 2008: CHRIS VAN HOLLEN AND TOM COLE

1. *Washington Post*, April 13, 2000, p. M1.
2. opensecrets.org.
3. Ibid.
4. "Bush's Fundraising Dinner Raises $15.4M," Associated Press, June 13, 2007.

5. Federal Election Commission, "FEC Summarizes January–June 2007 Political Party Fund-Raising Figures," Aug. 14, 2007.

6. THE FUND-RAISING PHENOM: DEBBIE WASSERMAN SCHULTZ

1. Americans for Prosperity Foundation, "Debbie Wasserman-Schultz's Porky Valentine to Her Colleagues," Feb. 15, 2007, Americansforprosperity.org.
2. *Palm Beach Post*, March 31, 2007, p. 17A.

7. THE REPUBLICAN STRATEGIST: KARL ROVE

1. *Washington Post*, July 23, 1999, p. C1.
2. *Wall Street Journal*, Aug. 30, 2004, p. A1.
3. "Historical Look—All 2nd Midterms," Republican National Committee document, November 2006.
4. Harold W. Stanley and Richard G. Niemi, *Vital Statistics on American Politics, 2005–2006* (CQ Press, 2006), p. 28.
5. Speech at Washington College, Chestertown, MD, April 18, 2005.

III. POWER OUTSIDE THE SYSTEM

1. Paul C. Light, "The New True Size of Government," Robert F. Wagner Graduate School of Public Service, August 2006.
2. Overview and Building Site and Building History, Ronald Reagan Building & International Trade Center, itcdc.com.
3. *New York Times*, Dec. 8, 2006, p. 14.
4. *Iraq Study Group Report*, United States Institute of Peace, p. 6.
5. Ibid.

8. THE ADVOCATE: HILARY ROSEN

1. *Washington Post*, March 22, 2007, p. A11.

9. THE SOCIAL SECRETARY: LEA BERMAN

1. White House Office of the First Lady, "Guest List for the Luncheon in Honor of the Visit of Chinese President Hu Jintao and Madam Liu Yongqing," April 20, 2006.

2. "East Room Art and Furnishings," whitehouse.gov.

3. White House Office of the Press Secretary, "President Bush and People's Republic of China President Hu Exchange Luncheon Toasts," April 20, 2006.

10. THE NETROOTS WARRIOR MEETS THE ESTABLISHMENT: ELI PARISER AND KYLE McSLARROW

1. *Journal News*, White Plains, N.Y., April 18, 2004, p. 1E.

2. "net neutrality alert," Ben Scott e-mail to Adam Green, April 4, 2006, 9:40 p.m.

3. "Your Own Personal Internet," Wired Blog Network, June 30, 2006.

4. "Interview with Eli Pariser: Director of MoveOn," MotherJones.com, June 29, 2007.

11. THE LOBBYIST: ED ROGERS

1. *New York Times*, Oct. 26, 1991, p. 33.

2. "Barbour Griffith & Rogers: Firm Profile Summary 2006," open secrets.org.

3. *Washington Home & Garden*, Fall 2006.

4. "Spies, Lies and KPMG," *Business Week*, Feb. 26, 2007.

5. Letter from Representative Henry Waxman to Gordon Dobie, March 22, 2007.

12. THE INDUSTRY MAN: BILLY TAUZIN

1. Michael Barone and Richard F. Cohen, *The Almanac of American Politics 2004* (National Journal Group, 2003), pp. 709–12.

2. *Wall Street Journal*, Oct. 25, 2006, p. A1.

3. "Pharmaceutical Research and Manufacturers of America, PAC Contributions to Federal Candidates, 2006 Cycle," opensecrets.org.

IV. ROLES REDEFINED

1. "Bush Spends Thanksgiving with Extended Family in Crawford," Associated Press, Nov. 28, 2002.

13. THE POLICY ADVISER: ELLIOTT ABRAMS

1. "President Bush Visits Prague, Czech Republic, Discusses Freedom," White House Office of the Press Secretary, June 5, 2007.
2. "Deputy Assistant to the President and Deputy National Security Adviser for Global Democracy Strategy Elliott Abrams," White House biography, usinfo.state.gov.
3. "About Ethics and Public Policy Center," eppc.org.
4. Joseph Laconte, "The Ghosts of Appeasement: Christian Realism and the Rise of Islamo-Fascism," The John Jay Institute for Faith, Society and Law, Nov. 16, 2006.

14. THE SPINNER: BRENDAN DALY

1. Taylor Marsh, "Reporting from the Capitol," huffingtonpost.com, Jan. 4, 2007.
2. Kagro X, "Big Day on the Hill," dailykos.com, Jan. 4, 2007.
3. *Los Angeles Times*, Feb. 8, 2007, p. A1.
4. *Washington Post*, April 5, 2007, p. A16.
5. Fox News Channel video clip posted at thinkprogress.org, April 5, 2007.
6. Representative Tom Lantos, "Within the Bounds," *USA Today*, April 6, 2007, p. A10.
7. Transcript of *The Big Story with John Gibson*, Fox News Channel, April 10, 2007.
8. *San Francisco Chronicle*, April 11, 2007, p. A14.
9. "White House Says Lawmakers Should Not Go to Iran," Associated Press, April 11, 2007.

15. THE POLITICAL OPERATORS: JIM JORDAN AND TERRY NELSON

1. Matthew Continetti, *The K Street Gang* (Doubleday, 2006), pp. 18–19.
2. *Wall Street Journal*, Dec. 7, 2006, p. A1.
3. "Wal-Mart Is Taking the Lead on Environmental Sustainability," wal-martfacts.com, April 3, 2006.
4. *New York Times*, May 12, 2006, p. 1.
5. *Washington Post*, Oct 12, 2006, p. C2.
6. *New York Times*, Oct. 26, 2005, p.1.
7. *Wall Street Journal*, April 9, 2007, p. A1.

8. *Los Angeles Times,* Aug. 18, 2006, p. A1.

9. *Arkansas Democrat-Gazette,* March 10, 2007, p. 33.

V. CHANGING THE SYSTEM

1. James Reichley, *The Life of the Parties* (Rowan & Littlefield), 1992, p. 43.

2. Neil MacNeil, *Forge of Democracy* (David McKay Company, 1963), p. 209.

3. Committee on House Administration, *History of the United States House of Representatives* (U.S. Government Printing Office, 1994), p. 306.

4. Ibid., p. 315.

5. Burdett A. Loomis, "From the Framing to the Fifties: Lobbying in Constitutional and Historical Contexts," Carl Albert Congressional Research and Studies Center, University of Oklahoma, Fall 2006.

6. David McKean, *Tommy the Cork* (Steerforth Press, 2004), p. 59.

7. James Sterling Young, *The Washington Community 1800–1828* (Columbia University Press, 1966), p. 78.

8. Charles Peters, *Five Days in Philadelphia* (PublicAffairs, 2005), p. 5.

9. Michael Barone, *Our Country* (Free Press, 1990), p. 279.

10. MacNeil, *Forge of Democracy,* pp. 278–79.

11. William S. White, *Citadel: The Story of the U.S. Senate* (Harper & Brothers, 1956), p. 24.

12. J. Stanley Kimmitt, oral-history interviews conducted Feb. 15, 2001, to Oct. 9, 2002, Senate Historical Office.

13. Don Oberdorfer, *Senator Mansfield* (Smithsonian Books, 2003), p. 506.

14. Barack Obama, *The Audacity of Hope* (Crown, 2006), p. 36.

15. Transcript of Governor Schwarzenegger's Second Inaugural Address, Jan. 5, 2007, Office of the Governor, Sacramento, California.

16. THE NEW REPUBLICANS: SAM BROWNBACK AND PETE WEHNER

1. Koszczuk and Angle, *CQ's Politics in America 2008,* pp. 398–99.

2. Michael Barone and Richard F. Cohen, *The Almanac of American Politics 2004,* National Journal Group, 2003, pp. 709–12.

3. "Sen. Sam Brownback Plans to Withdraw from the Race for the Republican Presidential Nomination," Associated Press, Oct. 18, 2007.

4. "Pete Wehner—White House Deputy Assistant to the President and Di-

rector of Strategic Initiatives," President George W. Bush: Resources for the President's Team, results.gov.

5. Pete Wehner, "Spirited Debate: Religion and American Politics," University of Pennsylvania Fox Civic Leadership Lecture, March 29, 2005.
6. *Washington Post*, April 21, 1996, p. C7.
7. Wehner, "Spirited Debate."

17. THE NEW DEMOCRATS: MARA VANDERSLICE AND JIM WEBB

1. Perry Bacon, Jr., *Washington Post*, June 5, 2007.
2. James Webb, *Born Fighting* (Broadway, 2004), p. 343.
3. Ibid., p. 9.
4. Ibid., p. 8.
5. James Webb, "Why You Need to Know the Scots-Irish," *Parade*, Oct. 3, 2004.
6. *Washington Post*, Sept. 4, 2002, p. A21.
7. Jackson Landers, "Jim Webb Defends the Second Amendment," Rule .303 blog, Nov. 2, 2006, rule-303.blogspot.com.
8. *The Virginian-Pilot*, Norfolk, Va., Oct. 28, 2006, p. A12.
9. Robert Timberg, *The Nightingale's Song* (Simon & Schuster, 1995), p. 457.
10. George F. Will, "Already Too Busy for Civility," *Washington Post*, Nov. 30, 2006, p. A23.
11. Democratic Response of Senator Jim Webb to the President's State of the Union Address, Jan. 23, 2007, transcript at webb.senate.gov.
12. Kagro X, "Yeah, He Had a Gun," dailykos.com, March 26, 2007.

18. THE DEAL-MAKERS: BERNADETTE BUDDE AND ANDY STERN

1. *Wall Street Journal*, Feb. 26, 2007, p. A1.
2. "Union Members Summary," Bureau of Labor Statistics, U.S. Department of Labor, Jan. 25, 2007.
3. Matt Bai, "The New Boss," *The New York Times Magazine*, Jan. 30, 2005.

19. THE TAX MEN: CHARLIE RANGEL AND JIM McCRERY

1. *Chicago Sun-Times*, June 2, 1994, p. 20.

INDEX

ABOUT THE AUTHORS

JOHN HARWOOD is the chief Washington correspondent for CNBC and a political writer for *The New York Times*. Harwood began his career in 1978 at the *St. Petersburg Times*, where he served as state-capital correspondent, Washington correspondent, and political editor. In 1989 Harwood was awarded a Nieman fellowship at Harvard University. He subsequently spent sixteen years at *The Wall Street Journal* beginning in 1991, covering the White House, Congress, and national politics. In addition to CNBC, Harwood offers political analysis on MSNBC, *NBC Nightly News*, *Meet the Press*, and PBS's *Washington Week*. He lives in Silver Spring, Maryland, with his wife and their three daughters.

GERALD F. SEIB is an assistant managing editor and the executive Washington editor of *The Wall Street Journal*. He writes the paper's "Capital Journal" column and is a regular commentator on Washington affairs for CNBC and the Fox Business Network. Seib is the recipient of numerous awards, the Merriman Smith Award, the Aldo Beckman Award, the Gerald R. Ford Journalism Prize, Georgetown University's Edward Weintal Prize for his coverage of the Gulf War, and the William Allen White Award of the University of Kansas among them. Along with Harwood, Seib was part of the *Wall Street Journal* team that won the 2002 Pulitzer Prize in the breaking news category for its coverage of the September 11 terrorist attacks. He lives in Chevy Chase, Maryland, with his wife and three sons.

ABOUT THE TYPE

This book was set in Electra, a typeface designed for Linotype by W. A. Dwiggins, the renowned type designer (1800–1956). Electra is a fluid typeface, avoiding the contrasts of thick and thin strokes that are prevalent in most modern typefaces.